The autho[r]... 1/16 ...2/... first page, ...ght which is both deep[ly] [per]sonal, but also has wider collective significance. Written in an accessible and honest way, this book addresses the suffering of our troubled times, dismantling false beliefs and encouraging us to align ourselves once again with the ancient ways. He offers a cosmology that supports the reality that darkness, illness and affliction may be the very portals through which we enter, individually and collectively, into an initiation, a rite of passage, a healing. A brave work, to be celebrated and savoured.

Melanie Reinhart, teacher, astrologer and bestselling author of *Chiron and the Healing Journey*

A courageous and sincere exploration of how to travel the shamanic path in 21st century England. With our ever-increasing global ecocide, this book addresses the problems and associated dis-ease of our being apart from Nature rather than being a part of Nature.

Dr David Luke, senior lecturer of psychology, Greenwich University and author of *Talking with the Spirits: Ethnographies from Between the Worlds*

This book is a heartfelt exploration into the soul sickness that afflicts the modern world with very real healing solutions inspired by ancient cultures. Through the author's personal story we are touched to discover that what we may have seen as pathological inside of us, actually holds the key to our transformation, both individually and as a culture. A heart-warming work.

Jamie Catto, teacher, author and c[reator] of the multi-award winning, Grammy nominated global philoso[phy]

Jez Hughes is a remarkable healer, [p]sy...

The Heart of Life – Shamanic Initiation & Healing, recounts the need in our modern era for initiation and re-birth. He talks about ancestors, death and initiation in a fresh way; educating the reader about the importance of remembering our ancestors. Our modern world is out of balance. The root of this could be our fear of death and disconnection with the natural world. Jez talks in a frank way drawing on personal experiences to show the importance of spiritual/ shamanic initiation as a bridge into the unseen world, thus allowing for greater spiritual transformation and acceptance of death.

I recommend Jez's book for all people searching for meaning amidst the chaos of western living.

John Lockley, Sangoma (Traditional South African Shaman), spiritual teacher & ceremonialist.

This is a book of the heart, spoken by one who has a deep understanding and personal experience of knowing. His is the story of the divine spark that flows through all of consciousness, reaching those willing to surrender and become one with nature through the teachings of the ancestors and ancient ones. In this book you will become immersed in the sacred ways of the shaman, the one who knows, learning that you are the one that has locked away and hidden those life changing teachings. Jez will lead you to the edge through his deep personal healing awareness, to become once more whole and healed.

Barbara Meiklejohn- Free, best-selling and award winning author of *The Shaman Within* and *The Shamanic Handbook of Sacred Tools and Ceremonies.*

In *The Heart of Life,* Jez Hughes rightly says that many people have no context in which to place the spiritual experiences they have and don't feel connected to the earth. He offers a context that may appeal to many people. Hughes also suggests that it's loss of meaning that creates soul sickness. I agree. People want to find meaning. This book may well bring people to where they can begin the journey.

Elen Sentier, author of *Elen of the Ways, The Celtic Chakras* and *Following the Deer Trods,* and other books on the British native tradition.

The Heart
of Life

Shamanic Initiation and Healing
in the Modern World

The Heart of Life

Shamanic Initiation and Healing
in the Modern World

Jez Hughes

MOON
BOOKS

Winchester, UK
Washington, USA

First published by Moon Books, 2015
Moon Books is an imprint of John Hunt Publishing Ltd., Laurel House, Station Approach,
Alresford, Hants, SO24 9JH, UK
office1@jhpbooks.net
www.johnhuntpublishing.com
www.moon-books.net

For distributor details and how to order please visit the 'Ordering' section on our website.

Text copyright: Jez Hughes 2014

ISBN: 978 1 78535 026 9
Library of Congress Control Number:

A CIP catalogue record for this book is available from the British Library.

Design: Stuart Davies

Printed and bound by CPI Group (UK) Ltd, Croydon, CR0 4YY, UK

We operate a distinctive and ethical publishing philosophy in all
areas of our business, from our global network of authors to
production and worldwide distribution.

CONTENTS

To Ali, my love
To my parents, for your love
To the invisible ones, for my life

Acknowledgements

Thank you to Andy Thomas for your encouragement for this project, which kept me going when I wanted to give up. Thank you to Andy Wood for friendship and brotherhood throughout my journey. To Donna Waugh for friendship and love. To Helen Sewel for astrological insight and guidance. To Tara and Boag, for friendship and laughter and to James Clifton for friendship and deep connection.

To Rodrigo, Don Santos and the Wixaritari nation for friendship, teaching and sharing your beautiful medicine with us.

To Pete Bowley and Sara Saunders at Two Feathers for support and community. To Siobhan and Darren Thomas for sharing your beautiful woods with us. For everyone who has come through the trainings and those who have supported them: Christian Timony, Beverley Peter, David de Sousa, Gabriel Lewry, Katy Dunne, Erica Shorter, Simon Welsh and Wendy Quelch.

To Daniel Stone, Simon Buxton, Ken Little Fish, Miguel Chiriap, Don Jaun Currico and many others for your teachings.

To Mervyn and Louis for your art. To Melanie Reinhart for encouragement and taking the time for lovely feedback. To John Lockley for shamanic chats and sharing. To everyone who has been for a healing and shared your soul.

To my family for love and support, Jon, James, Charlie, Emily, Vanessa, Pat and Jim Hughes. To Louise and Paris Jefferson. To everyone at Moon Books. To Iris Rauch for the light you shined in life and death. To Bejou Baile de la Perrier for being there when I needed someone the most.

To all the indigenous people around the world who have generously shared your ceremonies and sacred ways. To the plants that sustain and teach us.

And lastly to my beautiful, strange little family, Ali, again for all your support and love, Ditta and Scrilly and to Maya Bracknell- Watson for being you and teaching me.

Preface

There is a spirit that runs through everything, an invisible force that animates life. Like with the physical body, which is animated in a lifetime yet becomes apparently lifeless in death, this spirit orchestrates and conducts the physical phenomenon we call reality. It has been called many names, and many maps and guides have been set out on how to contact, connect with or embody it. Great treatises have been written on the routes we must take in order to fully realise this spirit that exists both inside and outside us; and what it expects of us when we do connect to it.

From ancient religious testaments to modern books that act as road maps for the soul, we have sought to educate ourselves: to train ourselves to think and feel in certain ways; to trick the mind and instincts that apparently rob us of our connection; to give of ourselves, to sacrifice; to make sacred; to meditate; to become disciplined in our actions; to ingest plants; to fast; to be in silence; to be in movement; to correct our bodies; all to somehow come closer to that mysterious force.

Yet, as many have observed, a butterfly that dances on the summer wind, a butterfly that asks no questions of itself, nor has any expectation, embodies, apparently effortlessly, the spirit of life more completely than we can imagine. So why the complexity? If it's that easy, why don't we just become like the butterfly? Why do we as humans seem to separate ourselves from nature, noting and celebrating how unique we are from the rest of creation, and then invent ever more complex ways to reconnect? It seems a crazy way to be carrying on.

Some will say, it's because we have been given the opportunity to become *conscious* of creation, of life, others might suggest we just took a wrong turn a couple of millennia ago, saw ourselves as somehow above the rest of nature, and in a way started believing our own hype. There's a great expression in football referring to someone who seemingly knows everything there is to know about the sport, without ever having played it: 'He talks a good game'. Perhaps we just started talking a good game a while back, and forgot how to live it.

Or, could it be that this is all part of the adventure that we call life? That, as Martin Prechtel has noted about Mayan cultural belief; it's not that we are born into 'Original *Sin*', but rather 'Original *Forgetfulness*'. It is human nature to forget where we have come from, what we are a part of; thus the adventure, the central plot in the great drama of human story, is to find our way back to this knowing. To re-experience that birth again and again, each time garnering a greater understanding and *knowing* of who and what it is we are actually giving birth to; who we really are and what we are really made of.

This process has a name and is what has been known for millennia, throughout cultures dedicated to a greater exploration of the mystery of existence, as *initiation*. For it is through initiation, whereby established ways of being are left behind to be replaced with ways that are more integrated with the surrounding fabric – familial, societal, ecological and spiritual – that we are able to come closer to the raw essence of life. To die and be reborn, stepping beyond that which we thought we knew to be true and into something greater, a part of a greater whole.

This then, is a story of initiation; initiation into experiencing existence in all its facets, both awe-inspiring and terrifying; when the secure cellophane packaging that we wrap around life in order to keep it safe and sterile has been unwrapped and discarded. For, it seems only really possible to get to the heart of the matter when we are willing to let go of that which protects us. Like a great love affair, in order to touch and be touched, we must at some point become naked.

This is also a story, however, about what happens when the rituals and necessary structures that support initiation aren't in place. It shows how people may seek to replace this primal need to go to the edge of themselves and beyond in the most disharmonious and destructive of ways. What happens when uninitiated behaviour runs rampant through all facets of human society and endeavour. The tangled mess that this results in which, no matter how rational and reasonable we become, can seemingly be impossible to extricate ourselves from.

In this context, initiation then becomes a necessary and potent tool for healing; healing the most excessive and destructive elements of human behaviour, both personal and collective, too much of which we have seen in recent times. So, ultimately, this is a story about healing. In a time when we could be facing our greatest challenge to the precious gift that is human life (the world will survive beyond us) there then arises the greatest need for us to initiate ourselves into the heart of what it truly means to be alive.

Introduction

When I was 14 I returned home from a school trip to the theatre to experience something that was to have an extraordinary effect on my life. After getting into bed normally my body suddenly was taken over by convulsions. At the same time my eyes started rolling around the back of my head and I found myself locked into a strange fit.

I cried out desperately to my parents who, worriedly, called the doctor immediately. It took a while for the doctor to arrive as my body continued to shake uncontrollably and my mind raced desperately out of control. I was convinced that this was the end and I was dying. Something was slipping away from me and, try desperately as I could, I couldn't hold on. I was sweating and shaking, couldn't breathe and could barely see. It was like a great electrical storm had emerged from within and was going to smash me on the rocks, extinguishing my small life before it had time to even begin to get going.

Then, as suddenly as they had appeared; the convulsions and eye rolling ended and I was left lying on the bed. It was then that things got very strange. As I lay there, I experienced a feeling of what I can only describe as absolute ecstasy, alongside a profound peace. I was looking out of my eyes, and somewhere deep in my awareness, I was still a 14-year-old boy, confronted by the worried faces of my parents and the doctor who had since arrived, but something else was taking over my whole being.

It was as if I had suddenly emerged from somewhere else and was now looking at, or rather experiencing, a world I had never witnessed before. I was possessed by that ecstasy. Everything was shining new; as though someone had turned the lights of reality on to make everything Technicolor, super alive and super vibrant. I remember sitting, then kneeling, up and becoming immersed in the football posters that covered the walls of my room next to the bed. My face, an inch from them, drank them in as they seemed the most profound and extraordinary things I had ever perceived. I could hear my parents' voices, trying to get me to lie down again and apologising to the doctor when I wouldn't, saying I wasn't usually like this, but it was as if the sound of their voices was a million miles away, coming from another world almost.

The world was new, and I was somehow no longer separated but connected to it through that feeling of absolute aliveness that coursed through my veins. It was a total experience of oneness with all of life through a feeling of profound love. It is as simple and yet as difficult to describe as that.

I couldn't speak for a long while, as long as the experience lasted, until gradually I came back to some sense of normality and my parents were able to lay me down again and finally I got to sleep. The closest I have since related to this experience is through the taking of very powerful mind-altering substances, be they either in plant or drug form, but I had taken nothing. The preceding fit, I can't as easily draw a comparison to. To be honest I have since experienced a wide array of hallucinogens and other substances, both in ceremonial and recreational contexts, and nothing has ever come close to that experience. The doctor, I am convinced now, presumed I had taken something.

The next day I felt profoundly scared. This experience wasn't supposed to happen. There was no context for it or any explanation that could get near it. I was a normal lad from a secular upbringing who was fairly popular at school and who really had only one thing on my mind, and that was to become a professional footballer.

This was not such a far-off dream as I had already signed schoolboy forms for a team in the top flight of the English league. My path was set out. My parents, probably as unnerved by the whole thing as me, put it down to an adverse reaction to the cough medicine I had been taking at the time. And it was left at that.

I never described to them the feeling of ecstasy or what I had experienced after the fit. I felt ill at ease with the whole thing, almost embarrassed and, like them, wanted to forget it as quickly as possible.

But the experience wouldn't go away, as a few months later the fits returned, not to the same intensity, but rather through waves of panic that would take over my whole being. My body again would shake and I would be convinced I was dying. But, unlike the first time, I would never get to the point where everything would calm and the feeling of ecstasy would take over. I became locked in the terror.

A few times I was rushed to the accident and emergency department and one time was kept in intensive care for a couple of days as my temperature had risen to dangerous levels. I remember I had to talk to my family through a telephone as they stood outside the window of the room, like in prison scenes in films. Looking back, it almost felt like I was indeed locked in a prison, that of my body, which would rebel in these strange ways at times I could neither control nor predict.

Yet the doctors could never discover anything medically wrong with me. So I would return home and again get on like they never had happened, but always with that strange, haunting awareness that anytime, for no reason, reality would shift and I would find myself again in the same cycle.

After a couple of years, these episodes faded, until an experience with the drug ecstasy in my early 20s culminated in me lying in A&E again and prompted their terrifying return. These then lasted on and off throughout my 20s and into my early 30s. It was through seeking healing for the debilitating illness that grew out of these experiences: intense panic attacks, partial epileptic seizures, constant terror/anxiety, obsessive thoughts, minor psychotic episodes and psychological breakdowns that set my journey in motion to heal myself.

I was stubborn and strong willed by nature. I didn't trust Western medicine and, anyway, it hadn't been able to help when I was younger. But I was also intensely private and ashamed by the strangeness of what I was experiencing, so I kept most of it to myself and sought to somehow find a context and meaning whereby I could get to the root of what was happening and somehow heal the extreme edges of the symptoms.

For, there was always that nagging thought that would tug at my consciousness; that one time a fit of terror had preceded the feeling of the most profound beauty that I had ever experienced. They must then have some purpose.

After many years of exploring many different spiritual and healing pathways, some that helped and others that made things a lot worse, I settled on a love of ancient, indigenous world views and embraced a shamanic pathway. Eventually, about two-and-half years into an intensive training and after having spent three weeks in the Mexican desert, I felt the intense return of all my symptoms.

It was then, using all the techniques I had learnt, that I was able to discover that these experiences – the debilitating fear and attacks – were a doorway to greater level of consciousness, one very different from that of everyday thought and action. When I discovered this, in a single moment, I stopped fighting the symptoms and instead allowed them to propel me through that doorway. It was then that I again discovered that place of pure ecstasy and connection that I had at 14, but this time with conscious awareness.

It was a beautiful, haunting night I will never forget in a back road town somewhere in Guatemala. I had been through an intense time of learning in the desert then had been on the road for several weeks and had many adventures, including jumping the border and being held up at gun point by an armed and masked attacker. More of these stories I will explore later in the book.

From that moment on, when I rediscovered the place of unity with all of life, the symptoms eased and they didn't return. I was cured, for I had discovered the purpose of my sickness and indeed found the healing I sought. My 'illness' had become the key that connected me not only to a sense of wholeness with life, but also to the mysterious workings of my own soul.

I can now see that this was my initiation. It lasted a long time, on and off around 15 years and was incredibly painful, but at its culmination it had ultimately served its purpose, for it had connected me to a reality far bigger than that which I was willing or able to comprehend previously. Along the way, it had taken me through and beyond the edges of what I understood as normal or real, outside the comfort of my familial and societal environment. Indeed, it had taken me to the edge of madness and beyond.

Yet I did discover a far deeper sense of meaning and purpose than I ever could have had without the experience. I also learnt a lot about what makes people sick, in their souls, and what kind of pain this sickness can lead to. Without this experience I wouldn't be able to do the job I do now, which is to assist others when they find themselves in that 'dark night of the soul' when disease and illness take over.

It was finding that sense of meaning and purpose that was perhaps also one of the main proponents in me finding wellness again. When we are sick, it is often as if our whole world is torn apart. In that context it's very easy to lose meaning. Ironically, it's the loss of meaning or purpose that can then keep us sick for longer than is necessary and it's the journey back to these essential needs of human existence that many times provides the healing.

I discovered that going through what I had experienced, the madness, the disease of my spirit, was in many cultures recognised as a legitimate and common calling to a certain path – that of healing, of becoming a shaman. I then had a context for what had happened. I was no longer alone, or mad. There was no need any more to feel deep shame and weakness because I was unable to function in the everyday world. Somewhere, deep down, I must have known this anyway, that there was a reason for what was happening for, as I have mentioned, what had happened spontaneously to me at 14 had shown that through the doorway of extreme agitation lay exquisite beauty. But, I was not able to trust this process, or myself, and thus got caught in the between place, the place of madness, disconnection and intense fear.

In many ways, the world on a collective level is going through something of a similar phase now. Many people are waking up to the possibilities of unity and connection, of healing, and yet there is an equal amount of people clinging desperately to an old way of being. This is natural and human, as any transformation, especially one so big as to affect the fundamental way we view reality, creates resistance.

It also can create impatience on behalf of those waking up to the change as it takes a long time to integrate such transformation; it is often evolution as opposed to revolution before it can be grounded into our everyday lives. But we have to move forward together, because at our core we are all one, so this conflict between waking up to a new reality and holding on to the old is an important part of any transition.

To heal this conflict in the outer world we have to heal it in ourselves first. Indigenous cultures understood this well, this is why they had initiation, to guide individuals in the community into a gradual phase of waking up to realities far wider and beyond their individual lives, while at the same time being held in the safety of the community. Everyone could then move forward together.

We have lost these old ways and now, perhaps more than any other time in history, we need them to assist us in the other crisis we are facing, which is loss of meaning. This is what is creating such soul sickness in our times. Without connection there can be no meaning, apart from transitory ones that we distract ourselves with, such as the latest gadget or gossip or relationship. Thus, we need to get connected again, but in a way that doesn't completely blow our systems apart, as happened to me when I was younger.

This then is a major intention of this book; to provide a framework where we can be guided on a process of initiation into all the wonders and healing powers of the universe and, in doing so, we can rediscover the exquisite bliss that lies at the heart of life.

So what is initiation and what does it mean to initiate ourselves? Initiation is an opening, a flowering of all our latent potential and a focussing of this potential into something that we were born to become. In the process of initiation we become like the artist's clay and are moulded by something greater than ourselves into definition, we are given form and context.

We are also given a glimpse into the future and deep past and are able to make sense of these stories in the context of the present. But, more importantly, we are able to see into invisible realms normally hidden to our everyday consciousness and it is in experiencing these realms that we are able to perceive the natural order of things, of which we are a part.

Thus, our normal anxiety of separation that occurs at birth and haunts us through our lives is placated and we are able to respond to life from an integrated and mature place. All the apparent contradictions that play on our minds and imagination – how we are given this gift of life only for it to lead to the vast unknown of death, that every happiness can lead to sorrow and every beginning to an end – can be resolved as we understand that this is all part of some great plan, some great unfolding.

Initiation allows us, as a small leaf growing out of a bud, to perceive and understand the whole tree and, in this understanding, know our place upon that tree. To know who we are, where we have come from and what we are here to do; to truly know our nature.

So, with all these potential rewards, why then do we avoid initiation in the modern world? Well maybe for the simple reason that the kind of perspective that we are talking about, the unveiling of the invisible world, doesn't come easy. There are certain safeguards that stop us from knowing this world too well – our connection to the physical world to begin with. On some level we are hard wired not to know what lies beyond our bodies or everyday life, for this is a place we visit upon death, and death is seen as the antithesis of life. Really it is the complement.

In many senses, life *is* initiation. The greatest two initiations we will ever face are natural and affect everyone – birth and death – the ultimate definitions of life. All the other processes either build upon, or towards, these monumental events. However, there are ways to be born and ways die, beyond the merely physical occurrences in themselves. The way we deal with birth and death in the modern world, the clinical or hidden nature of it, says a lot about our relationship to initiation and in particular our relationship with what we call the invisible world; what cultures for millennia have called the world of spirit.

This world, that which cannot be perceived with our normal senses, is alive and well and even though it is largely ignored in modern, secular culture, still has a profound effect on our life here.

Initiation always has at its centre, a relationship between the visible and the invisible.

Life describes this process well, as we were all invisible at some point, as a spirit, a thought in someone's head or feeling in their heart, or just as an instinct that brought two people together, and yet somehow we made that long journey into the beings we are now. And some day we will all be invisible again, from nothing to something and back to nothing again. Nature is constantly exhibiting this journey.

This is where shamanism fits in.

So, what is a shaman? The term was originally from Siberia,

from the Tungus region, and translates roughly as 'he who sees' or 'he who knows'. This name was used by anthropologists on a much wider scale when they noticed that in most of the indigenous tribes they studied there would be a member of the community who acted as an intermediary between the human world and the world of spirit.

These 'shamans' would use supernatural and spiritual means to bring healing to members of the community by removing blockages and tracking lost souls; discover psychically by remote viewing where the game would be for a successful hunt; find lost things and people; communicate with the dead; organise and hold ceremonies; influence the weather for good crops; fortune tell and generally problem solve and petition the spirits on behalf of the tribe.

They also held the sacred knowledge of their people, which would be passed down orally, and they were responsibility for ensuring a balance between the world of spirit and nature and the human world. They were the doctors, priests, psychothera-pists, mediums, poets, storytellers and often leaders of their tribes. They were called many names, but anthropologists simplified this by calling them all shamans.

So the shaman's role, at its core, is to move and negotiate between the visible world and the invisible world and to ensure that a balance is held between the sacred and everyday life; that humans continue to live in harmony with nature and their environments. They are the great initiators, opening people up to the reality and magnificence of the invisible worlds. Even though we may no longer live as tribal people once did, I believe it is still essential for our survival that this balance is maintained. Thus, shamans will exist throughout time and in many different guises.

For me, the shamanic pathway is always one of healing; this doesn't change whether you are born into an indigenous tribe of the upper Amazon or, as I was, in a new town on the edges of Gatwick airport famed for its excessive amount of bypasses. If those strange beings in the invisible world call you to help them to bring healing into the world, usually through some kind of initiatory crisis, then eventually and often in the most unusual or roundabout ways, they will get their way.

As African shaman and elder Credo Mutwa says: 'We have less control over the course of our lives than we think we do.' Or, as a shamanic friend of mine once joked: 'The spirits are like the mafia, when they come knocking, you don't refuse!'

When I received the blessing of my healing from the shamanic pathway, or from those spirits – invisible, energetic beings that protect and guide me through my life, as they protect, guide and hold together the world of manifest reality – it became clear to me that I then had a duty to give back; to assist others in their own healing, as I had been assisted in mine. Not to do this felt like an insult to the ones that had brought me the healing and had cured me. This then began my real initiation and start of my learning how to use these ancient techniques of spiritual medicine; out there in the 'real world', not just in the confines of my own inward journey.

Thus, the material in this book draws not only on my own experience of initiation and healing, but also from the thousands of people who I have seen as clients, who have been generous enough to share the mystery and magnificence of their own souls and allowed me to bear witness to their healing and initiatory journeys.

These people have come from all walks of life, often knowing very little about shamanism and caring even less about it, having usually coming through personal recommendations, and yet something about its interpretation of the pain they were experiencing – the perspective it could offer – has often touched them deeply, helping to begin the healing process.

In many ways, as I've already mentioned, the whole of the modern world is going through an initiatory crisis at the moment, as is evidenced through the fear and insecurity that permeates almost every aspect of living, from ecological brinkmanship, to the constant warfare and random violence that surrounds us and the economic uncertainty and stress of living that cuts into everyday lives. These and countless other issues weigh heavy on our souls, causing much pain and heartache. In Britain alone, it is estimated that up to a quarter of the population is suffering from some kind of mental illness at any one time.[1]

And it is these invisible realms, the mental and emotional issues of the soul and spirit; that most traditional cultures recognise as being the precursors of the physical, thus problems on a soul level are often seen as the cause of *any* illness, including most physical ones. This is where the shaman would be called in to heal the invisible causes of illness.

This is what I feel is needed now, and is the gift that shamanism can offer us, for this is a problem that reaches much deeper than merely personal circumstances or wounding – right into the heart of the age in which we are living. To be effective in its treatment, I feel we need a perspective beyond the personal and psychological, which can address the whole nature of disease at the moment.

From a shamanic perspective, as with many other traditions, we are all connected, all part of a singular organism that is the earth. What affects a part of the organism will somewhere have its root cause within the whole. As holistic medicine seeks to treat the whole person; to bring true healing to individuals, we must then also seek to heal the wider living environment of which we are just a small part. Thus, healing, or even merely reconnecting to, the earth becomes essential to healing ourselves.

To take this further, not only do we exist in the context of the wider earth of which we are a part, we also live in a particular time, which history has brought us to. This history has a profound effect on the present, shaping the many belief systems that go a long way to explaining and diagnosing whether wellness or disturbance will prevail. This is how psychology can be so effective in describing why people act the way they do in the present, through past trauma or wounding, and how the repeating of this trauma in different forms can run through and provide the major narrative of people's lives.

A straightforward example of this is how often deep wounds such as abuse can run in families, as the abused become the abuser or seeks out the 'comfort' or familiarity of another abuser in their lives, until healing occurs. Thus the past needs as much healing as the present, in order to free us from the prison of repetitive wounding. However, it is not just personal histories that are important to recognise, for as we are all connected to each other and the earth as a living organism, so we are connected to all of history and carry the memories of the past, of our ancestors, deep within us.

Only when we have gone through these different stages of healing can we often come to ourselves, our own unique personal contribution to the whole, and explore how the personal stories that make up our character may be either blocking or assisting us in our lives. We live in a time where we take everything personally; it is the age of the individual. I have seen many people for healings, who have such a great grasp of their own personal histories and are very eloquent in the psychological patterns that are inhibiting or causing them pain, and yet they seem as incapable as ever of moving beyond the blocks or healing themselves.

This, I would suggest, is because everything is taken *too* personally and there may be pain that is present in their lives that has its root cause outside their own personal histories. This is where shamanic healing can be so effective, and this is where providing a context that goes beyond the merely personal is so important.

To assist us in this, I wish to explore the nature of our souls, or the invisible landscapes that make up our being as three interrelated and interlocking entities.

The first part I call the Body Soul (or earth soul). This is the part of our being that resides in our bodies and connects us to the whole of life here on the earth and through that the universe. In many ways it is the part of us that is so wounded in the modern world through our disconnection from nature and the strange and often destructive relationship we have with our own bodies. It is typified by our obsession with the way the human body looks and preoccupation with the material world – possessions, money, security etc.

It is the part of the soul that paths such as shamanism and other nature-related disciplines that have sprung up over the past 50 years or so are intimately connected to, and can assist us in healing. This is where the organism as a whole is felt, in our bodies, and the destruction to any part of the earth will be experienced in this aspect of our being. Thus there is a need to heal our environments if we are to heal ourselves. This process begins by reconnecting to the earth. Upon death, this part of us will return to the earth to feed life here.

The second part I call our Ancestral Soul. (or blood soul). This connects us, initially through our bloodline, to the human history of which we are a part. All shamanic cultures honour their ancestors. This is partly due to the fact that they can offer an intimate and direct connection with the spirit world, for it is much easier to connect with an invisible being that exists now in spirit, if you knew them and had a good relationship with the being in this world.

Also, indigenous people recognise that we are on some level a sum of our ancestors and we hold the memory of their lives, their triumphs and failures, their gifts and blessings in our blood. This blood, as it pumps through our bodies, connects us directly to our hearts. If there are any unresolved grief or pain or wounding patterns that our ancestors carried then we will inherit them, as sure as we will inherit their DNA. The Greeks understood this well in their tragedies, whereby curses would fall on certain houses or names through the actions of their forebears, with their descendants facing cruel fates through no fault of their own.

Various tribes of the North Americas also understand this. They extol the virtue that before you act in your own life, you should think of the consequences that your actions will have on those at least seven generations in advance. Of course, this has had a very practical use as well, ensuring that thought went into the preservation of societies and cultures for long periods of time and that generations didn't act in selfish, destructive ways.

From both a practical and emotional level, this aspect of our soul is also deeply wounded. With the past century's unprecedented warfare, violence, speed of change and upheaval; the reverberations of which we are still reeling from, there is much healing that is needed. Upon death this part of us will return to the 'ancestral pool'.

The third part our being I call our Dreaming Soul. (or personal soul). This is the part of us that is of our own unique essence and I believe travels through many different lifetimes and incarnations in many different forms and realities throughout the universe. It is the part of us that is truly timeless and which a lot of spiritual paths emphasise. It is that which provides meaning and purpose to our lives while also connecting us to the spirit of all life, the creative force within the universe that has been called many different names.

However, to truly experience and get to know this aspect of our being, we must also get to know and heal the first two souls. This is why, for me, healing can be such a complex and difficult process. And it is why so many people who come to me for healings, who may have their whole personal histories worked out and have had extraordinary opening and expansive experiences whereby their own personal souls have touched the spirit of all life, can still be suffering, as I was for such a long time.

If the person is carrying wounding in their Body Soul, carrying the pain of the world as many people are, or a whole load of ancestral burdens, then these will affect that person's ability to be truly healed. For some people, there might not even be the chance to understand who they truly are or why they are here, because their personal souls are buried under a whole load of ancestral and collective burdens.

Also, it is very difficult to integrate the experiences that this part of our personal soul can offer us, if we are not fully connected to the earth and orientated within ourselves. This is why there is such a fine line between spiritual inspiration/exaltation and madness. The individual can be blown open and then apart by experiencing too much, if the necessary foundations are not in place. In the modern Western world, because most of our traditions for initiation and opening spiritually have been lost or destroyed, this is a very real danger.

Another pitfall is people create their own kind of half world of non-embodied spirituality, creating what psychotherapists call the 'spiritual bypass'. This is where people look to certain forms of spirituality as an avoidance of their own pain, usually held in their bodies. And yet, when we do heal the first two aspects of our being and connect with and fully embody our Dreaming Soul, then the riches of the universe can truly open up to us.

These three souls correspond to the three worlds that are prevalent in most shamanic and ancient cosmologies. The Lower or Underworld corresponds to the Body Soul. Religions have laid a heavy moralistic and judgemental perspective on this world and called it hell. It is a world of primal forces and is often full of helping spirits that come in animal form; the main power centre that we access this world and part of our soul through, is the navel. By doing this we are able to orientate ourselves in space.

The Ancestral Soul corresponds to what shamans call the Middle World – the spiritual or invisible equivalent of the manifest world of reality we experience with our senses. The power centre we connect with this part of our soul and world is the heart centre, as this is the place where we connect with others and ultimately this world. This enables us then to be orientated in, and have an experience of, time.

The Dreaming Soul corresponds to what shamans have called the Upper World, or what religions, again with a heavy moralistic perspective, have called heaven. The power centre we connect to this world with is through what Eastern traditions have called the Third Eye, which is shamanically known as the 'Strong Eye'. Because of a focus on individual consciousness and in particular transcendent religions and philosophies over the past 2,000-3,000 years, this part of our soul has been over emphasised, I believe, at a cost to the other important aspects of our beings.

What we are a part of (the Body Soul) and where we have come from (the Ancestral Soul) have been overlooked in favour of where we are going to or why we are here (the dreaming aspect of our being). We have sought either to get to heaven and paradise or to get off the karmic wheel without fully embodying all that we are on earth and realising the precious gift that is our life when all aspects of our being are integrated.

By perceiving the world through this energy centre and part of our soul we are able to experience timelessness and begin to orientate ourselves within it.

I share this as what I have discovered, or have been shown, on this journey into the invisible landscapes and how the nature and make-up of these landscapes of our soul can either aid or hinder the healing process. What I present, however, is in no way put forward as any kind of definitive 'truth', or even in anyway particularly original (there are many cultures and paths whose belief systems include the presence of more than one soul in the human). I first came across this idea in Robert Lawlor's excellent book on Australian Aboriginal culture, *Voices of the First Day*. At one point he compares the Egyptian idea of three souls, similar to what I outline here, with that of the Aboriginal cosmology.[2] I have just been guided to build upon and integrate these ideas into a living, breathing cosmology that makes sense in the modern world and can assist us in a healing and initiatory journey.

I present these ideas then merely as a small map of some of the territories that can assist us in connecting to and healing the invisible realms, along the way to physical, emotional, mental and spiritual wellbeing. In the end though, maps are just maps and quite often need to be thrown away in order to look up and experience reality as it is, as they can only describe the landscape. Ultimately we are all one, and energy is just energy. However, to assist us in exploring these realms, a map can sometimes be useful, if it is not held on to too tightly.

It appears to me that more than ever we need some kind of orientation in space, time and then timelessness to connect us to the world and ourselves once again, so that we are able to deal with the challenges that lie ahead of us, from a grounded and centred space. When I look around and perceive the world, the over-riding sense I have is of disorientation, of things spinning out of control, as if the train of the modern world is careering dangerously close to the edge of oblivion, with no one knowing quite how or why we got here and, more importantly, how we could even begin to get back to some kind of equilibrium.

Re-orientating ourselves can help us to become confidant in ourselves again, no longer giving away our authority to so-called experts or theories of existence that are constantly changing with the latest fashion of thought. We can become able to answer those questions that healers and visionaries over millennia have seen as essential to human health and wellbeing: 'Who am I?' 'Where do I come from?' 'Why am I here?' Getting to know and connecting with these three aspects of our being can assist us in all this, through the simple and yet monumental act of exploring our souls and the invisible landscapes that make up the reality we inhabit.

Chapter One

The Earth's Navel – Healing the Mother

If you were to ask an indigenous villager or community member where the centre of the world is, or its birthplace, they would invariably answer that it is that mountain over there, or that lake, or that rock, or that tree. They would also probably have a great number of stories that confirmed this to be true and cemented it in their mythology.

Reading such stories I could never understand such claims. If Lake Titicaca, on the border between Bolivia and Peru, really is the birthplace of creation, what of all the other places that claim to be the same? How many actual centres or 'navels' of the world could there really be? Surely a centre is a centre; there can only be one? More importantly, where was mine? It took me a while to realise that human beings have an innate need to be connected to the centre of the world; it is where we come from.

Somewhere, deep in our being, lies the memory of being in the womb, going through the most extraordinary transformational process, literally growing from a seed into the being that we are; this complex web of thoughts, limbs, emotions and spirits. That magical, alchemical process we have all been witness to and an active part of, which if we could remember would surely bring us closer to the mysteries of creation.

The birth of life – what greater feat is there in the universe? What greater initiation? And all the while this is happening, when we are being 'dreamt' into existence, or dreaming ourselves, we are in the centre of another person's being, our mother; connected to her through the umbilical cord at our navel. As soon as we are born, this cord is cut and we no longer truly exist at the centre of the world, we have been born into another.

Psychologists, beginning with Freud, have spoken of a desire to return to the womb being a primal urge within the human, particularly male, psyche. Indeed, many have associated the ecstatic spiritual or mystical experiences as being merely echoes of what we felt in the womb, especially those that describe oceanic feelings of oneness with all.

These people suspiciously view these experiences and sometimes the whole of spirituality itself as really the desire to regress psychologically back to the womb, to a state where we were floating in a watery kingdom, not separate or alone as we are here, and with all our needs and desires being met by our mother.

But what if an ongoing experience of being at the centre of existence, not separate from a greater life than our own, one that supports and feeds us in our every basic need for growth, was essential to our wellbeing as humans? What if that extraordinary experience of initiation, the very growth into being within the womb, was meant to be re-experienced here on earth albeit it in a different, more expansive, way – a way in which this connection was not to another human, i.e. our mothers (or partners or lovers and other surrogates), but rather to the earth itself?

If this was the case, then it would make sense, or more importantly be essential to basic primal needs of survival, to know where the navel of the earth was. It would also be essential to have a meaningful relationship with it, both physically through being able to travel there and celebrate its existence, and spiritually/metaphorically through story, myth and ceremony.

What if this need to orientate ourselves, to be able to grow out of our connection to the earth, was one of the essential parts of being human and alive on this planet? To explore this further, we can look at what perhaps happens when that connection isn't there; a situation we very much find ourselves in now in the modern world.

It isn't too hard to observe today the spiritual malaise that

seems to infect modern life as we become more and more disconnected from nature. This is reflected in the physical environment
that surrounds us. Consider the changes the earth appears to be
going through as extreme weather patterns or events become the
norm; the loss of so many creatures to extinction and the
destruction of the world's forests; a pile of rubbish the size of
Britain free floating in the Pacific Ocean; pollution on a level that
we cannot even properly comprehend; the wiping out of so many
of the indigenous peoples who do live close to and in harmony
with nature; a nuclear plant in Japan that was brought down by
an earthquake and is poisoning the water; poisons going into our
food supply; polar ice-caps melting and endless predictions of
catastrophic consequences alongside counter arguments that it's
all being made up to keep us in fear.

Images and words relaying these phenomena are being
constantly fed to us. All this I feel weighs heavy on our souls and
has the cumulative effect of disorientating us and compounding
our distrust for nature, for the story now appears to be, even
among those who want to heal the environment by bringing
attention to what is going wrong, that nature is going to either let
us down and not be able to sustain us, or wipe us out as an act of
restoring balance. Either way, it doesn't look too good for
humans.

I spent a long time working for an environmental
campaigning organisation when I was younger and the burn-out
rate among those who worked there was huge. There was also I
noticed a lack of care that people took of themselves, the problem
was always 'out there' and like great warriors they would put
themselves to war with those that were causing the damage.
Unfortunately the destruction that is being wrought on our
environment is felt in our own souls, especially the Body Soul
part, and when we're at war with the destruction we can also be
at war with our own selves.

To explore this further I'd like to describe a healing I did once for a woman who was in the late stages of cancer. She had suffered a lot of loss in her life including a very difficult relationship with her mother. The feeling of distrust and rejection she felt around her mother was very big; it became clear that it needed healing as the spirits guided me to open a channel of communication particularly around forgiveness with her mother's spirit. She was now in the Otherworld, having died previously. This woman had campaigned tirelessly for environmental rights and had achieved extraordinary things in her life; she was a real inspiration to so many people.

I remember someone, who was also on a similar path, talking after the healing about how he feared she had gone past the point of no return, after facing so much pain in her life, around recent discoveries they had made about the real state of the environment. How desperate the situation was and that in many ways it had taken away her hope.

I remember feeling an overwhelming sadness in that moment, similar to what I had felt in the ceremony and healing. The grief I felt wasn't about death or the illness, in many ways the grief *was* the illness. It was about disconnection, a disconnection from a mother's love that is there to support and hold us when we are feeling lost and small and unable to cope with so many problems, our own or the worlds.

It is this unconditional mother's love that is so essential to our wellbeing as humans, it literally keeps us alive. We may not have had the blessing of that from our own birth mother; many people haven't and this usually isn't anything deliberate on the mother's behalf. They may have not felt that deep security in themselves that would have enabled them to give unconditionally, for we can only give what we feel inside ourselves. Or we may have experienced that love, but at some point when we become fully human and adult we have to leave that security behind; we have to separate from our human mother's love.

This is what initiation is about. In indigenous tribes it was often carried out in a big way around adolescence, to ritualise this separation. At times this would be dramatised in spectacular ways as the group of initiators would come and literally tear the young people away from their mothers who would be kicking and screaming. The more they protested, the more the young people would know they were loved. This was all done in a semi-theatrical way as the mothers knew their children would be safe and would return, but they had to act as though they were losing them forever, because in a way they were. When they returned they would be no longer children, but adults in their own right.

However, the important thing here is the initiates were not just separated from their mothers and left alone in the world. This is the perception in our Western individualistic consciousness; that we are somehow alone in the world to battle it out and survive. We will explore the nature of this perception later, but it is a perception that keeps us clinging on to parental or familial ties for too long into adulthood.

In contrast, in indigenous cultures, the love and security that was provided by the mother was replaced by teaching the young people to connect with the earth as their true Mother. All the ceremonies and rituals would ultimately be about emphasising this relationship, so the young people knew that whatever they did in life, wherever they went, they would have this relationship with the Mother to fall back on when they needed it. They would be safe.

They would also be taught the responsibility they had towards the Mother as a being that needed constant feeding back and respecting. This also involved learning about how to respect her limits that provided danger in the environment. However, ultimately the earth, the Mother, was seen as a nurturing, loving force. We have lost that, we are disconnected at our navels from that vital support system.

Many people who take on the world's problems do so in a way that assumes a responsibility for them. This is understandable as they look around and often think that no one else is taking this stuff seriously or even acknowledging it: 'No one is taking responsibility for what is happening, so it's up to me then. I need to get the message out there.' For anything to change we need people to be doing this. It's essential that we are to wake up to some of these realities of how our destructive actions are affecting the planet we reside on. Many people are being catalysts for this.

However, when I go into the energy bodies of many of those who are involved in such activities, the darkness and conflicts of the world are often held in there and alongside this darkness are usually feelings of helplessness and heavy emotions such as grief or rage. It is these emotions that are frequently holding the conflicts in place.

Thus, the battle 'out there' is reflected internally. Often, the important thing is that it hasn't been resolved inside. This means that finding resolution or solutions in the outer world becomes extremely difficult, as the outer world will always reflect what is inside. This isn't to say outer action isn't important, as it is vital if we are to change things. To enhance it though, we can also bring ourselves into inner harmony.

This is one of the tenets of shamanism; nothing happens in the world of everyday reality before it has been 'dreamt' first, i.e. before it has existed in the invisible world of spirit. Spirit comes first, and then it manifests in the physical world. What is alive in our internal energy bodies will be what we then attract in the outer world. It is our imaginations that give birth to the world of form. We will explore this in much more depth in the final section of the book. Indigenous people know this simple truth very well. As John Perkins notes in *The World as You Dream It*, they often look at us in the West or the modern world and say that we have forgotten that all life is a dream and therefore we are creating a nightmare.

I have always had this tendency to let the world's problems

weigh heavy on my soul; most healers or people attracted to this path do. An example of this was back in early 2000, at the beginning of my shamanic journey, when I found myself in the desert in Mexico having gone through quite an intensive spiritual exploration with a group of people. Everyone was very tired, including our teacher, and talk got around to the state of the world. This was a time when the Mayan prophecies around 2012 were reaching popularity and as we were in Mexico and had visited many Mayan sites, they seemed especially relevant.

Most of the talk around the prophecies was emphasising some kind of cataclysmic change, something along the lines of half, if not more, of the population being wiped out and the other half getting instantly enlightened, but having to leave the earth to exist on some other plane. I just felt an overwhelming sense of sadness and helplessness at all this talk. I liked the earth and didn't want to leave even if enlightenment was on offer and I certainly didn't want to be wiped out!

To try to resolve these feelings I took myself off deep into the desert to be alone. Except I wasn't alone out there in the wilderness, I was far less alone than I felt inside the camp. There's something truly magical when you can get so deep into nature that everywhere you look (and in the desert you see for what seems like forever) there is no sign of human life or human impact on the environment.

Out there, in that vast wilderness, feeling small and vulnerable, I just broke down with all my frustrations and grief over the destructive path that seemed to be set forth for the world. This was compounded by all the environmental work I had done and the fear for our future this had engendered.

However, as I expressed to the earth all the pain and sadness that was in my heart, I was suddenly struck with just how beautiful and vast the world really was. There was something in the threat (real or perceived) of losing the world that paradoxically connected me once more to it. It was my grief that took me into it, as grief often can.

I realised in that moment that there was still so much of nature untouched, like this desert, and through a connection with that vast landscape my heart burst open as I could feel the invisible power of it surge through me. I was just a tiny part of the world, yet the power of the whole of nature was also within me. I knew then that this power could heal itself, there was easily enough of it to transform our environments and remedy the damage caused by humans. We just have to know that power within ourselves first and not be scared of it.

I then had a vision that I wanted to be part of this healing, not in a grandiose way of saving the planet as I had always dreamed of, but rather in helping people to experience and be healed by the power of the nature that I could feel flowing me. It was this vision that led me to do the work I do today.

If we are able to heal ourselves and our connection with the earth, then we can heal the earth. Or, more accurately, become a part of *its* healing. In that way we don't have to take responsibility for the problems of the earth, because the problems really live inside us. We're not the bosses of nature, nature is our boss. Or, rather it is our Mother and if we can surrender and really learn to trust our Mother, all can be well because everything will then follow its own natural course.

Indigenous cultures understand this subtle and interdependant interaction between the outer environment and inner world of humans very well.

As John Perkins also notes, many cultures would practice 'singing up the sun' in the morning and this process continues today, especially after all-night ceremonies. In this simple action of singing a sacred song to help the sun rise, they would then become part of and immersed within the creation process of the world. They would celebrate and be reminded of the awesome power of the earth, the extraordinary miracle that is a new day.

I have done this many times. I have stayed up all night facing all the mysteries and strange fears that the unknown of the night can bring, touching the raw essence of my primal nature, then calling to the sun as it rises in the morning, feeling its warmth and life-giving properties, and feeling as if I was witnessing and present at the very dawn of creation. Everything is renewed in those moments. I feel reborn and the world feels reborn with me.

Some ancient cultures believed that if they didn't continue to be active in this process of welcoming the sun with their song and renewing the world, then the world would die. I used to consider this idea a lot without being able to understand it, as my rational mind would argue that we've stopped being part of such a process of 'singing up the sun' millennia ago and yet the world is surviving fine.

Then something in me realised, as I looked around, that a part of the world has died, both inside and outside us. It may take time for the physical, manifest reality to catch up, but when we stop 'feeding the sacred' as Martin Prechtel puts it, through this active process of renewing ourselves and reconnecting to the creative power of nature, then life and nature (the sacred manifest) will stop feeding us. This is both a practical and a deeply spiritual consideration.

This is where our disconnection from the earth and from feeling it feed us through our navels is also felt. There are many people, perhaps the majority, who seem to ignore that the world has any problems at all and are completely cut off from its pain. Yet, it is being this cut off that causes so many of our modern illnesses and problems.

To explore this we only have to look at our relationship with those everyday necessities that keep us alive. We stand on the brink of the potential for many food, water and power shortages in the not-too-distant future. Particularly regarding food, people are talking of a slowly ticking time bomb as the world's reserves are depleted from over-farming and unexpected weather patterns. So why do we continue to farm the earth in such destructive ways or consume and waste so much food when we know that this is unsustainable?

A part of the answer may be that on a simple psychological level the relationship between what we ingest in terms of food and the wider environment of which we are a part has been lost. Our food comes in neat packages from a supermarket that we can travel to in our car, surrounded by other humans, without even coming close to nature in the whole process. We can then forget very easily that it is nature that has essentially provided us with what sustains us. We think it's the human who supplied us. And, as already has been mentioned, humans can be very forgetful. It is this that gets us into the most trouble.

When we do forget this relationship, it then becomes very easy to dismiss or ignore entirely on an unconscious level the fact that our negative impact on the earth could have a negative effect on our own wellbeing – the intimate relationship between the two having being lost. There is that famous quote attributed as a Cree proverb that sums this up well: 'Only when the last tree has died and the last river has been poisoned and the last fish been caught will we realise we cannot eat money.' Such simple profundity cuts to the heart of the issue we face.

We have to get back that relationship, because no matter how much we can understand intellectually that our actions could have consequences on our environments, unless we truly can feel the relationship between nature and ourselves and our dependency upon it, know it both conscious and unconsciously, it becomes very difficult to act upon.

Ideas have to be felt, in the heart or in the gut, before they are truly acted upon with any conviction for change, for it is the heart and the gut (through the navel) that really connects us to the earth and this part of our soul through our connection with our own bodies. And it is our bodies that contain our very measures for survival. Otherwise, everything becomes just more information for the brain to struggle to process. The mind devoid of its relationship with the body has only limited power. And it is here we can get overwhelmed and start to feel completely helpless.

I remember one time helping to skin a deer that a bushcraft friend of mine had brought back to our home, having recovered it dead from the roadside. The body was still warm and, as we cut into it in a respectful way, I felt an overwhelming reverence for this creature that retained its beauty even in death. Seeing and touching the blood and all the organs – the heart, lungs, kidneys and liver – I was struck on a fundamental level how similar I was to this deer. Also, seeing where the car had made impact and the resulting trauma wound where the blood had darkened intensely, I was aware how fragile life is. I was also aware, in a visceral way, of how the memory of trauma, be it physical or emotional (for the darkening was a result of the deer releasing so much adrenaline) is carried in the blood and can infect the whole system as it travels around the body.

I found it an intensely spiritual moment as we gathered all parts of the animal – the skin, bones and sinew – to be used for making tools later and the meat to be cooked as a feast for friends. When blood is in your hands and you can feel how death gives birth to life, then avoidance becomes more difficult.

On a personal level, if this relationship between nature and what we consume isn't truly felt, then it can feed a kind of insatiable hunger in individuals. When we eat, part of what we are seeking is sustenance from the earth, as we got from our birth mothers when she shared her milk with us or further back, what we received through our navel in the womb. It was far more than just a physical act when we were fed by our mother. The act of unconditional giving and love (hopefully) was a vital ingredient. (Sometimes we received a whole load of other emotions that our mothers may have been holding onto through that connection, many of which it can take a lot of healing to release.)

Yet when food comes out of a packet and is totally divorced

from any connection with nature, or the very concept that we need a connection with the earth to sustain us isn't even there, that essential invisible ingredient of love and nurturing is missing.

The level of hunger in the modern world is enormous despite being the most fed we've ever been in history. People are constantly trying to fill these holes in themselves with food, drink or other physical substitutes such as sex, money or consumer goods. We are, as a society, quite addicted. Why else would we always need more of everything, usually far more than we could ever need? Yet, have you ever noticed how good food tastes, how the most simple of meals can be so nourishing, when we are outside, camping for a few days, or on a beach or park in summer? This is even more true if they are cooked on an open fire.

What constitutes the physical components of what we experience in life is only a small representation of a much larger reality and when it comes to healing the soul, can only go a small way towards effective treatment. It is what lies beneath that is important. If we are to heal this relationship with the earth, our own bodies and effectively face the problems that seem ready to beset us in terms of changing environments, we are going to have to begin this process of recentring ourselves on the earth again, through our navels and this part of our souls. In this we have to open up to that sacred relationship with nature, to feel and then understand the role she plays as our Mother, the true provider of our sustenance and welfare.

Chapter Two

Acknowledging and Healing the Wound of Separation

I feel there is first something important that we need to acknowledge, and that is that life is a wounding experience. From the moment we are born, the experience of pain is never that far away, from the first gasp of life and the scream that invariably accompanies it, throughout our existence.

Every person will suffer loss at some point in their lives: of those they love, their ideals and dreams, faith, innocence, their illusions, perspective, belief in themselves, belief in love, at times even their minds or souls. And eventually everyone will lose the precious gift that was gifted them at birth, their lives. This is one of the simple and hauntingly beautiful aspects of life as a human, we are all aware on some level that we will one day die.

All will be gone, all will eventually be lost. Great civilisations, cultures, species all will at some point return to the earth. This is something we cannot insulate ourselves from. No matter how great our technologies, no matter how much we cut ourselves off from our emotions and no matter how many times we turn our face from it. This truth is there awaiting us every time crisis invades our lives and we're reminded how fragile life is and just how much things are really out of our control.

It is in these moments that the fantasies we create or buy into, that sell us the illusion we'll always be safe, come crashing down. The illusion is that pain won't be ours as long as we believe enough in one thing or another: our parents, our children, our nation state, our religion, the afterlife, our philosophies, our leaders, our jobs, the products that we buy, ourselves as individuals.

When this illusion is crushed, quite often our minds turn to existential worries and it is in these moments that I often see people for healings. In the face of loss, be it of a person, a relationship, a belief system, a job, a self-image, health, it is amazing how quickly people's thoughts turn to those primal fears we all carry within us. It is as though any loss can quickly destroy that illusion of invincibility we may hold about ourselves.

If I was to peel back the layers of the individual stories of those who come to see me for healings in these situations, there are two main fears that stand out. The first is that of losing one's mind, usually when the emotional trauma being experienced is overwhelming. The second is of losing one's physical health; for when people are in the highly emotional states that loss brings, they usually become highly sensitised to their body and any symptoms of pain become exaggerated and very fear inducing. Also, loss reminds us intensely of our own mortality. Very often there is a mixture of both as people swing between these two painful extremes.

The above symptoms may go on for years to the point that when people seek healing; they may not even connect what they are going through to the loss or trauma they have experienced. Often they judge it as some kind of medical problem, a lack of the right chemicals in the brain or an inability for a part of their body's organism to work properly. This is no surprise as the DSM-5, the psychiatric model/bible used to diagnose mental illness, now officially recognises 'excessive grief' as a mental disorder. The amount of anti-depressants prescribed when people are in mourning is huge, which suggests that culturally we see it as a brain problem that can be fixed.

However, it is the shaman's job to look deeper. When I see people who are going through intense personal crisis in their lives and have very real fears for their mental or physical wellbeing, it usually doesn't take much probing to discover that the trigger was some kind of past loss or trauma and an inability to deal with the resulting pain.

There is a place that exists in people's energy bodies just above the navel that I like to call 'the void'. This is a very real place though it is not often felt or experienced as it can be buried under a lot of distractions. However, when people are going through the intense healing or initiatory crises we are describing, it often becomes very prominent. It is an intensely dark place energetically, a bit like I imagine dark matter or black holes might feel like. Indeed this void very much has the feeling and quality of a black hole about it, as it suggests something so primordial, mysterious and endless. Part of my job as a healer is often to heal people's relationship with this void and at times take them through it.

However, understandably, their resistance to it is huge. It is a place that going to on an emotional level feels beyond the fear of death even, it is the fear of complete annihilation. This is the place that people often face when they are going through a healing crisis. It is as though they are suddenly awakened to the certainty that they will have to at some point face this place, in life or in death. And it is the avoidance of the void that keeps people locked into a place of existential and emotional trauma.

I remember having to go through this void on the fourth time I undertook a burial ceremony. This ceremony involves digging a grave about two feet deep, and then being put inside. The grave is then covered by wooden slats, with blankets on top of these that shut out all light and then a whole load of earth piled on top of the blankets until you are completely encased under the ground. The purpose of it is to reconnect to the earth, the Mother, in a deep visceral way.

The idea of spending a night completely encased beneath the earth, however, is one that fills me with dread as it can be intensely claustrophobic and it doesn't seem to get easier over time. I was doing this burial to prepare myself for taking other people through this rite as I hadn't done one for a while and wanted to re-experience it personally. I had a shamanic friend of mine, my best mate, to hold the ceremony from above ground and support me.

The mistake I made after having been in the grave for quite a while, was to fall asleep. I had actually been enjoying myself up to that point feeling that Mother's love all around me. However, when I awoke I was completely bewildered as to where or who I was. There's something intensely unnerving about opening your eyes on waking and because of the absolute blackness still not being able to see anything. I was gripped by a primal terror. This went into my body immediately and triggered what I could feel as the beginning of one of the violent fits that had haunted me previously. In a moment of pure instinct I screamed to my friend to let me out.

Luckily and before I had the time to somehow force my way out (it's amazing what strength we can find in those moments) he was there immediately to remove the mud and wood that formed the lid of the grave. God knows what my face must have looked like because his looked pretty shocked as he reached in to help me out. I couldn't be still though, such was this terror gripping me, and I literally had to run around the woods for a while like a mad man, before finally heading back to the fire he had built to support me from.

I couldn't speak for a long while until the adrenaline wore off and I came back to some kind of human awareness. Luckily, my friend just sat there, supporting me without attempting to bring me back or rescue me from the place I had gone to and after a long time and in a moment of exquisite healing, he just asked simply: 'Do you want an apple?' We both suddenly burst into laughter as he handed me the ripe, red fruit as the intensity of the situation gave way to absurdity. Man, did that apple taste good!

As I sat there, regaining my sense of self, with the sugar from the fruit and the warm flames of the fire calming me, for all the life of me feeling like I was never going to set foot in another grave or even think about doing any kind of shamanic ceremony ever again; I was suddenly struck by the realisation that I had to go back in, that there was something I had to face in that grave. I was quite calm as I told to my friend, his face then repeating the shocked look that had greeted me when I'd got out. But he didn't question me and instead led me to the grave and reburied me.

The fear was intense as I was covered over again. Another unnerving sensation is hearing heavy clumps of earth raining down of the lid of your own, albeit temporary, coffin. Yet I knew I had to face that fear and as I lay there, my body beset by terror, and time began to meld into a singular moment in the darkness, something in my awareness brought me to the void. I knew then it was facing this deep sense of annihilation, lurking in the shadows of my consciousness, I had been running from a lot of my life. I also knew that in that moment, I had no choice; this is what I had to face.

So, I did what I always do in situations like this – prayed for my life; prayed to spirit to somehow help me. I then turned all my attention, all levels of my awareness, to that void; surrendering any hope, belief or control, to face that pure blackness and the madness I felt that lay within it. It is a madness that had haunted me for a lot of my life.

Paradoxically, as has happened before to me, in an act of total surrender I travelled through the void, through the meaningless and nothingness and darkness, the sense of annihilation I had known so well in times of pressure and emotional meltdown in my life. Then I experienced, on the other side, what I can only describe as the face of God – pure light and pure love. I was overtaken once more by pure ecstasy that coursed through my being.

This cycle of facing and going through the void, then experiencing unity and oneness, is one that has framed a lot of my spiritual journey. It is what began it all and has been my biggest

teaching. It seems to me, again and again, that through disso-
lution comes oneness, but this is something that has to be experienced over and over and cannot be learnt theoretically. Or, to put
it another way, God always seems to show up in the strangest of
places.

This is what makes the burial ceremony so powerful, but it
can go even further and heal debilitating physical illnesses. In
2013 a participant (C) on the initiations I run came to the course
with multiple illnesses and physical disabilities: fibromyalgia,
ME, hyper-mobility, chronic pain syndrome, chronic fatigue,
degenerative disease of the spine, ADHD and hypothyroidism.
This meant that C arrived in the woods where the trainings are
held only being able to walk with the aid of two canes. She
couldn't sit for more than 20 minutes without falling into sleep
and her body was in constant and debilitating pain. Although
relatively young, her life was only going in one direction, of
greater physical disability and she was understandably scared
where this would lead. She was on a cocktail of drugs and
constant medical supervision, but nothing seemed to be proving
effective.

C also, as is often the way with these illnesses, had been
through a very dark time emotionally and psychologically in the
previous year, culminating in a suicide attempt. This course,
which takes place over six months in the depths of the woods
with very little home comforts and which involves a stripping
down of the soul, was then going to be very challenging for her
on every level. However, she was determined to explore the
underlying causes of her illnesses to heal herself and follow her
dream of exploring this pathway more deeply.

When it comes to the burial, everyone has to dig their own
grave, which is a mental and physical challenge in itself. I offered
to help C, but she refused even though she was in incredible pain
doing so and could barely make the necessary imprints in the
earth. Part of the intention of the burial is to leave everything

that we're hanging onto, everything that makes us sick, in the ground. To give it back to the Mother so that she can take our 'shit' and transform it into fertiliser. C later told me she had taken this intention deeply to heart and that every time her spade hit the earth she committed to leaving all that was making her physically sick in earth, to rid herself of her illnesses.

After a long night she completed her initiation, but when we helped C out of the grave in the morning, almost immediately her whole body completely seized and she couldn't stand, as would often happen, as this was one of the symptoms of her illness. I could feel her intense disappointment as we held her paralysed body upright at the mouth of the grave, for this was exactly what she had gone in the grave to release. She was angry and in her despair, shouted to the forest: 'I was meant to leave this fucking crap in there!'

However, after taking a moment to calm herself, she then took deep a breath and with a focus of will I've rarely seen in my life, said: 'No, this isn't going to defeat me! I am going to walk out of this grave.' I and my assistant offered to carry her, but she refused. We stood, as if frozen in time for what was probably only a moment, but seemed like a lifetime, and then something quite magical happened and her whole being suddenly relaxed and let go and she started walking, gingerly, towards the fire that had been burning all night to support those in the ground. She made it unaided to that fire.

From that moment, C threw away both canes she was using, and walked on her own. A couple of months later she had halved her medication and by the end of the course she was being signed off by her doctor, who couldn't quite understand or believe what was happening. Indeed, by the end of the six months she looked like a completely different person, as she was. She was also able to get her driving licence back, which had been taken away due to the fact she could be affected by a seizure at any time. She had got her life back, which previously had been heading in only one direction, that of more and more disability.

C was able to do this and heal herself so fundamentally, not just through the power of the ceremonies. These supported and held her in her journey providing the necessary framework, but mainly it was because of her intention to face, go through and release the pain that was manifesting in her body as debilitating physical sickness.

She had to face her void of nothingness; it had literally taken over her whole life and was threatening to consume her. Yet, at the same time, she had absolute faith in the power of shamanism and in the invisible power of the Mother to heal her, to literally take the sickness from her. And so she was healed.

When people are facing their own voids it often calls for them to have the deepest faith. A lot of the time that is all that they have. Faith lies at the core of all spiritual healing and spiritual healing, I would say, lies at the core of *all* healing.

The Lakota Holy Man Fools Crow, one of the most powerful medicine men of the 20th century, talks a lot about this in the excellent book on healing, *Fools Crow: Wisdom and Power*. He outlines the main difference between the Indian and the white man when he says that the Indian 'believes to see' where the white man has to 'see to believe'. It is an important and fundamental difference, as the believing to see takes enormous amounts of faith.

It is that lack of belief, in magic, mystery and the miracles that faith can bring that affects us so much in the modern world. We will explore the power of belief and faith for the positive and negative in the upcoming chapters. This is why healing in this way can sometimes take longer than conventional medicine because people need to be shown that such magic exists and healing is possible. Trust has to be built up, which can take time. This is especially true when people are going through intense crisis because, even if they may have had some kind of faith at different times in their life, when they are beset by the pain of loss or sickness, when they are facing their void, this can be tested to its limit and often is lost. It is almost as if when we need it the most, our faith goes missing.

Why is this? Part of the answer might be that one of the perennial rationales used to justify a disbelief in the existence of God, or indeed in any benevolent force in the universe, is that if God exists how come there is evil, pain or suffering in the world? It's much easier to believe in God when things are going well. Yet this question, naïve as it is, is only relevant if we have been sold the illusion in the first place that life *shouldn't* contain pain or suffering. Where in the world did this illusion come from? It certainly couldn't be based on any empirical data or even a faint observation of the evidence!

We find it increasingly difficult in the modern world to accept that life does contain suffering and a whole host of negative experiences without jumping to the conclusion that something must be wrong somewhere. You can see that in the way we jump from one relationship to the next or one distraction to another, desperately seeking that strange phenomenon called happiness that will in our minds insulate us from our pain.

People make a lot of money in all kinds of different arenas, including the spiritual, selling this idea. We see the presence of pain as proof that we are either alone in an uncaring universe, or that somehow we have sinned and upset the benevolent force and therefore must spend our whole lives atoning for it. A lot of religions have been very much based on this principle.

But what if pain was a vibrant, necessary and deeply meaningful part of existence? What if we allowed pain to take us deeper into life, closer to the void and closer then to God (or whatever name you might have for the love at the heart of life)? It is our scars, worn proudly, that mark our initiations and bring us closer to the earth, closer to life. As a woman will bleed every month in order to be able to have the opportunity to give birth to life, so must we all suffer and give something of our essence in order to become closer to, and a part of, the magical, creative source.

A lot of indigenous ceremonies are based upon this principle. Take the Sun Dance as practiced by various North American tribes, for example. In this festival, one that is undertaken to ensure health and vitality for the people of the tribe as a whole, warriors pierce themselves and then hang from a central sacred column by these piercings until their skin is ripped off. They also fast and dance for four days continually. It is in their great sacrifice that the warriors petition the creator to look kindly upon the rest of the tribe for the following year and although it is physically, emotionally, mentally and spiritually gruelling, it is seen as a great honour to be chosen to undertake this ceremony.

This follows the basic principle that for anything to live in this world, something has to die or to give of itself, that something could be a fruit, an animal, a vegetable or a human. This is the cycle of life. Thus the warriors give of their blood, they sacrifice their wellbeing, and through that process they die and are reborn – to assist the community to also die and be reborn so it can be renewed.

Almost all shamanic ceremony, the way I see it, should involve this basic principal of giving something of ourselves – often our sweat, tears, blood, fears, physical endurance, time or just simply our love. For, when we do give these things willingly and freely, so the value of life increases manifold. It is no longer something we are separate from. We have an emotional and visceral bond with it, felt deeply in our bodies. We know what it costs us. We have felt and grieved each loss and through continued sacrifice we remain an active part of the creation process.

This is not done out of guilt, however, which is the essential point. This way of sacrifice has been manipulated too much by religions. Guilt usually separates us from our emotions and our bodies. It has the same Latin root as 'beguile', which means to deceive usually through subterfuge. When I encounter excessive guilt in energy bodies it is usually covering and hiding much more potent emotions such rage or heavy grief.

Therefore when we give of ourselves through guilt the giving isn't really done by our whole being, it is done by the part of us that is feeling guilty, which is hiding part of our true emotional self. Instead our sacrifices should be acts of love, then we can give fully and completely of ourselves. This, in turn, allows the universe to respond in kind.

To do this I feel we must acknowledge this pain of separation that greets us at birth, the pain of being cut off at the navel from our source – the pure essence of spirit that we were before we arrived in a human body, which can now be felt through the earth. Through acknowledging it and allowing the pain of it to seep deep into our being, not hiding or seeking to distract or cover it paradoxically, through the pain, we can then become more connected to that we have been separated from.

The pain can then take us closer to the earth and by becoming closer to the earth we are able to feel the spiritual sustenance that connects us once more to our source. As one of my teachers said to me: 'Nature is the visible face of spirit.'

Every birth contains the seed and pain of death; every death contains the seed and ecstasy of birth, and vice versa. Life then becomes sacred on its own terms, without the conditions of redemption or some kind of end to suffering, for there is no end point, just a continuing cycle. This is the way that we might perceive it, were we to examine nature, and use the cycle of the seasons, the continuous way nature gives birth to itself and is dying, as inspiration.

This is another paradox of being human, we live as part of nature, subject to its rules: the limits of our bodies; death as a definition of life. Yet we're constantly influenced and pressured by our restless minds and spirits, our imaginations, the parts of us that know no limitation. In the modern world, while we underplay the power of our thoughts and imaginations in helping to create the reality that surrounds us, we seem to be at the constant beck and call of their fluctuations. How to exist within the parameters of these apparent conflicting opposites then becomes the exploration and food for our journey into healing and initiation. It is the grit of the road.

Chapter Three

Reconnecting to our Wild Instinctual Natures

In accepting and getting to know the nature of life here on the earth and allowing our wounds to take us into a deeper relationship with it, we can then allow ourselves to come closer to that much-maligned part of us: our wild, instinctual nature; our primal self.

To begin with let's consider this viewpoint: when a pack of wolves hunt then tear apart their prey in an ecstasy of bloodlust, this is as sacred an act as when we build temples and worship in them. More so in fact, for when the wolves kill their prey, they are helping to keep in balance the delicate ecosystem that sustains life here. Wherever wolves have been hunted out of existence, deer and other prey of theirs overpopulate, destroying much flora and fauna, which in turn has a knock-on effect, taking the food and habitat of a lot of other animals and insects. The world then becomes a lesser place.

In contrast, when we build our temples, we are taking from the earth the raw materials and changing the environment. If this isn't done with sensitivity, then it could begin the process of expansion, ever upwards and onwards fed by that part of the human spirit that struggles with limits. Our temples may come in different forms nowadays yet they still are the places we go to worship, even if it is to the gods of commerce and money. It is remarkable how the towers and skyscrapers mimic the ascendency of church spires, as if we're always trying to get as close to the sky and heaven as we can and as far away from the earth as possible.

Whose then is the more sacred an act? The wolf, sustaining and ensuring the balance of life or the human who seeks to take and build? Perhaps both, in their own ways, both seeking to, in different ways, keep the spirit of life alive. But whereas the wolf will not judge, nor seek to destroy absolutely the human, the human is very capable of doing the same to the wolf.

In fact the human, driven by hate, can murder quite efficiently six million of his fellow beings. In those moments we say that people lose their 'humanity'. However, I would suggest the opposite; that they don't lose their humanity, rather they lose connection to their animal and earthy natures. A counterintuitive view maybe, as we usually project human violence onto nature, people are said to be 'acting like animals'. Yet the murdering of six million, as with a lot of acts of modern warfare, is usually undertaken in very cold and clinical ways.

When this happens, all the anger, hatred, resentment and desire for vengeance that drive these acts remain buried under a mask of so-called 'civilisation' and are justified through rhetoric and rationale. This means that these destructive forces, which take people over and compel them to commit such acts, can be so incredibly long lasting and still remain unfulfilled. There is something in their nature that means they eventually eat up their host and so can never be fulfilled by any action 'out there' in the world.

No matter how many lives are destroyed, no matter how much 'blood-letting' occurs, the inner hatreds are never relieved, because they are never directly addressed. The poison is never released as it is always seen to be 'out there' and is projected upon whoever the enemy is. It is interesting that a figure like Hitler was literally being eaten up as his whole body was racked in constant pain; he was addicted to amphetamines and other drugs that masked the symptoms.

In contrast, pure aggression – as the wolves embody on their hunt – tends to be short lasting and burns itself out quite quickly. It has a very specific use in nature, as mentioned before by keeping the whole of creation in balance, and once the object of their desire, their hunger, has been sated, there is no need for the wolf to carry on killing. Even if it isn't, the wolf will often give up and wait to fight another day. If humans were able to embody ritually some of these forces, it could be the same and they could be released much more quickly.

Indigenous peoples recognise the potential for these natural destructive emotional energies fed by the survival instinct getting caught in the human. This is because they can mix with the human mind, which can confuse these instincts of aggression and domination and then add to them 'stories', which can eventually lead to whole belief systems being built around these stuck energies.

Take, for example, the need to embark on ethnic cleansing to rid a society of the 'disease' that is attacking it from within, or the lesser everyday racism and fear-based ideologies that blight communities. These could be seen to come from these natural aggressive energies being blocked and then coming out in twisted, ideological forms, driven by hatreds and prejudices.

The real disease that these stuck destructive emotions cause, felt within, is then projected out there onto people who are different and therefore easy to fear. No amount of appealing to reason or educating people not to hate will release these energies, as they will always go into the shadow and infect the weakest in the society – usually the poorest or people on the fringes.

Alternatively, consider the belief that there is powerful group of people controlling the whole world that needs to be defeated, or, again on a lesser everyday level, the idea that there are poisonous people in our lives we have to rid ourselves of. Again, what is inside that is being perceived in the outer world? Whether these beliefs are 'true' in a real sense is irrelevant, as they may well be. It is the effect they have on the host, the one believing them, which is important, and that is usually to disempower them into believing that it is something 'out there' that has to be got rid of while the inner poisons are ignored or held onto.

Whereas an animal will relieve its destructive urges through instinct, we have to channel many of them through the mind and the socialisation processes that the mind gives birth to. Civilisation is one of those socialisation processes of the mind that has gone to an extreme. Tribal peoples, recognising this, created very specific ceremonies and rituals to ensure that, when these powerful destructive forces become stuck inside, as is normal and human, they can be released and the individual or society is cleansed.

Some of these ceremonies involve taking plants that will cause the person to vomit out the poisons continually or they may involve, through dance ceremonies of wild, ecstatic abandon, actually embodying some of these natural forces and then releasing them back into the earth. In these moments it is then possible to become a part of and at one with the destructive forces of nature as well as the creative forces. They are both honoured.

We will explore some of these ways in more detail later. When these ceremonies are observed or even taken part in by modern Western civilised people, they can be unnerving in their intensity. This is what anthropologists first discovered and found so abhorrent when they studied tribal peoples and what they considered to be their 'savage' ways. Even nowadays, people who study and practice shamanism still often overlook the darker aspects of indigenous spirituality and tend to want to practice a sanitised version.

In many ways there is a profound weakness/disease in the modern human, that in turning away from and judging the destructive side of nature so harshly we actually perpetrate acts of 'evil' on a far greater scale than the nature we judge. Part of the reason we see ourselves as somehow separate or different from the rest of creation is, I feel, because since the advent of Western civilisation with the Greeks we have turned away from that wild instinctual nature within ourselves. We have gradually turned away from our bodies and in doing so have disconnected ourselves from the rest of nature.

The solar power of logos has been the one we worshipped and, with the advent of Christianity, we then took that further by 'throwing God up into the sky and burying the Devil in the basement'. All aspirations have been about ascension, this has been the religious/cultural story for a long time. Everything to do with the earth and its natural processes within us was seen as dark and evil, while the heavens were worshipped.

It is often similar today when people talk of being 'spiritual', as it is 'light' and transcendent philosophies that are over-emphasised. Some people took this to an extreme around 2012 with the Mayan prophecies, when they talked about human beings going through a period of evolution whereby we would all suddenly and spontaneously ascend to the 5th dimension and have no need for our bodies anymore. Yet, if we are separate from the earth, it is easy then to feel alone in an alien universe as explored in the previous chapters, an existential worry that haunts the modern soul.

But why have we done this? Well, part of the reason may be that it is in the body that our most destructive urges live. The body decays and has to face death and the part of the human soul (our Dreaming Soul) that is locked in a battle for immortality by trying to defeat death, doesn't like this, so has separated from it. We turn our faces from it, in an attempt to deny the very fact that a part of us will decay very slowly and eventually be swallowed up by the earth from whence we came. We will be annihilated; this is the void of the previous chapter that lives inside us and needs to be faced. Again, many modern spiritual paths also continue this avoidance by emphasising the immortal part of our soul and the light and love that we also come from, while denying the 'darkness' of our earthy instincts and desires.

Physical death is an important act of life; we at times contribute to it. Doing so with forethought, or even just by following our natural instincts, we can contribute also to the delicate balance of the eco system we are part of. The irony is that in turning away from death and our so-called destructive urges, or a meaningful and bloody relationship with them, we have perpetrated far greater acts of violence on the human spirit and the physical world than ever before. It has come back to haunt us, as anything denied or repressed always does.

We must get to know and make a home for our violent expressive urges. Only then can we have any hope of mastering them. Or, indeed, finding some kind of peace and sense of home in the natural world. We are what we are, a part of nature.

Chapter Four

The 'Shadow' in Illness

When I was suffering from mental disturbances in my late teens and 20s, I developed a form of OCD or Obsessive Compulsive Disorder they call Pure Obsessional. This involved my mind being invaded by incredibly violent thoughts and impulses at moments seemingly beyond my control. I could be sitting there having a nice conversation with a lover and suddenly the impulse to grab a knife and stab them through the heart would take a hold of me. I would then have a mental image of myself alongside the physical sensation of doing it at the same time. Or, I would be on my own reading and the thought that I could slash my own throat would appear, alongside the horrible feeling in my throat of something cutting across it.

These thoughts and impulses would have the immediate effect of terrifying me. My body would be flooded with adrenaline and my mind would begin to race. Within moments I would be convinced that these impulses had a power over me and that unless I kept absolute control over myself, I would end up carrying them out and suffer the devastating consequences.

It came to a point, when I was younger, that I wouldn't be able to go into the kitchen, with its wide array of knifes on display, without my mind going into a complete meltdown and my body being racked with intense fear. The knives would haunt me as I tried to get on with just the simplest of tasks, as if they were somehow compelling me to carry out a murderous attack on myself or others.

This would then bring about, alongside the fear, the most excruciating feelings of shame. How could I have such thoughts or impulses? I thought of myself as a kind, reasonable person and yet having these thoughts would convince me that I must be evil.

Or, rather something evil lurked inside of me and unless I somehow got rid of it or pushed it down, it would take over and destroy my life. I became convinced I had to protect everyone, including myself, from these thoughts. And because I tried so desperately to push them down or fight them with logic and reason, these thoughts and impulses then began to gradually take over my whole life. They became obsessional.

Another type of these obsessional thoughts would come if I felt strange sensation in my body, like a tingling in my arm, which would then lead straight to the belief that I was dying. I would become convinced I had something seriously wrong with me, like a heart problem or something else terminal. It was as if the 'evil' would be about to strike from within and death could then take me at any moment. Unless I somehow held on to life or got rid of the disease inside of me, I would die.

It got to the point that I remember being terrified of going to sleep at night, as losing consciousness meant losing control and I became obsessed with the idea that I would never wake up again. I became hyper vigilant and it felt like whatever was happening around me – which was usually nothing out of the ordinary – I was involved in a battle of my life. Fear and death stalked me constantly and filled my body and mind with terror.

These moments would strike out of nowhere until they completely dominated my whole waking life. When it was at its worst, it felt like I was haunted 24 hours a day, as I would wake from what little sleep I managed with my first thought of the day being, 'How long before one of these thoughts or impulses will come?' Of course, then one would appear and the rest of the day would be a constant battle with them and the terrifying feelings they invoked.

This battle involved trying to push them away, or reason with them or pretend they didn't exist, or solve where they were coming from. Until, in the end, exhausted, I would break down and have one of the intense fits I described in the introduction.

These episodes would at various times go on for months and years at a time.

The enemy wasn't out there, but inside me; inside my mind. As anyone who has been haunted by their own mind in whatever way will tell you, when your enemy is your own mind, there is no escape. Your tormentor lives inside you. It can appear the most irrational thing in the world to those outside and, indeed, it is irrational. But it is the irrational that lives inside us that can cause so much pain and anguish, especially if we view it, or try to treat it, from a purely rational perspective.

This was why there was little treatment from Western medicine apart from drugs (which I was adamant I didn't want to take) or Cognitive Behavioural Therapy, which can be effective, but didn't work for me. I had to go on a journey to get to the heart of the energy that was behind this intrusion of madness into my life and in doing so, learn not to fear that energy. Because in fearing it, I was feeding it and making it so much stronger.

This was a long, lonely and at times incredibly painful journey, a 'dark night of the soul' if you like. It took patience (though at the time it felt like I didn't have any!) and a willingness to face my own greatest fears – death and/or going mad. I remember I became convinced as I watched programmes that had old people on the TV that I would never reach that age as I would either be consumed by death or madness long before I had any chance of reaching any kind of maturity. This would make me incredibly sad as I would watch as my life seemed to slip by and I had no control or mastery to affect it. And I was still only a young man.

I did have that power, but it was only by turning around to face my darkest demons and learning to surrender and trust that I would be held by something greater than me in this process, that I was able to regain that power. The irony or paradox was that the so-called 'evil' I was running away from, this devil of an illness, actually held the key to the cure for my soul sickness. It took me a long time to discover that on the other side of the fear that was haunting me was ecstasy and power; that the fear was just a gateway. If I stripped away all the stories that my mind had made up around this violent, destructive energy that had entered my life, and just faced the energy of it, the pure, unadulterated fear, it would no longer have a power over me.

Fear is incredibly powerful. This is why leaders manipulate it so much in others because they know it can be used to make human beings achieve extraordinary achievements. Look at what happens when a nation goes to war; the amount of energy that is created as humans build war machines of incredible magnitude and individuals transcend all of their self-perceived limitations in acts of incredible bravery and physical, emotional and mental endurances. Look what Hitler achieved. This may be why war or the intense drama of battle (now often transposed onto human relationships) is on some level appealing to the human spirit. There are many stories of soldiers finding and seeing God on the battlefield.

Those edges of fear and conflict also hold the ecstasy of fully being alive. Fear can wake us up and bring us into the moment, it is designed in nature to bring us into our bodies and all the pleasure and pain that they give birth to. It defines us as human, as opposed to spirit where we come from, and connects us with nature. Imagine a stag, high up on a misty hilltop, its breath loud and visible in the air, about to rut, full of power, full of adrenaline. It is full then of a sensation that we might associate very closely with fear. Fear connects us to our desire, which keeps the world giving birth to itself.

Of course, the deeper you go into it, the more you face and befriend the spirit of fear, you realise that beyond the bodily sensations, it is actually a trickster spirit; that fear as we know and experience it, is just another illusion. However, we cannot experience this by denying or repressing it. It is then we become most in thrall to it and build whole societies dominated by this repression.

Western medicine would say that mental problems such as those that affected me are caused by an imbalance of chemicals in the brain or a misfiring of certain synapses. The shaman, in my view, always looks deeper, exploring such themes as what is out of balance on a soul level that causes this to happen. It is a simple perspective that views the physical chemical imbalances as not a causal factor, but a rather a symptom of a deeper imbalance. Imbalance in the physical body is seen to reflect an imbalance of the soul, which can help us move beyond simple reductionist and rational responses to problems that are highly irrational. Because the whole chemical imbalance thing is only a theory after all and yet it is presented as fact.

Shamanism exists and has a base in the same irrational territory as these problems. The whole of the shamanic universe and world view is built so completely on the irrational (the existence of invisible beings that have such an influence on our lives for example). I feel it is then best suited to explore these irrational and invisible diseases of the mind as, to put it simply, it comes from the same place and engages with the same territory.

It is these problems, as mentioned before, that are reaching something of an epidemic in the modern world and they are not always directly obvious. The amount of physically destructive behaviour that causes so many health problems is far greater than the recorded mental disorders. Addictions, for example, lead people to not only destroy their own lives through alcohol, drugs, food, sex or gambling, but also the lives of those closest to them. These, in my opinion, have a similar cause – a mis-relationship with natural destructive/creative energies inside of us.

Another example is obesity, which threatens modern health hugely. It is surely incredibly irrational to eat in such a way that threatens to destroy the body through ill health. In many of these illnesses we are in the territory of the very modern disease of the human: through their destructive actions destroying the very thing that sustains their life, be it the physical body or the earth itself. To treat this effectively we must look deep into the irrational, into the heart of the Body Soul. But more importantly, I feel, we have to look at the destructive forces that are giving birth to such diseases and really get a handle on the fear that is at the heart of them.

I have been around a lot of mental illness in my life, my own, people very close to me and of course the clients I see on a regular basis. There is a strong strain of schizophrenia running through my family. Indeed, if I had allowed myself to be diagnosed at the height of my problems, I am sure there would have been an element of this much-misunderstood illness in there.

One of the major themes I've observed in people going through mental and emotional disturbances, when I observe them from a shamanic perspective, is the sheer destructive power that seems to take over their entire being. It is like a violent energy surrounds them. It is this energy that usually terrifies them and is at the source of their problems, as it was for me.

People can spend a lot of time and energy, as I did, trying to keep this destructive force under some kind of control or trying somehow to disconnect from it. This, in turn, can lead to extraordinary mental acrobatics. And it's these mental acrobatics that often create belief systems that further alienate the person from reality and themselves, leading quite often to the terrifying thought: 'I'm going mad'. This often indeed appears to be the case as the rational mind tries desperately to keep a lid on, or in some way understand, what is highly irrational.

Beneath it all is this destructive energy that cannot be kept under control as it needs release. This could be a highly personal thing. The person has sat on and repressed their own destructive instincts for many years as they didn't fit into the picture of themselves as kind, reasonable people. Or they were simply just terrified of them. This could involve the repression of powerful emotions such as heavy grief or rage that, when unable to be released, turn toxic. Or, it could be impersonal and the person could be absorbing an incredible amount of destructive energy from their environment. Some people are the proverbial sponges or scapegoats – absorbing everyone else's repressed urges that hang heavy in the environments and then acting them out internally. Very often it is a combination of both.

Traditionally this would be a role that the shaman would take. They would take on the harmful energies of the sick person in a curing ceremony and then release them safely back into nature where they could be reabsorbed and dispersed. They would also do this on behalf of whole communities, which is why if there was anything negative going on in the community, the shamans would often be the first ones to get the blame!

Part of their role was to be the psychic release valves of toxic, negative forces (often powerful repressed emotions or instincts) that blight both individuals and societies. Their training would then instruct them how to meet these energies without doing harm to themselves. A lot of people are still unconsciously fulfilling this role, but without the necessary skills to release the toxicity, thus they are being consumed.

Whatever the cause, the act of trying to control these forces turns them inwards and makes them self-destructive. This can in turn lead to immense shame that exacerbates the problem, as the person suffering is engaged in a huge secret battle to somehow defeat this force inside or outside them. Or they can be acted out in destructive ways to harm the people closest to those who are suffering, which is another form of self-destructive behaviour.

Alongside this often comes the belief that no one else could ever understand what they are going through. This is understandable in a way, because when a person is suffering like this, it can feel like they are engaged in a life-or-death battle for their soul. So who is going to understand this? The professional who diagnoses a chemical imbalance in the brain? This is where talking therapy can be effective as it releases this hidden battle and takes some of the power or the sting out of it.

However, just talking cannot often in itself remove the energy that surrounds the person. Diagnosing the problem and treating the symptoms through medication, although it can offer a temporary relief, doesn't necessarily cure the root of the problem either. What could help is if we look at it through the eyes of the shaman, or the 'one who sees' this energy, the invisible, irrational force that takes over the person's life.

I would describe this force as something that moves into people, like a spirit or a 'demon' that seems to change their whole personality while they are suffering from the illness. I've witnessed this many times, being close to people. One minute they're fine and then suddenly out of nowhere the whole energy shifts, a heaviness enters the room and the person I was just talking to is gone. Instead something else is in their place. The often quoted 'black dog of depression', first observed by Winston Churchill, is an example of this energy personified. It would be like this for me when I was in the midst of the illness. One minute fine, the next this darkness would invade my whole being and I knew that was it. I would be gone and engaged in an inward battle for at least the next couple of hours.

From a shamanic perspective, something is happening that can be observed from a wider angle of perception. On the invisible level what we might call our 'inner demons' are real. They are alive, albeit on an invisible energetic level. Every time I do a healing and go into a person's energy body I usually come across one or two of these. These so-called demons also exist in the outer environment; they are always there being fed by the collective fears of people.

They also, as destructive forces, hold an important place in the environment, as nature exhibits this creative/destructive dynamic constantly. The wolves embody them upon their hunt. They are an important part of the fabric of the reality we inhabit on earth. However, when mixed with the human mind, as explored, they can become incredibly destructive.

Every myth throughout the ages speaks of these aspects of the invisible world and how they interact with the human and natural world. The 'Devil', based on old pagan gods, was an amalgamation of a lot of these demons rolled into one entity. The problem being that instead of being honoured as he would have previously been with rituals and offerings, he was dumped in the basement and denied, repressed and fought at every turn. This ultimately just has the result of feeding him – for if the Devil represents our fears, then by fearing him we're actually feeding him the energy he thrives on – thus making him ever more powerful.

Whereas in the modern psychological age these stories have been often approached from the point of view of metaphors for our inner worlds or for psychological processes, I would suggest that these metaphors are real and they exist both inside *and* outside of us. A spirit teacher once said to me on this subject: 'The metaphor *is* reality and reality is a metaphor.' This is why story, poetry and song often bring us closer to the literal truth than any amount of rational analysis.

Thus, these devils and these demons literally exist; they are just invisible to most people most of the time. However, when chaos enters a person's life through some kind of trauma or breaking down of their idea of reality (this can be the end of a relationship, the loss of a job, home or material security, the death of a loved one, psychic openings through drugs or stress etc.) they can be left open and susceptible to these natural forces, these demons, both inside and outside of them.

These energies don't always create mental illnesses. They can equally become locked in the body and from a shamanic perspective manifest as physical illnesses. These are the viruses that we seek to destroy through increasingly powerful drugs or medical procedures. Yet by doing so we paradoxically end up just creating ever more powerful 'super bugs' or illnesses that we have to then go to war with again. Beneath it all, I would say, is simply the energy of fear and by fighting it we make it ever more powerful.

All this is the diametric opposite of what the shaman does in that the shaman learns to connect with and embody invisible, otherworldly forces that are beneficial to human health, which may live both inside or outside of them. These 'allies' can come in the form of plant spirits, animal spirits, elemental spirits, other nature spirits, ancestral human spirits, gods or the spirit of virtually anything that is beneficial to the human. In the Amazon, Steven Beyer reports how the shamans there work with the spirits of dead Western doctors to help them with curing the illnesses they now encounter – a nice turnaround of our traditional expectation that the indigenous have all the answers and also a sign of their pragmatic approach to curing.[3]

By connecting with these forces the shaman is able to raise their energy to a high enough power to face and kick or tease out these demons we have been talking about. They involve themselves on our behalf to cleanse and remove the offending spirits that are causing the ill health. Or, they are able to transmute the negative energy of the demon into something benign. The shaman is able to do this because they will have faced these demons inside themselves first. They know from personal experience what they feel, taste and smell like; the tricks they play to grab at or distract our attention and the energy of our fears that they feed off.

This is why the path of the shaman/healer involves intense initiations that cause them to face their darkest sides and the darker side of life. This is why they are known as 'wounded healers'. Training can help with this, but in a way the best training is the initiatory illness that they go through. That is why

I feel I went through the soul torment that I did and why probably my best training was the illness in itself. Many people have suffered in similar ways and had to face their own internal and external demons, I'm in no way unique. For me people who have suffered in this way always make the best healers; if they can move through their problems and heal themselves. However, quite often people who have suffered like this feel less inclined though to pronounce themselves as such, as they are often all too aware of their own frailties.

This is why I also feel those working shamanically can be of great healing benefit to the world as it goes through this current initiatory crisis. No amount of focusing on the love and light side of life is going to help this. We need people who have learnt to transmute their own inner demons, or at least learnt to live with them without taking them too seriously. We need these people who can raise their energy and become full of the healing powers to cleanse away some of the excesses of torment that a mis-relationship with fear has generated.

But the removal of these energies doesn't have to just fall to the shaman as, through understanding and strength of spirit, anyone can face these dark forces and most people will have to at some point in their lives. Most people who come to me for healings are indeed doing that, it is my job to assist them and guide them in this, and often literally remove the cause of the torment. However, until the person learns to face some of these forces also themselves, or the underlying causes of them, they can sometimes walk out of the healing and welcome them straight back in. This is why it is important that we all learn not to feed these energies too much with our fears. Indeed, it is what is needed on a global level at the moment I feel.

Let's take the often violent intrusive voices that haunt people with schizophrenia. I heard voices from when I was a child. Probably because I didn't see any problem with them, as they were there as long as I could remember and I never told anyone,

I wasn't so affected by them. Also, on the most part they were quite benign. I would only really hear them at night, just before going to sleep, they would start up and it would be like two or several people having a conversation across the back of my head. They were very distinct from thoughts, and the conversations could be about anything. Usually they were quite banal and they used to actually help me sleep as I would drift off listening to them as someone might a radio.

In a strange way there was something quite comforting about these voices as it meant that I wasn't just stuck with my own thoughts at night, which can be incredibly repetitive and boring. So they were a nice distraction and on some level it meant I wasn't really ever alone. It wasn't until I was speaking to a teacher of mine about someone close to me who was being affected by such voices in a negative way that he suggested that being open to voices wasn't always a good thing as you were 'bumping into all the disconnected parts of everyone'. I decided then to close off to them. Because they had never been a problem to me it was easy to do. I just decided not to hear them and trained my mind in this way by stopping giving them attention and they were gone.

When someone is suffering from schizophrenia, these voices can turn very nasty. It is anything but comforting and they don't appear to have the same power to turn them off. This is because, similar to when I was haunted by the obsessive thoughts, the voices appear to have a power over them and take over their whole being. They begin to dominate their life. It is in many ways, I feel, not the voices themselves, but the nature of the energy behind them that is the problem. It is the destructive energy that invades and destroys the person's life and will be evident in many other symptoms other than the voices or other hallucinatory symptoms.

The shame and fear of being 'mad' can also contribute to the downward spiral of illness. Just the label of being diagnosed as 'schizophrenic', with all of the incredibly violent imagery that has been generated in our culture around it can be incredibly terrifying for people, and deeply shaming. If they then completely lose touch with everyday reality, this is when things can go very wrong. However, it doesn't have to go this far, and often it doesn't.

I was doing a healing for an African lady a while back. She had moved from Africa in her late 20s, trained as a psychotherapist and counsellor and had worked in mental health for many years. We were talking about someone close to her who was struggling and I was explaining my perspective of energies or spirits that can take over people's lives and she said: 'That's *exactly* how we see it back home! If someone is hearing voices we go and listen to them as they could be revealing some important information from the spiritual realms. But I can't say that now when I treat my own patients as they would probably lock me up!'

There was an incredible irony that I, as a Western educated white man, was talking about the nature of illness from a perspective that was so inherent in her culture, yet had since been educated out of her in her work. I know that we now send psychiatrists out to a lot of places in Africa, to 're-educate' the natives from their primitive beliefs in dealing with such illnesses, which conveniently, if you were to be cynical about it, opens up huge markets for the drug companies.

Yet there are other ways to treat these invasive voices or other symptoms and getting to the root of the energy behind them is often the first step. That is not to totally dismiss the drugs, as there may be a time and a place when they are necessary and effective. I often feel that modern medicine alongside traditional can be the best combination in some cases. But what I am interested in here is exploring the root problem of these diseases of spirit.

This is also not in any way meant to diminish the potency of such powerful mental illnesses such as schizophrenia. I am aware also that so called 'spiritual' causality may not always be the best way to approach these things when someone is in the midst of such an illness, as it can add paranoia to an already enflamed imagination. Sometimes people need in the short term the promise of medication and a rational approach to what is an extraordinarily disorientating disease.

There is a huge difference in hearing voices or having other experiences of other realities bleeding into your everyday life and retaining some sense of reality, than being totally engulfed in psychosis. This in many ways marks the difference between the mystic and the madman, a fine but important line. Or the shaman and the mentally ill. There is, however, also a huge cross-over.

If we were to approach something like schizophrenia as an extreme example of an underlying disease in our society; that those suffering the mental torment are the ones actually taking the knocks for the whole of the culture as they are the ones open to the invisible forces behind the reality we inhabit, then we may see it differently.

This would involve 'listening' to what they are saying, like the African lady suggested they would in her culture. However, this doesn't mean getting caught up in the detail or story of what is being said, as this may just be a whole load of personal and collective fears and paranoia. But, instead, listening in a different way and feeling the energy that is behind what is being expressed. What is the nature of the pain? How is this pain being acted out or being held by the collective at the moment?

We may then begin to understand or deal with some of the underlying causes of the symptoms, both on a personal and collective level. This can mean we can get closer to healing many other problems that exist along a similar spectrum, even if they may not be obviously related. We can also get closer to the underlying symptoms of our cultural pathology and psychosis.

Fear, which most of the energies that create illness (these 'demons' we've been discussing) are an offspring of, looked at from a shamanic perspective has a spirit to it. It is alive and it exists both inside us and in the outer world. This spirit isn't going away, it's too vital for life. It is our job then to somehow 'befriend' it, so it can become an ally, rather than an enemy. When we do befriend it, the struggle ends and the power it has over us is diminished.

To explore how to do this further let us explore how belief systems have built up around these natural creative/destructive energies and how these belief systems can keep them locked into the individual and collective consciousness, creating the demons that destroy so many lives and in a way threaten the survival of human beings at the moment. To do this we have to look at the prevailing myth, the belief system that is prevalent in the modern world.

Chapter Five

The Prevailing Myth – Healing the Father

Belief systems or cosmologies – the way we view the universe and describe how it functions – are incredibly important as they tend to hold the whole culture of a people in place. Richard Tarnas, astrologer, philosopher and academic, author of *The Passion of the Western Mind* and *Cosmos and Psyche*, describes it beautifully:

> Why is cosmology so important? Because a cosmology is a container for everything that happens within a civilisation – all the thinking, the assumptions, the actions, the strategies, the economics and politics, the ecology, the self-image of the human being, one's role in the larger scheme of things and in every specific situation one finds oneself in.[4]

Ancient cultures understood this inherent power of a society's cosmology well, which is why there is such an emphasis on story and myth. These not only provide the moral and cultural learnings for the people, but also literally, albeit on an invisible energetic level, hold the society in form. This happens through the repeating of these stories, usually about the creation of the world, which creates an energetic resonance similar to when we might sing up the sun in the morning as described before: the invisible energetic framework holding reality in space and time.

We become part of creation in the stories we tell ourselves about life and then creation mirrors this back to us. It is the part of the human who is able to define his surroundings and through defining them, actually affects the way that they manifest. Our thoughts interact with the Great Thought that is the Universe and both give birth to the reality we inhabit.

A simple and practical metaphor for this is the architect who draws up the blueprints for a building. These come from his mind and imagination and thus are invisible, yet with application the plans become a reality and the building is built, changing the environment and the visible world completely. Most magic just follows this simple principal, this ability that the human possesses in a more obvious way than most other creatures in nature, to draw from the invisible world and create in the visible.

Sometimes it's possible to manifest in different ways, which is literal magic. Sometimes the imagination of thought holds reality in place or changes it in subtler ways, creating the zeitgeist that actually gives birth to an age. This usually comes from the masculine part of our natures, though this isn't limited to men or women. However, in the past two thousand years or so, maybe back further, the belief systems have been created largely by men. Let's then explore the root of some of these systems of thought in the modern age.

We all begin life in our Body Soul as a seed and, as I feel there is the memory of being in the womb somewhere deep in our being, if we track this back further there is the memory also of being that seed and its initial burst for life, racing to conjoin with and fertilise the egg. This is the Father aspect of ourselves which balances the Mother we explored in the previous chapters. This is a part of us that had to fight hard in this race for its very survival and in doing so, this will to live and to be born, has already beaten extraordinary odds stacked against it; such is the miracle that it has been part of. To put it simply: it won the race for life.

This will to live, to go through the eye of the needle, beat the competition and give birth to one self is retained within us, to ensure our survival in a world that at times is dangerous to our very existence. Nature has this in abundance, the will and ability to adapt, survive and at times even prosper in the most unlikely of circumstances. We have it too. It is the creative and protective force that runs through all of life. It is also one that can be destructive as only through the death of many other potentials, does this seed live.

I would suggest that some people a few centuries ago observed this phenomenon, albeit from a different perspective, and then made the extraordinary statement that all nature is then just a 'survival of the fittest' or the best adapted – what I would see as a re-enactment of that initial race. Yet to view this in such absolute terms, useful as it may have been to introduce the concept of evolution and break away from the intellectual prison of religious dogma, may just say a little more about our inflexible minds and need to be black-and-white about things, than the nature of the reality itself that is being observed.

I don't know enough much about the theory of evolution to argue as to its validity or not. However, when I connect with nature personally and spend time communicating with it in ways that I have been taught, I don't get a sense of 'competition' being the overriding force. I can feel that power of growth and evolution, what we could call the male aspect, but I often feel also an equally if not more powerful force that is quite the opposite. As many other scientists have observed that co-operation and interspecies communication has a huge part to play in nature's growth and survival – the feminine aspect. And what is 'survival' anyway – the absence, denial or defeat of death? If nature is indeed the visible face of spirit, the manifest reality of a much deeper essence as I experience it to be, then the whole survival thing takes on a completely different context, as what is there to survive?

Another, related aspect of the cultural myths that make up our cosmology is a kind of Cartesian-Newtonian reductionism that basically states that all nature is dead matter. This is further explored by Richard Tarnas as he quotes British philosopher and mathematician Bertrand Russell, who sums up well this rational based scientific view of nature as compared to humans:

...Nature, omnipotent but blind... has brought forth a child (man), subject still to her power but gifted with sight, knowledge of good and evil, with the capacity of judging all the works of his unthinking mother.[5]

Apart from the quite obvious psychological inferences of this statement, which could be read to ascertain the feelings that Russell has towards the feminine, this also contains the modern secular belief system that human beings are the only life form in the universe that possess consciousness. This is a belief that cuts into the heart of what we think about ourselves and separates us from our animal earthly natures as the 'unthinking mother' has no consciousness.

It also separates us from any sense of faith that there are aspects of the universe that are looking out for us in a benevolent way and can actually cure us if we need it; that this 'unthinking mother' is able to listen and respond to our deepest wishes and desires. This is the faith that is so often missing when people seek healing.

It is a remarkably arrogant position to take. Humans are the only beings in the *entire* known universe that possess any kind of awareness (but not unlike the religious position it grew out of that stated humans were the only ones to possess a soul). This position in many ways sums up for me the isolation that the rational mind feels surrounded by, but cut off from, the rest of consciousness.

In simple terms it has the effect of desacralising the world and nature, nothing has meaning apart from human life, and even meaning in human life is relegated to a very lowly priority in our existence. Yet this arrogant position, one that was supposed to replace the too egotistical anthropomorphic approach of religion, is one that the modern world has chosen to believe about life.

Rather than exploring whether these cosmologies are 'true' in any existential sense, which really is somewhat impossible, personally I agree with Robert Lawlor who, again in *Voices of the First Day*, states that the only real way you can evaluate whether a belief system that describes the nature of reality has any worth or not is to view how it is used practically and affects the societies it rules over.

If we know the nature of the cosmology and where its weaknesses or contradictions to health are, it can then be easier to diagnose the nature of the disease that may be affecting the system as a whole. Shamans, I believe, have to know the nature of all the energies that can take people and societies over to have any hope of being of assistance in healing them. They must get to know the poisons to be able to treat them.

The birth of the current cosmology coincided with huge 'advances' in Western civilisation as the scientific revolution took hold. It freed us from the prison of a corrupt and dogmatic religious determinism. Yet, a lot of those so-called 'advances' are now creating the problems that we face as the technological and industrial revolution threatens to destabilise the whole of human life on this planet. Our inventions have become dangerous to our survival – a great irony considering the theory they coincided with and how they are often used to justify our position at the head of evolution.

This philosophy of the origins and nature of life also coincided with, and in some cases was used to justify, some of the most horrendous extremes of violent racism and predatory behaviour in Europe in the late 19th century through to the 20th century. This can be seen through the expansion of European empires, dividing the entire continent of Africa into segments as a prize for those 'fittest' and culminated in the rise of Fascism and Nazi genocide. The 20th century was the most bloody in human history as human beings became efficient and adept killing machines.

Of course there have always been wars and empires and again it is remarkable how similar the cosmologies of religion and rational science are when used to justify these acts. The story used to be with religion that we were introducing the rest of the world to the one true God, thus saving them from themselves. Then it became, through science, as the most evolved human the white man is just following natural law and dominating the rest of the species. By ridding them of their crazy, primitive ways and building railways, 'developing' their countries and educating them we're helping them 'evolve'. Thus again, saving them from themselves. Subtly, this still goes on with all kinds of 'development' projects, be they money or charity motivated.

Might it then be helpful to ask whether this cosmology that we have been living under has any inherent fault lines in it? When Nietzsche said that 'God was dead' in the 1880s, he was articulating the very real fact that as intellectual Western people, we no longer had a relationship with the universe that was based on anything sacred. The world was just a dead lump of mass to be explored and exploited. It became, what sociologists have termed 'disenchanted', the magic and mystery were ripped out of it.

This was the intellectual climate or cosmology that gave birth to the modern age we now exist in. Richard Tarnas again expresses what can occur from this belief system:

A disenchanted world view empowers the utilitarian mindset, so that efficiency and control, power and profit, become the highest values governing the society. In such a world, literally nothing is sacred, because the whole has been desacralized: everything can be objectified and commodified, ancient forests are nothing but potential lumber, mountains become mining projects, children's minds marketing targets. Our relationship to the universe becomes I-It rather than I-Thou. The need to fill the spiritual hunger of this cosmically isolated consciousness, combined with the imperatives of corporate profit and personal greed, produces a techno consumerist frenzy that is cannibalizing the planet and threatening to crash the entire Cenozoic Era.[6]

This is the prevailing belief system that informs modern consciousness. Whether we actively seek to believe in it or not, it is there underlying everything at the root of our culture and is reaffirmed constantly through what we are taught at school from a young age and witness through our media. In many ways it has created a kind of 'secular fundamentalism'.

It is prevalent in our philosophy of capitalism that rules the way we govern society, often including spirituality. Thus, even this can become market led and achieving the spiritual 'goal' of enlightenment becomes just another thing to aspire after or crave, to possess or to sell.

In many ways the prevalence of this belief system is becoming even stronger, as the past 40 years of aggressive capitalism have seen. In this period we have seen the rise of what have been called 'the super-rich' – the top 1% of the population that owns nearly 50% of the entire global wealth, creating an inequality the like of which we have never seen before in human history, as some economic historians are noting.

Concepts such as equality, social responsibility and welfare have all been swallowed up by a market-led philosophy that consistently propounds the belief that competition and survival of the strongest or fittest is the only way a modern democracy can prosper. Everything, from school league tables to NHS targets, is based upon this highly flawed strategy.

This is constantly supported by any rational analysis that supports the prevailing belief system. The 'rational' is worshipped in equal measure with material wealth, which is seen as the only accurate measurement of human prosperity.

These beliefs are taught and ingrained early; they are in the air we breathe through the psychic environment and I would venture they exist in the Body Soul and not the rational mind. Because of this they can be very difficult to dislodge. I have experienced this, having been on a spiritual journey for a long time and witnessed all kinds of incredible out-of-this-world experiences, including spirits manifesting in physical reality, being picked up and having a spirit walk with its arms around me through a crowded pitch black room and all kind of other visceral experiences; it has still taken my mind years of deprogramming to accept these experiences as reality. And that's even when I wanted to believe in them! I'd read of all the books, primed myself for these experiences and yet when they did occur, I still couldn't quite believe them as they challenged so fundamentally the prevailing belief system I had been indoctrinated with from a young age.

It was my unconscious/Body Soul that still had to go through a cleansing period before I was able to accept the reality of the invisible world as a truth, I was able to trust my experiences. I see this again and again with my students. Imagine then how hard it must be for those that don't want to believe this stuff in the first place. Or, worse still, the sensitive people, like those we explored in the previous chapter, who are open to these powerful otherworldly forces and yet have to contend constantly with the belief that what they are experiencing is simply 'madness'. Yet what they are experiencing or expressing, the destructive energies we've explored, are at root, the shadow side of the cosmological vision that our whole culture is based upon. They are simply expressing our cultural pathology.

Real change, real healing, will take us time as a species because we have to begin by altering the cosmological vision we have of us in relationship to the universe. We are all a part of that cosmology, whether we ascribe to it consciously or not, as cosmologies hold an immense power over us on a personal level.

So how might this vision affect us when it comes to personal healing? One way is the aforementioned lack of faith and the fear of the irrational that this rational-based cosmology engenders. We have to learn to 'believe to see' again. There have been endless studies on the power of the placebo that confirm how belief affects human health. In fact, recent studies have shown that even when patients are told they are taking a placebo, they still respond in the same way and show real physiological improvements to their condition. They get better even though they know the pill they are taking contains no real medicine![7]

This, I would say, happens because the belief system is so strong in our culture that when you are sick you take a pill and get better, that just the act of swallowing the pill stimulates the body's innate system to heal itself. In fact, statistically the placebo is the most powerful drug ever invented by Western medicine!

Shamans have always utilised this fact; that the belief of the patient has more power in healing than the conscious mind. Hence when they would remove the invisible destructive poisons we discussed in the previous chapter from a person's energy field, they would then produce a physical object – a stone or piece of glass or something – to show the patient what they had removed and what had been causing the illness.

Anthropologists saw that this was sleight of hand and then labelled the shamans fakes. However, what the anthropologists didn't acknowledge and the shaman understood, is that part of us has to be tricked into believing something has been removed (which it has, albeit on an invisible level).

After all, shamans when they were sick would seek the same healing from other shamans and even though they understood the sleight of hand part of the healing it would still be effective. The part of us that holds belief systems is deeper and often a lot more powerful in its influence than the rational mind. We have to train this once more to have at its core a sense of wonder at the mysterious power of the universe that cannot be quantified or qualified, to make it sacred once more, in order that we may again begin to 'believe to see'.

Another way the prevailing belief system and cosmology can

affect us on a personal level is that it is based around this need to constantly seed and win the battle for life and then to hold on and preserve it at all cost. Thus, when any illness enters our lives it is immediately, on a deep level, seen as some kind of failure, that we have somehow lost the race. In this story death is then seen as the ultimate failure.

Thus, when people seek healing they are often doing so from a position that presumes that they have got something fundamentally wrong in life. Often people who have suffered serious illnesses talk about how their illness among others becomes a taboo subject. People around the person whisper about the illness or only talk in grave ways about it. There is also the cultural pressure for the person suffering not to talk about it in any intimate detail. Unconsciously this might be because it shows a clear sign of weakness, which culturally must be hidden or masked at all costs. It is like the people afflicted are exhibiting the weakness or sense of vulnerability that everyone fears the most.

This is especially true of mental illnesses and labels such as schizophrenia entrench this pattern. Indeed, what was once considered normal human behaviour – i.e. the intense, uncontrollable and at times excessive grief that comes from personal loss and tragedy has been pathologised. Likewise this has been done with the creative energy that involves intense highs and lows, or the seeing of visions or hearing of voices. The offending brain chemicals that are seen as causing the problem are then blasted into submission by increasing powerful drugs.

This treatment has, at its root, this cultural cosmology of a survival of the fittest, or best adapted. Everything outside of this vision, everything that is superfluous to 'evolution' is rejected and then placed into the shadow – the storehouse for everything rejected and repressed. The most sensitive or psychically open in society will then carry this shadow on behalf of everyone else.

The problem with seeing any illness as primarily a sign of failure, of the body or the mind, is that it is an incredibly disempowering place to start any kind of healing journey from. It means that people often can be consumed with feelings of unconscious guilt and shame about the illness, which suppress the body's natural healing responses. This is similar to a religious position whereby the person suffering might believe that they have been guilty of some kind of horrendous crime that God is now punishing them for.

Nowadays, it could be the universe, 'bad karma', their own body or life in general – whatever people choose to believe, that is responsible for the punishment. This can also lead quite naturally to the feeling of victimisation that comes from being persecuted, which is another, inherently weak place, to begin any healing journey from. For when your persecutor is your own mind or body (or God) the healing journey is laced with and crippled by this internal conflict, between persecution and victimisation.

Another, perhaps more healthy way of viewing any illness is that it can come into people's lives for many different reasons. It may even in fact come as a gift, a blessing that takes a person deep into themselves and reconnects them with a sense of who they are again. This can happen on a deep soul level, rekindling something that may have been lost for many years previous to the illness.

Illness can cause people to re-evaluate their attitude and relationship to life and those closest to them. It may be the Body Soul's way of communicating to the person that they can live a different life, one that on a deep level they've always craved, but were afraid to step into. It may even just provide a deeper meaning and sense of gratitude for life, no matter how short lived. Many people who have gone through or are in the midst of major illnesses talk of these things. How then can this be a failure? Even if the illness ends in death, but the life before that death is lived to the full?

Illness can also gift remarkable visions and insights about the nature of reality. This is because it can crack open our mind to the vast magnitude of consciousness usually hidden to everyday awareness when we are fit and healthy, which is another reason why the 'shamanic sickness' is so important in indigenous cultures.

For anyone on any healing journey there are two fundamental things that will assist them. The first is faith and the second is to feel empowered to explore the nature of their sickness without feeling it has marked them as being different or somehow having failed at life. Our cosmology, in my belief, needs to be changed to enable this to happen. Otherwise, we could unconsciously create the very thing we are all running from and trying desperately to avoid: sickness.

In fact, I would say this is already happening. In the UK nearly half of the population is now on prescription medicine at any one time.[8] Even taking into account an aging population, these are extraordinary statistics. This would suggest to me that we are quite sick, and yet no one is talking about it. On both personal and collective level, we have to not only change our belief systems, but also get to the very depths of where they come from and what natural process may be causing them. This can bring about long lasting change.

There is great power and energy in the place where our cosmological vision of life is locked, in the race for life. Thus our achievements as a civilisation and what we have built and created in the modern world are extraordinary. It feels to me like we are constantly going through that tunnel, bursting forward with the power and right to be alive, driven forward by our beliefs, to make our creations live, to constantly give birth to every thought or idea that enters our minds or imaginations, to build everything, driven by the desire/need to win.

'Life, life, life!' becomes the mantra – give birth to it, prolong it and hold onto it desperately once it is yours. We have focused our intent very strongly and utilised this force that runs through all of nature, a force of extraordinary magic and power.

Many indigenous cultures look then at Western civilisation and say that our magic is in fact too strong. That we have given birth to too much in the world, things that were not meant to be born here as they affect and impact too much on the environment and create dangerous imbalances in nature. We have not balanced this with the other, receptive and passive acts of being human. We have not balanced this Father aspect with that of the Mother. We have got so locked up in our thoughts and creative processes that they have then taken us over.

By being subsumed in this primal place of the race for life, the shadow side of it, the destructive nature of the survival process, has taken us over. It is seen in every missile or bullet we fire, every skyscraper we build: the imagery is so blindingly obvious of where this intent is coming from when you look at it. This is part of the 'destructive' energy we have explored that takes people over when they are sensitive and too open to the collective pathology.

The Shuar, an indigenous tribe from the Ecuadorian Amazon, famed in previous times for the shrinking of their enemies heads, have a belief I was told, that it is the male's role in the tribe to embody this destructive force. They are great warriors who fight and kill their enemies. Ultimately this is seen as a good thing though as the inter-tribal warfare keeps the human population down and ensures that they never outgrow and threaten the natural resources of the jungle. The eco system is then preserved.

However, the men, if left to their own devices, have a tendency to be taken over by this force too much and can end up destroying the environments surrounding them. Thus, it is the women's role in the tribe to control the men, to ensure the damage doesn't get out of control and start threatening their society. The females are seen as having the real power and needing to exercise it the most. Thus, a lot of shamanic cultures are matriarchal in their power structures.

Because of our cosmology we have also forgotten the sacred nature of giving birth: to ideas, objects, other humans, and how much this affects both the living world of creation and the invisible world of spirit that is the source of the inspiration of these things in the first place. All things come from nothing and will return to nothing in the end. Giving birth to too much creation, as Martin Prechtel observes, creates spiritual debt:

> Shamans are sometimes considered healers or doctors, but really they are people who deal with the tears and holes we create in the net of life, the damage that we all cause in our search for survival. In a sense, all of us — even the most untechnological, spiritual, and benign peoples — are constantly wrecking the world. The question is: how do we respond to that destruction? If we respond as we do in modern culture, by ignoring the spiritual debt that we create just by living, then that debt will come back to bite us, hard... Shamans deal with the problems that arise when we forget the relationship that exists between us and the Otherworld that feeds us, or when, for whatever reason, we don't feed the other world in return.[9]

In many respects it feels like we have built up an extraordinary large debt, and the times we are living through promise that part of that debt is overdue and payment is about to be enforced. Nature is biting back, hard. Yet, we are able, as creators of that imbalance, to heal it. But first we must move beyond an inherent desire for death and destruction that this will for life has inadvertently created.

Chapter Six

The Will for Life Becomes a Desire for Death

The will for survival has become an overused tool, yet it remains locked in the unconscious, in the Body Soul. It has taken us too far in a certain direction and in doing so it has taken us more and more into its opposite, the desire for death and annihilation. For every birth, there has to be a death and when one thing is overemphasised, nature always seeks to create its opposite in an attempt to counterbalance itself.

When we look at modern civilisation, it doesn't take a great leap of imagination to view it as some kind of lemming-like tumble over the cliff in collective suicide – ecological, political, social or economic. Many have observed the modern human in many ways as acting like a virus that invades then destroys its host, thus destroying itself in the process. In an age that praises and prides itself on its rationality, that doesn't appear to be a too logical way to carrying on. So how does the will for life become a desire for death and destruction? And, more importantly, how do we heal this?

One thing that ancient philosophies teach us, whatever their context, is that life is circular. The earth is a globe, as are the sun and the moon, our planet tracks a circular course around the sun, as do the other planets in our solar system, albeit in elliptical orbits. Nature follows cycles, the seasons demonstrate this, as do we from birth to death to, depending on your sensibilities, rebirth.

If you set off far enough in one direction around a circle, there's one thing that is pretty much guaranteed, you will end up coming back to where you began, from the opposite direction. Human beings do this quite naturally; people favour a side of their body so that when there are no points on the horizon to navigate by, like in dense woodland or desert for example, they will walk in circles.

Thus it is in politics, when historians note the further around to the left you go, the more to the right you become and vice versa. I have seen this often in so called 'spiritual' circles; the more that people talk about and are focused upon sentiments such as 'love and light' or 'peace' the more of the opposite kind of emotions such as fear, jealousies, aggression or power struggles become paramount.

There was one great story I heard from a friend of mine who lived at a famous spiritual retreat/community. He bemoaned the fact that no one would ever face up to the shadow sides of themselves at this place. No one was dealing with their 'shit' he said and yet he could feel it everywhere; the suppression of grief and rage, the fact that no one could talk about fear except in disparaging terms, all these natural aspects of being human somehow became unacceptable in this community.

Through becoming unacceptable they then almost became tangible in the atmosphere, the proverbial elephants in the room on a mass scale. Instead, the focus was on love and compassion and, ironically enough, acceptance! Then one day, right below the main community hall, the sewerage system for the whole community exploded, having been blocked for quite a while unbeknown to anyone. This sent cascades of human shit into the centre causing quite a stir. Whoever said nature doesn't have a sense of humour!

In terms of life being circular and the dualistic nature of the universe – light-dark, night-day, birth-death, man-woman – we have a simple logic or pattern for why things will turn into their opposites – the paradoxical nature of the universe. The Chinese Yin and Yang symbol portrays this beautifully and simply. So when we seek life too much, we risk meeting and being consumed by its opposite, the will for life becomes the desire for death and annihilation.

Living within the tension and containment of opposites and not seeking one over the other is very important and it's something we in the West often struggle with. In seeking absolutes, such as concepts of truth or certainty, we have lost the ability to embrace contradiction. Accepting that good can exist within evil and vice versa is a simple example of this. This duality is one of the lessons we're here to learn about, for we have to learn to live within it before it can be transcended. Living within the tension of these opposites is essential to survival. Put simply, South African shaman Vusamazulu Credo Mutwa says:

> Inside each soul are two worms, a red and a blue worm, and they are always in conflict with each other...the red worm represents evil, all the vices and weaknesses of a person. And the dark blue worm represents all the good, virtues and strengths of a person.
>
> Every soul must have both good and evil... Without a perfect balance, the soul will die. If, for instance, a man should only be good, he would have no reason to exist. If he were only bad, he would be automatically be destroyed. Overly good people never live long. The two worms are always quarrelling inside each soul, and if one worm seriously damages the other, the soul can no longer survive in the world. Survival requires a balance between good and evil.[10]

So if we are to follow the logic of the circle, in trying to preserve life; that which is so precious and yet appears so threatened now, instead of constantly running towards life and the will for survival, maybe we could turn around and instead go back towards and embrace death, destruction and annihilation. Maybe we need to face bravely and consciously the void that lives inside of us. We may then learn through experience one of the most powerful and difficult lessons on any spiritual path: surrender. In this way we may just find our way back to life. This might be the initiation we are going through as a species right now.

The other side of fear is power and if we constantly run from or are controlled by fear, then we have a mis-relationship with that primal power. We are either running from our power or controlled by our desire for it. This means it can be used against us and manipulated by very clever people who we then become in thrall to. Or we use it against ourselves, and become self-destructive in order to simply set ourselves free from that control, that seeming our power has over us. Either way this primal power, the power of our connection to the earth, becomes an enemy, as opposed to an ally.

Beneath this power is, of course, love, as love is beneath and the other side of anything; despair, rage, deep grief, sexual desire, joy. Yet, the less we seek this love, the more we let go to ourselves, the more its presence becomes suddenly tangible. This sets us free, as every route leads unto it. There is no one path we have to correct ourselves into following. It is our birthright.

But how can we do this in a sane and safe way? How do we face up to these inherently destructive and/or primal sides of ourselves? Well it is possible to do this, alongside the spirit of life and expansion. We can feed both those worms inside us and ensure that the balance of nature is kept in a harmonious aspect within us.

This has to be done spiritually as well as materially and is the beauty of the shamanic path as I understand it, as it embraces our primal selves, recognising the raw magical power that these parts contain. If we are to be able to fully challenge and change the existing paradigm, which uses this primal force in such destructive, unconscious ways, it is important that we are able to become conscious of and have some kind of mastery over these forces. Otherwise even spiritually it can all become about being

more 'evolved' and feeding and tapping into the cultural pathological obsession with 'progress'.

It cannot just be about good intentions, the shadow side of life
has to be acknowledged and in many ways honoured. But there
is a difference between honouring these urges and continually
acting them out. What can help us here is the containment of
ritual and ceremony alongside connecting to invisible forces that
can teach us how to deal with these energies. We have to
embrace death, ritually, symbolically, with our hearts, minds and
emotions. We have to embrace and go through the more
destructive elements of our Body Souls and, more importantly,
change the belief systems that have built up around these.

These are the forces that affect us personally through illness
and disturbance and collectively through the struggle we are
going through to ensure our 'survival' on this planet. We have to
heal our relationship to 'Father Sky' – to create cosmologies that
embrace the mysteries of the universe again and recognise the
sacredness of all of life. When we can bring Him into balance
with the Mother beneath our feet, then real change in the world
can occur as we, as humans, stand between and unite them both.

One of my favourite passages of writing of all time sums it up
perfectly. It comes from Lakota Medicine man John Fire Lame
Deer's autobiography in a chapter entitled Getting Drunk, Going
to Jail:

I'm no wino ... but I am no saint either. A medicine man
shouldn't be a saint. He should experience and feel all the ups
and downs, the despair and the joy, the magic and the reality,
the courage and the fear, of his people. He should be able to
sink as low as a bug, or soar as high as an eagle. Unless he can
experience both, he is no good as a medicine man.

Sickness, jail, poverty, getting drunk – I had to experience
all that myself. Sinning makes the world go round. You can't
be so stuck up, so inhuman that you want to be pure, your

soul wrapped up in a plastic bag, all the time. You have to be God and the devil, both of them. Being a good medicine man means being right in the midst of the turmoil, not shielding yourself from it. It means experiencing life in all its phases. It means not being afraid and cutting up and playing the fool now and then. That's sacred too.

Nature, the Great Spirit – they are not perfect. The world couldn't stand that perfection. The spirit has a good side and a bad side. Sometimes the bad side gives me more knowledge than the good side.[11]

Chapter Seven

The Power of Ritual and Ceremony

The body, which contains the Body Soul along with all the traumas and wounds it holds, responds, in my experience, to two things – love and fear. It's really as simple as that. Fear, as already explored, helps to keep us alive and safe here in the world and can create the desire for life and love helps us to open and connect to others here and in the Otherworld, which, in turn, keeps us alive in the material world. One contracts the other expands. They both are necessary for our wellbeing as humans.

These are the two worms, this is God and the Devil and this is the polarity that creates life here; both are sacred. The problem seems to me very often that we spend a lot of time running away from one (fear) and towards the other (love) and yet the more we do this the more we seem to run into fear and away from love, such is the paradoxical nature of the universe.

I would say there is a third force that contains and transcends both of these polarities and that is Universal Love, a kind that is unconditional – the source of which we have called God/Great Mystery etc. Without the polarity of opposites, this Universal Love does not have the ability to create even though everything comes from it and will return to it; it is the tension of the opposites, the duality that gives birth to the world. Learning to exist within the tension of the opposites and finding ways to at times transcend them into Universal Love brings healing.

The greatest way to experience and live these forces, in my opinion, is through the container of ceremony. Ceremony can happen when two or more people come together with shared intent. As we've explored, human beings contain and can embody both highly creative and destructive forces. In the modern world, because of the lack of ceremonies ritually, relationships have become the container for a lot of these energies and have taken the burden of them.

Romantic love in the West was assigned a mystical status in medieval times through the troubadours and romantic poets. A lot of people now point out that these were really talking of a love affair with the divine as opposed to human love; however, relationships have developed a kind of mythical status in our culture in terms of the stories we tell ourselves about them.

The problem may be, and the reason so many are breaking down now, is they cannot hold the strain of such powerful energies. We need ceremonies to take the strain off them. The real beauty and power of ceremonies, as I experience them, is that they can literally give birth to the world (as two people can when they make love with the potential of giving birth to new life), recreating ritually and energetically the fundamental conditions, the primal forces that gave birth to life.

To harness these kinds of energies, we need a strong container, otherwise they can get a little out of control. Ceremony is always happening, human beings are constantly ritualising their lives. The difference between now and a time when ceremony sat at the heart of human culture is that a lot of the time the ceremonies aren't held with conscious intent. They are more often created unconsciously as we attempt to bridge that gap of meaning in our lives. This can lead to problems as often the forces unleashed within spontaneous expressions of ritual may not always find a safe home. To explore this, we can look back to times when this has happened in an intensive way.

Let's begin in the 1960s when so much of our modern culture was born. Through the revolutionary cultural explosion that occurred in that decade, the most extraordinary 'happenings' or convergences of people sprang up. A lot of these were around music and festivals and of course the lubrication of LSD and they became like Dionysian, ecstatic rituals. The rock stars of the time were like gods on the stage, orchestrating the audience in this celebration of everything that was locked down and repressed by the dominant culture. Free love, free sex and psychic abandon were the order of the day, alongside political revolution and the overthrow of the dominant ideology in a complete revolution of consciousness.

As can be seen though the astrology of the time (Pluto conjunct Uranus), an astrology that is being mirrored for the first time since that period right now, there was a creative/destructive force that swept through the Western Hemisphere and the rest of the world in that era and it was the young who were attempting to bring it into being.

Viewing it shamanically, I would say that those rock stars on stage didn't become like gods, but rather were taken over by energetic and archetypal forces and so in those moments on stage they *were* gods, quite literally. These were the ancient ones coming back to life, brought forth through the cracks in reality that the LSD (based on and similar to shamanic teacher plants) was creating. This was the invisible world pouring forth into this world.

Yet, the sheer power of these otherworldly forces was enough to destroy many individuals, especially those who embodied these gods on stage. For they would not realise that when the ceremony had ended, the power of the gods would also leave them. So, even though the performers felt invincible up there, when the energy was gone they were but human again and all the physical and emotional limitations of the body that could be transcended onstage would eventually catch up and either send them mad or worse.

This is why so many of these heroes and heroines burnt themselves out completely and ended up dead. Their ego or personality got attached to the archetype they were embodying and they thought that they were that power as opposed to just a vehicle for it.

This is often the role that the artist plays in Western culture, hence the stereotype of the creative genius who while creating great masterpieces simultaneously destroys themself. These artists embody both the creative and destructive forces of life, but without the holding or container that a traditional culture might offer.

Again, looking shamanically, it appears that they are not destroying themselves, but rather in some way being eaten by the otherworldly forces that create the art they are producing. These creative/destructive forces are too much to handle for a single human being if their ego or personality is too weak to be a container and gets attached to the forces. This is why spiritual paths that involved opening up to these forces consciously involve incredible discipline and the artists that do survive and prosper are the ones who themselves employ strong self-discipline with their art – they create their own containers.

Being in the midst of creative inspiration is a lot like the feeling of being so completely in love – they both contain their own very real potential for madness. Indigenous cultures would often look suspiciously at both, if they are taking over the person's whole life. This is because they were aware that those afflicted were not actually being taken over by the object of their desire or by their creation, but rather by incredibly potent and powerful forces from the invisible world.

The container of ceremony, out of which most if not all art has emerged anyway, is always necessary. The ancients, such as the Greeks, who understood the phenomenon of gods embodying humans well, would fill their dramas with the tragedies of a person either consumed by the will of a god or in battle with that force and what happens when the laws of gods of the natural world aren't adhered to or honoured. The theatre they created had a ceremonial, healing purpose – as a vehicle for the catharsis of these energies on behalf of the audience watching.

We too, as the audience, can easily confuse the person who is unleashing these powers, i.e. the artist, with the god itself and end up distracting ourselves by our obsession with who they might be, rather than what they are bringing forth. So then, in our hunger to consume that which comes from the invisible realms and is beyond the everydayness of life, of which we are perpetually starved due to the lack of conscious ceremony in our lives, we end up devouring the artist themselves. The human worships the human, not the force behind them, until they are sacrificed.

This is seen in the rise of the 'cult of celebrity' we are now seeing. So many famous people have fallen down this track. We could look at the life of Elvis as a great example of this. Not only did he embody the potent forces from the Otherworld that kickstarted a sexual revolution, he in many ways then lived the excess of his nation and predicated, through his life, the path it was and still is on.

The dominant Christian mythology is based upon a different archetype, but one that follows the same course – the man/god who carries the sins of the populace. These people not only hold the spiritual inspiration of their people but then they carry the 'sins' – the negative, destructive energy and are eventually sacrificed. We will explore this more later.

What happened in the 1960s was without the conscious container of ceremony. Everything was left and encouraged to run free as a counterpoint to the oppressive control of dominant society at that time, which meant that it turned naturally a little dark and destructive as the whole counter-culture revolution got lost or defeated in a mess of overdoses on drugs, sex and violence. The shadow of these uncontained energies became dominant. The forces that had been unleashed began to consume the very people who had unleashed them.

What was lacking then, and hopefully is growing now, is the ability for people to hold the space of these gods and to ceremonially invite them here, without blowing their systems apart or being eaten alive by such powerful forces. For what happened in the 1960s, when a lot of the modern spiritual movements were also birthed including our take on shamanism, could be seen as a microcosm of civilisation's interaction with these primal forces.

When there are bursts of growth in civilisations, when great empires rise and fall, it is as though these primal archetypal forces, these gods of the different worlds are bursting through and overtaking whole nations of people. Civilisations and empires, from the Roman to the Mayan, seem to follow this similar arc, whereby the expansion and growth is eventually turned inwards and they end up consuming themselves, acting in such ways that are ultimately destructive.

What 'possesses' people to rise to great heights only to implode from within? Why build such temples, ancient and modern, such pantheonic statements to the universe that we, human beings, exist? Well maybe human beings do become possessed and when they are overtaken by such energy they then feel the need to somehow express and create in the world what they are being taken over by.

This kind of embodying of potent, natural forces was, I believe, utilised by some of the most powerful leaders of the 20th century. The mass rallies of Hitler could be said to have had the same ceremonial, magnetic quality, albeit with a different intent. Outside the arena and time, we may look back at television footage and wonder how this crazy looking man with the hysterical movements held people in such a thrall. What the cameras cannot capture I'm sure is the invisible intensity of the force that he was embodying, a force strong enough to move a whole people to extraordinary lengths, both terrifying and appalling in their magnitude and execution.

According to a lot of research into the occult practices of the Nazis, including their use of powerful ancestral symbols, much of this may have been done half consciously. As many other leaders have discovered through all kinds of different means, when you are able to stir up that level of emotional power, be it hatred, revenge, fear or rage, people will follow you seemingly to the end of the world.

The power of emotion fuels ceremony because it fuels human beings to go beyond the realms of the mundane. It also binds people together. This happens in families, in love relationships and in the mass of collective ritual, where the one disappears into the whole and becomes so much more than a mere individual. It is in these moments we are no longer alone in an alien universe, no longer separate. The unleashing of emotion, whether it's the love that two people share or the collective rage of a nation, is a powerful force. And it is one that often needs a full understanding of its source and also needs containing or it risks running riot or being manipulated for negative means. I believe it is a human need, as fundamental as our need for food, to feel and experience collectively the power of such emotional forces that are created in ceremony and to come together in unity. This need can easily be manipulated though by some powerful magicians of consciousness and intent. The rise of abusive 'cults' with charismatic leaders can also fall into this category.

I feel indigenous cultures have always been somewhat wiser here. They understand the need to engage with and channel these emotional forces, but they do this in a way that *ritualises* them and expresses and contains them through the power of ceremony. They keep them close to the earth rather than building them upon the earth! This may in the end be the main role of the human, to co-create reality in this way so that life continues to grow, is continuingly giving birth and renewing itself again and again through the power of these primal archetypal forces channelled through ritual and ceremony.

Everything can be expressed in ceremony if it is held in the right way, especially the tension of the opposites that create life here – fear and love, contraction and release, destruction and creation. They find release within ceremony by consciously bringing in that third element of creation, Universal Love. It is connecting and unleashing this third element that lies at the heart of all ceremony.

However, to release this Universal Love in a creative and expansive way – to get to the heart of it – we often have to go through the tension of the opposites on earth. This love is sacred and to unleash it on earth we have to respect the polarities that create life here.

Every shamanic ceremony I have experienced that was worth anything, that actually touched something deep inside me, always involved the intensity of this opposition – sacrifice and suffering leading to immense beauty, pain or fear leading to love. If you are being buried alive in a grave in the middle of woods, this is obviously going to engender quite a lot of fear, yet at the same time spending a night being held by the earth is an experience of great beauty and wonder. In my experience no one really wants to get in, but then in the morning they don't want to come out again.

Another example is the North American tradition of the sweat lodge, one of my favourite ceremonies, whereby a wooden bender is built, covered with blankets and then hot rocks are brought in that have been heated up in a fire and water is poured over them to create steam. This can involve facing intense physical discomfort through the heat from the rocks. Sometimes it is so strong that it literally sears your bare body. People also often face fears of being out of control in a darkened enclosed space and yet the sense of community and love and the presence of the spirits in the lodge can heal almost any disease.

One of the incredible and magical parts of this ceremony is that it recreates the very conditions at the beginning of life. The rocks are the seeds heated in the fire to create the primal power of the masculine, which then are brought into seed the feminine bowl that is the lodge, the womb of the Mother, and water is poured on to create the magical steam – the breath of life.

Everyone in the ceremony has the opportunity to participate ritually in the primal conditions that give birth to life. Inside, the lodge becomes the universe at the beginning of time in which, in the pitch darkness, the void is created and then filled with the magical healing presence of the spirits and the creator at the source of life. In the midst of the sweat, the discomfort, the prayers and celebration, life is renewed and healing happens.

Another example of intense ceremony is working with teacher plants (which we will explore in the next chapter), which can and usually does involve vomiting and at times facing horrendous inner demons and conflicts and yet can at the same time catapult us into worlds of absolute, striking ecstasy – and bring healing to almost any known ailment. It was the same when I spontaneously touched the spirit of all of life at 14; I had to go through convulsions and a fit first.

Nature, in my experience, nearly always asks a price, as does spirit, and each experience of the invisible world involves some kind of cost. This is why ceremony and ritual are so important, to make sure that debt is paid, the debt we all have to the gift of life. This is why the ancient act of offerings are also important within these ceremonies and rituals, be they literal presents for the gods in the form of tobacco, food, drink, coins or our creations; or the giving of ourselves in some way – our blood, our sweat, our tears, our sheer physical, mental and emotional exertion.

It is as though we as humans must constantly remind ourselves that we must give back to life if we are to receive, we have to feed life to be nourished in turn. For, when we forget this, as we have done in so many ways, we end up taking so much more than we could ever need and destroying the delicate balance of existence in the process. Again, this is not just a moral consideration, but a deeply practical one.

An example of this is the Wixaritari nation (Huichol) of Central Mexico who traditionally would walk a 500km pilgrimage to collect their sacrament peyote, which was and still is at the heart of all their ceremonies. Nowadays, because a lot of the land on their pilgrimage is privately owned and inaccessible, they have to travel by car. Yet it is still a trip done when fasting and involves many physical challenges including sleeping out in the freezing winter desert without any shelter. They are trying at the moment to reintroduce the old ways of walking by foot on the pilgrimage. The pilgrims then return home, after paying homage and offerings to their sacred mountain that the cactus grows at the foot of, bringing back the sacred plant for the community's use that year.

By then it is fair to say that they will have earned, through a lot of hard physical and emotional endeavour, the right to commune with the beautiful offerings peyote has to share. This essential part of any ceremony is something we can easily forget in the West with our tendency towards instant gratification. This is why pilgrimage has its role in some many traditions and is often at the source of many miraculous healings.

This principle was also at work in the story of C when she dug her grave. In many ways that work coupled with her intention created the healing at least as much if not more than the night she spent in the ground. This is one of the reasons why I hold my trainings in the woods, even though the centre has to be virtually rebuilt every year as opposed to a nice retreat space, which I could just turn up to.

The ceremonies I feel are so much more powerful because they are earned through a lot of physical endeavour and, not being a naturally practical person, with emotional and mental challenges along the way. When people come on the courses they are constantly challenged by the environment. We had one weekend in March when it didn't get over 0 degrees and didn't stop snowing. The only accommodation we have is in tents and some people coming had never even camped before. But they were the ones who loved it and didn't want to go home. It's certainly very hard to ignore nature and our real place in it when it you're freezing and have to dance semi-naked in the middle of the woods for a ceremony!

To truly touch the heart of life and to let in the healing spirit of that central element of Universal Love that sustains life here, and that all of life is born out of, we need to learn how to exist and dance within the polarities of existence. Ceremony is the place we can do this, not only to learn this dance but also more importantly to stop the conflict and drama between these extremes being acted out in the world.

The fact that wars have such a fascination in our culture, especially the world wars of the past century, hints at the power that these great rituals have in the human imagination when they are acted out on the world stage. People often look back at times like the Blitz, when England was constantly being bombed by the Germans, with some kind of fondness, talking of the spirit that it engendered among the people amidst the tragedies and hardship. There is no accident that it is often called the Theatre of War. This conflict, acted out, has its basis in ritualistic human behaviour, which is why such conflict, beyond moralistic concerns, is so appealing to a lot of people.

Ritual and ceremony have never really gone away in the modern world, the main difference now seems to be the conscious *intention* behind such acts: either, on the negative side, to manipulate masses into destructive and politically motivated behaviours, or more benignly but perhaps equally as corrosive in the long term, as some kind of entertainment or distraction; rather than sitting at the centre of our existence as they once did.

It seems that, although we may have ignored or overlooked the power and importance of ceremony and ritual to human wellbeing, its power hasn't diminished. In fact it may mean we're actually more likely to be in thrall to such powerful forces of group emotion and invisible powers, which can then become dangerous to our lives.

This is where we can learn so much from indigenous peoples and the earth birthing and saving power of their ceremonies. Ceremony, through our Body Soul, connects us with the whole of life and reinforces our relationship with all the creatures we share this planet with. The spirits of animals are often invoked in ceremonies, whereby we as shamans can merge our spirits, our consciousness, with theirs.

Through the power of the drum, costume and movement I can open up my awareness and become consciously the stag. I can feel what it feels like to be the animal, how it moves and relates to life. In that moment of communion, I can feel the ecstasy that comes from losing my human consciousness and being once more primal and animal, connected to the whole web of life. No longer separate or alone in the universe, no longer forgetful of my origins; through the stag I can travel back to the ancestral spirits that created life.

The animals are our elders; they came before the human and are closer then to the source. They still hold the memories of what it is like to not 'leave the garden', or in other words, not become disconnected from the earth. When they are able to show me this in ceremony I then receive the huge spiritual power of the earth in my being – in many ways it is like plugging into the mains again and recharging the whole system. When this relationship is emphasised and re-emphasised through ceremonies, it becomes much more difficult to act in a destructive way towards other species on the planet, as the sacred nature of the relationship is cemented through these intense, meaningful experiences.

This is the purpose of such ceremonies, to remind us of that relationship we have with the earth. To honour and celebrate that relationship and the many other beings, be they rock, tree, bird or animal, that we share this planet with and who we also share a common heritage. This is making the world sacred again; building a hugely meaningful and soulful relationship with the land of which we are a part, fed by the emotional ties created in ceremony. It is remarkable when you spend some time working with a piece of land like this; the aliveness and spirit that the land begins to exude becomes tangible as it is brought back to life again.

In this way ceremony also acts as a healing for the earth's body, which is like performing acupuncture to release trapped energy, or to charge up the spirit of a place. The earth holds onto memories and traumas that have happened on it, the same way that our energy bodies will hold on to the memoires of pain and trauma until they are resolved and released. Sometimes when you are doing ceremonies in such places you can feel the sickness that is held in the earth and it is our job, as shamans, to release and transform these energies, as it is on individuals.

The world is not just physically polluted at the moment, it is also psychically polluted. If we can heal it psychically, then the physical will follow. This is how we can remain empowered and confident, even in the face of environmental destruction that is happening on a mass scale. There are certain energy points on the earth's surface that act as portals or entry points to the Otherworld. These are the sacred lands of indigenous peoples and where the ancients on these lands built their sacred sites. They are birth places for the world. When worked with energetically these places can bring incredible healing to the planet as a whole and start the process of re-imagining a fecund and bountiful world once more. This is the purpose of ceremony, where conscious intent and the purposeful channelling of powerful, ancient forces can literally bring the earth back to life, at the same time as containing and releasing the more destructive elements of nature that we as humans embody.

Chapter Eight

Learning from the Plants

Among the great teachers in the power of ceremony and healing are the plants. This in particular is true for what shamans call 'teacher plants' – those that not only heal the body and rid it of physical toxins, but also at the same time give insight and clarity around the belief systems that are locked inside and causing the poisons to accumulate. They can heal all that we have been describing in the past few chapters; they can heal the Body Soul and our relationship to it.

They also connect us to the Otherworld of spirit in profound ways. They are not the only healers in this and I believe if over relied upon or used as a substitute for other ways of connecting with the sacred and ourselves that may require more patience and discipline, they can actually be counterproductive. They are gateway medicines, they open up doors for us into the invisible realms of spirit; people can often mistake the gateways for the medicine itself and believe without the plants that door is shut. However, once opened, it can always be gone through. Thus teacher plants need our profound respect and honouring if we do choose to invite them into our lives for healing.

Many books have been written about how such plants have helped authors find God or enlightenment, in fact the plants themselves are now called entheogens (meaning to experience God or the Divine within) as opposed to the old name of hallucinogens (to experience hallucinations).

However, the cultures that have cultivated these medicines for thousands of years don't tend to use them in this way. They, as cultures, saw the sacred in everything all of the time anyway. There wasn't the separation we have in our belief systems between matter and spirit or simply the lack of faith in an invisible force that sustains life, thus they had no need to go searching for God with the plants.

I personally prefer the indigenous way of using these medicines, which tends to be on a whole more practical. This is essentially for healing the body, mind and spirit, or for reversing ill luck, which in itself shamanically is usually viewed as a disease of the spirit through a loss of power. This may involve a restoration of faith and an experience of the numinous. However, for me, just searching for this doesn't have to be the intention, but rather the by-product, if necessary, of seeking healing.

The reason I say this, is that too much seeking of a transcended reality with the plants can have the effect of creating a lot of ungrounded people, going from one 'experience' to another, which is something I have witnessed. Because the plants are so powerful, it is important, I feel, to stay grounded when working with them. As with any ceremony, it isn't actually the experience of other worlds you have when in an altered state that is the most important thing, but rather how you can integrate these experiences into your life. Too much seeking the divine can create another form of spiritual bypass.

I have used the plants sparingly in my own journey, as the healing they tend to stimulate can take a long time to integrate. The real work is done in many ways after working with the plants, when what they have revealed to me or healed within me has to be grounded in my everyday life. If you are jumping from one plant experience to the next, as many people do, where is the time for the integration? It is easy then to become just a tourist and use the plants as an escape visa from everyday life, like any spiritual high that can be experienced in the short-term, because these plants can indeed connect us with the third force of Universal Love that sits beyond and contains the tension of the opposites here on earth.

But, in my experience, we cannot stay just in that bubble of love, floating above the tension of the opposites that create reality. There's not the power to always be effective there. We have come to earth for a reason and most of us have a job to do or a role to play here, that means we have to get down and dirty where life really happens, 'being in the midst of the turmoil' as Lame Deer put it.

Also, I feel that visions and connections to the Otherworld need hard work, discipline and sacrifice and can be worked towards in other ways. Personally, some of my most powerful experiences of being opened to spirit, including them manifesting physically, have come without the use of any plants. I think it's really important to cultivate both, so that when we are touched by extraordinary experiences with the plants, we are able to integrate them into some kind of reality, we have a framework for them that is grounded in everyday practice, and this will also mean we can go further with them.

Saying that, there are many people who use the plants on a regular basis staying grounded and are able to integrate the experiences and healing into their lives. Like everything there is no one way that is right with this, it's just important to be aware of potential traps. Use of the plants tends to polarise the modern shamanic community, as there are a lot of people who don't go near them, seemingly on a point of principle, which I don't fully understand. They also can have great opinions on the use of plants within shamanism without ever having experienced working with them ceremonially, which seems to me more than a little absurd, a bit like judging and telling everyone what India is like having read a lot about it and seen it on TV, but never having been there.

This is probably because they see other people talking about them in certain way or getting carried away with their effects. However, it also may be about control on a deeper, unconscious level. As mentioned before, the plants are very powerful and, when we do work with them, there will always come a point when we have to surrender completely to the process. As a

Peruvian Ayahuascero from the Cocoma tribe said to me once: 'You can lie to yourself, you can lie to everyone else, but you cannot lie to the plants.' I had an experience in a ceremony with a Shuar Uwishin (shaman) with the medicine Natem (ayahuasca) once that threatened to destabilise me, but turned into an extraordinary healing journey that might illustrate this.

I had travelled quite a long way to this ceremony and was quite sick, having some kind of chest infection that meant I could hardly breathe and was coughing a lot. I was also for some reason extraordinarily nervous, almost as if I could tell that some big healing was on its way. Having experienced being open to and overwhelmed by the raw intensity and power of the invisible world through spontaneous so called 'psychotic' and visionary experiences throughout my life and having being affected deeply by these experiences, to the edge of madness, I've always been naturally quite wary of anything that will open me up so much to the Otherworld, as the plants can do. I feel some of this fear is important for respect and because of that I felt that the plants had treated me kindly in the past. I also am aware that at times I have to go 'back into the fire' to cure myself.

Although I had worked with ayahuasca before, all my oldest fears about getting lost in the Otherworld and madness seemed to be returning in their intensity before this ceremony. This wasn't helped by not feeling great physically and it was April and the ceremony was being held in a tepee and it was snowing. You could say that my resistance to the ceremony was fairly huge.

Eventually I began to relax into it though, and accepted the medicine gratefully when it was passed round. However, this temporary good feeling wore off very quickly. The ceremony quickly took on the feeling of chaos for me as the shaman kept disappearing outside to vomit (he was taking on and releasing the sickness of everyone else) and for some reason I began to lose all my trust in him being able to hold this space having never worked with him before.

This compounded the feeling that maybe I should have waited until I was physically stronger to take the medicine as through the sickness I hadn't really slept for a week. I started to become overwhelmed by my fears, which I then projected onto the ceremony and the shaman holding it. I felt completely out of control.

To make things a lot worse the medicine then started kicking in, in a way I hadn't experienced before. To begin with there was this incredibly loud noise that sounded like a helicopter around the back of my head. I kept looking over my shoulder and yet no one was behind me and the shaman wasn't even playing any of his instruments. It was coming from nowhere and in my sensitive state the sound starting to get a bit overwhelming, adding to the feeling of chaos. At the same time I was beginning to get intensely disorientated, drunk-like and nauseous and I couldn't stop swaying from side to side.

Then, to top it all off, as the shaman started to go around the circle cleansing everyone and singing, strange beings started to manifest physically in the circle. I had my eyes wide open and it was light in the tepee from the huge central fire, yet they were as real as everyone else there, as they started weaving in and around the circle. How they moved though appeared to be outside of time, as though the reality I was witnessing suddenly became split, between them and their movements and us; frozen in time.

I was aware of this strange paradox, of the meeting of these disparate worlds, which felt completely unnatural and unnerving. The medicine hadn't completely taken hold yet though and what was trying to take hold of me I was resisting, so I still retained a lot of my normal perceptual awareness. I was caught between the sheer craziness of the situation and my desperate attempt to regain control over the reality I was perceiving. It was a struggle I was bound to lose.

The beings were humanoid shape, but not at all human with

large alien/canine type heads. They were like nothing I had ever seen, or imagined, before. With everything else that was going on, that otherworldly sound that I couldn't get to stop, the intense nausea and disorientation and my not trusting the ceremony, the arrival of these beings was beginning to feel like the last straw. I was intensely frightened and soon this turned into anger that this was happening at all, that I had brought myself to this. This wasn't how ceremony was 'supposed' to be, it should be nice and orderly at least and make me feel safe, my rational mind was telling me as I tried desperately to cling to some kind of tangible reality.

To make matters a lot worse one of the humanoid beings then appeared around me and kept reaching into me, as if he (it had the feeling of a male) was trying to grab hold of me and take me somewhere. I could feel him very physically brush past me and touch me on the shoulder then reach his arm into me. I just kept desperately pushing him away as there was no way I was going to let myself be taken off by this strange being that had manifested physically in the world. It felt like he was trying to reach into my soul and if I let him take it that would be the end of me – that it would be death or madness or something worse. I was angry, disturbed, scared and felt completely overwhelmed and alone.

Finally, I regained some kind of sense of myself and remembered what I would do in my everyday life when feeling in trouble, which is to call out to one of my spirit teachers. This teacher has been with me consciously for most of my shamanic life, but probably a lot longer. I have developed an intensely personal relationship with him through countless ceremonies and healings. We had to go through years of distrust on my side for this to happen. I find it hard enough having a relationship with a person in this world, let alone an invisible one! Yet this teacher and friend had told and showed me things on many occasions that I could never have known otherwise. I'd also felt his presence around and within me many times when I really needed to not feel alone.

So, in that moment, I called out for him and as soon as I did, he was there and to my intense relief he manifested physically as well. I then felt his hand placed firmly and lovingly in the middle of my back, behind my heart, and his head behind my shoulder, where he usually appears. I immediately stopped swinging wildly from side to side and was still as I felt this huge surge of power come into me.

I was suddenly calm and focussed, all the nausea, fear and anger disappeared in a moment as I leant back into his arms and felt him holding me up. The strange being that had been around me reappeared and reached down once more, yet now he seemed completely different, no longer threatening but rather gentle and loving. It is amazing how much power our projections have, even of beings from other worlds. As he leant in my teacher then said: 'It's okay, go with him.' So I surrendered completely and let this strange being take me by the hand and lift me out of my body.

I've felt myself consciously leave my body completely on only a few occasions, even after a lot of years of attempting it through dream work. One time, through an intense personal trauma that left me not particularly wanting to be in the world, I left spontaneously after I had awoken from an afternoon sleep. What struck me that time was the very speed of flying around the room, which was so disorientating that I felt my awareness desperately trying to get something to hold onto, to get back into something.

It is very different from an inward visionary experience and yet a small part of your awareness does remain with the body. It is like your awareness is suddenly split in two and you realise how possible it is to fully exist in two different physical locales at one time; to be both dead (out of the body) and alive at the same time.

On that occasion, as I was flying around the room, all of a sudden I experienced an opening to another world. A partner who had recently died (the reason I was in such grief and not particularly wanting to be in the world) walked through. I remember pushing all my intention to join with her and with that flew, with the immense speed that my soul was travelling, straight towards her.

However, at the last moment something came towards me and physically knocked me off track and in an instant I was back in my body with a voice in my head saying: 'It's not your time yet.' The experience was as real as anything I've experienced in life and the idea of leaving the world, which had been going through my mind a lot, was gone from that moment onwards.

Back in the ceremony, I left my body with this strange being, yet this time there wasn't the same disorientating feeling of intense speed. I was calm and the instant I left, I was filled with the most immense feeling of joy, love and peace. My new guide then led me into physical realms deep in the Otherworld.

I travelled through time and space into worlds that I had never even imagined existing (they far were beyond my imagination), full of the most complex geometric designs; worlds beyond form but full of light, colour and the strangest of beings. They appeared, then unveiled themselves as my attention was placed upon them; intricate, precise and seemingly perfect in design. As I travelled through these worlds I was consumed by and immersed in the most intense, light and magical feeling of absolute and Universal Love. I knew I was beyond the realms of death, that finally I was fully immersed in that place beyond the fear and noise of existence.

At one point I was shown the world where I was from and all the life forms, all the ancestors that had existed and have yet to exist, how the illusion of time is propelled through space on the back of an incredible force that is Universal Love; held by these beings that come from some distant world somewhere on the same continuum as ours, yet at the same time one that holds ours together. I was shown how they have mastered the art of existing and influencing different physical and non-physical locations and that in this place all the paradoxes and contradictions of life disappear. Or rather, they don't disappear, but are reconciled.

In that place, I then felt suddenly the imprint of a painful personal dilemma that I had been struggling with in my awareness. This involved the prospect of not being able to have my own children, which I had always wanted and physically craved with my partner, who was the love of my life and felt like my soulmate. Yet having children with her was a physical impossibility.

The contradiction of the universe seemingly giving me what I had wanted for so long (I've always been a romantic) and at the same time denying something else I wanted dearly and had thought about most of my life (I'm also very family orientated) had caused me a lot of personal anguish.

However, as I felt the pain of this, I was also able to see the smallness and seeming irrelevance of my dilemma. And because I experienced this understanding at the same time as being held and surrounded by this Universal Love while consciously being aware of the spirit of life flowing through me (as it flows through everything and always will) I was able on some level to grasp the sheer enormity of time. I realised such things as these personal dilemmas and heartbreaks that can consume us, on a certain fundamental level are so irrelevant. Even our lives, which we invest so much time and energy in, are not really that meaningful in the midst of the great life force that is creation.

It was instant healing for me, as I felt a huge weight lift off my soul. There were then many other experiences, beyond the realms of words, before I finally returned to my body, the tepee and the rest of the ceremony.

Apart from the obvious bliss of experiencing these worlds and the incredible healing I received from that ceremony, there are two things that feel important from the whole experience. Firstly, that in the midst of the chaos and incredible uneasiness at the beginning of the ceremony that I could very easily have got trapped in, I was able to call on all the shamanic training I had undertaken. This meant that all the years of fully learning to trust an invisible teacher assisted me in not losing my mind. I know that many people, especially those of sensitive disposition and who aren't fully grounded or connected to life here, have been burnt by the experiences that these plants can open us to and have ended up ill mentally. They are not to be messed with. This is true for any spiritual pursuit that connects us with the Otherworld in powerful ways.

The second point is that this experience wasn't just a wonderful enlightening experience for me to think or write about. I now work with those beings that came to me in the ceremony, as I do with the spirit of the plants in the healings I do. For once a relationship like this has begun you don't have to be actually ingesting the plants to be able to work with them spiritually. Once doorways have been opened in the spirit world, they can always be travelled through and once relationships have been formed they can always be developed.

When in healings I feel the presence of something seemingly irresolvable that is causing intense pain to the person, or I sense fear of death so deep that it is stopping the person from actually living, I call on the presence of these beings. Sometimes they just come anyway, and the love and perspective from their world is transmuted through my hands into the person. They conjoin with the person's energy field, going through the resistance and cause their whole being to relax, which is when I am able to reach in and remove the energetic poison they have been hanging onto. This for me helps me integrate the medicine.

Interesting enough, the night after this experience there was another ceremony, which I approached completely differently. I got cocky and thought I had somehow now mastered the plants because I'd been shown so much and had such a profound experience. I thought of myself as some kind of master psychic traveller of different dimensions and the fact that I had been gifted these secrets of existence meant I was special and had a 'special' relationship with the plant. I was also craving and expecting a similar experience, maybe to be shown even more. I had conquered my fear and was ready for Mother Ayahuasca to simply reveal her secrets for me to revel in. When this didn't happen immediately I got impatient and ended up having a second dose, something I hadn't done before as I'm quite sensitive to the plants.

I lost my respect in that ceremony, everything about how I approached it was wrong, as I was treating the plant like some kind of ticket to other dimensions that wasn't delivering, forgetting it is a being that needs the upmost honouring, spiritually and physically. The plant duly bit me back. The experience that night couldn't have been more diametrically opposed to the one previously. I remained completely in my body, which was the whole night racked with nausea and pain. I had hardly any visions at all, though I was trying my hardest to make them manifest, and had to face the reality of my internal battles, seeing them completely played out in my mind and all the poisons that were locked inside of me.

I spent the whole night purging and incredibly uncomfortable. Yet I learnt an incredible amount about myself that night, as much as the previous one, as finally in the morning, I realised the whole battle I had had was a reflection of what was occurring in my Body Soul for most of the time in my life. I also learnt how not to approach ceremony, of any kind, and was rightly brought back down to earth with a huge bump.

This is the incredible power and beauty of the plants, as anyone who has worked with them will tell you – their intelligence to give us exactly what we need, how and when we need it. It really is uncanny sometimes.

How can this be so? I believe it is because they're our parents, they gave birth to us or rather, as the plant said to me once in a ceremony: 'They dreamt us into being.' I realised after the ceremony that this is both a mystical and practical point because on a fundamental level, without the conditions of life that the plants created, mammals and humans would never have existed. On the invisible level, although it isn't so obvious, the plants also have the same creative powers to imagine things into being that humans do. More so in fact; they just do it in a different way. They have their own unique spirits and intelligence. You only have to work with them a few times to realise this, in the way they can give us profound answers to our most intimate and bewildering personal problems. Again, this challenges the whole cosmological vision of humans being somehow at the top of the evolutionary chain and this is why they can be so powerful in shattering our culturally held belief systems. This is why they are such powerful agents of healing and change in the modern world, and are so needed.

The plants are closer to the spirit of all life, they go back further in time. We have come further away from the source and along the continuum and this is why they can teach us or, rather, *remind* us what being connected to that original source, that creative spark of life, feels like. So, if you are sick in any way and you conjoin your imagination of being well with the power of the plants' imagination – remembering it is the plants who gave birth to you, who continue to sustain your life and are closer to the source of all creation – then there is a strong chance you will be well. It's as simple as that. Anyone who works with the plants will tell you, they can assist you in healing anything and they consistently do.

The teacher plants show us how to connect and do this in dramatic ways, which can be useful as human beings can need their 'head broken open', to paraphrase the title of one famous book on the subject. However, all the plants have the potential to heal us in this way. People continually cure themselves from all kinds of illnesses with diet and herbs, including very serious or so-called incurable ones.

What helps in these cases, what I feel is the vital ingredient, is that the people believe in the power of the plants to heal them with their whole beings – they 'believe to see'. And yet so-called experts spend enormous amounts of energy trying to tell everyone that this can't be proven. The way I see it is if it works in one person that's proof enough of the *potential* for healing and that is the potential that we need to harness. We need to feed it, not seek to destroy it with rational doubt.

Another important point is the way this belief or intention interacts with the spirit of the plant doing the healing, as it directs it. Even those in the West interested in the potential healing power of the plants can get too caught up in the chemical components that are considered to be doing this healing. This is a blind alleyway I believe, and again indigenous people are so much wiser here. They will emphasise not just the whole of the plant in the healing, as reductionism interferes with its spiritual power, but also the way you interact with its spirit.

When a shaman administers any plant for healing purposes, they will always have spent a lot of time singing, praying and generally petitioning the plant for its help. This is why, in teacher plant ceremonies, beyond the ingestion of the plant, the songs that the shaman will sing are so important. These songs are probably more essential than anything else to the healing power of the ceremony, as they direct and literally give the ceremony its power.

This interacting and petitioning the spirit of the plants also explains how in the Amazon, several tribes will use the same tree or plant to treat completely different ailments. Thus, for one tribe, a certain tree will be used to cure respiratory problems while for another it will be used for digestive problems. This is because each tribe has a different relationship to the spirit of the tree and directs it for different uses. The Wixaritari, realising that all illness is of a psycho-spiritual nature, use just one plant, the peyote, to cure *any* illness, such is their love and reverence for this powerful teaching plant.

I know personally quite a few people who have cured themselves of physical conditions with homeopathy (which I feel works very much on a magical system) or herbal medicine and yet there are whole books dedicated to the fact that this is all quackery. Personally I'd like to take some of these so-called 'experts' and give them a strong dose of a teacher plant and then hear them expound on the limited powers or unproven nature of plants to heal! In fact I think it should be a prerequisite of medical training, just in the spirit of fairness, to balance out all the rational dogma that is also taught.

If you want to be an expert on traditional (alternative) medicine at least engage with it first rather than disputing it on principle. I don't go around telling doctors that anti-depressants don't work because I don't believe in the rationale behind them, because I've seen at times they do. I just disagree on the main reasons *why* they work.

If a person is getting better, then the reason why isn't even relevant. We should rejoice that things do work and engage in ways to harness the real, but often latent, power that human beings have to heal and cure almost any known disease, with the help of natural herbs.

As Terrance McKenna explores in his excellent book *Food of the Gods* the plants/drugs that a society favours can tell you a lot about it. In the modern world we have caffeine and sugar, both strong stimulants to ensure that the workforce is kept constantly alert and active in an adrenaline-fuelled state. (In a lot of high-pressure jobs such as the banking industry this might be supplemented by cocaine.) Then we have alcohol, which is used as a destressor or distraction from the harshness of the lives that this relentless industry has created. As McKenna points out so excellently, plants are hugely influential over societies whether we choose to acknowledge it or not. Plants that promote mind expansion or a slowing down and appreciation of nature are counter to the dominant society's ethos and desires and will therefore be suppressed/outlawed.[12]

Shamans, medicine men and women, witches and healers have always worked with plants. This seems to me one of the constants running through human history. Modern shamanism, taking its lead from academia, has emphasised the shaman going into different states of consciousness (often using the drum to do so) as central to the shamanic experience and thus also the teacher plants that can assist in this. This is a huge part of shamanism, but we can also work with these special beings that are the non-teacher plants. It's not just about altering our consciousness (that's the glamorous stuff to us spiritually starved people from the West) but being close to and embracing all the medicines of the earth.

For it is the plants that can heal our Body Soul, they can rebalance us while also changing the very belief systems we have about reality. We just have to believe in them and allow their healing and nurturing love into our lives.

Chapter Nine

Integrating the Body Soul

We have separated ourselves from nature and in doing so we have disconnected from a fundamental aspect of our beings – that of our Body Soul. I have explored some of this disconnect and suggested some ways back in, though the ideas here are in no way suggested as definitive. In fact, I have probably asked more questions than I have answered. This appears often the way forward when working with spirit – finding and asking the right question then being open and patient enough to wait for the answers.

The Kogi tribe of Columbia call the modern Western man 'little brother', emphasising our seeming immaturity and lack of eldership in the world. It seems to me that in growing out of ourselves – our archaic and indigenous past – we have forgotten how to grow *into* ourselves. We are like perpetual teenagers, forever pushing limits and not caring for the past or the future, or even much for the present. Not knowing where we have come from, where we are going to or where our home is. Just determined that we're right, have got all the answers and need to prove to the world how big and powerful we are.

Major initiation in indigenous cultures came during teenage years for a reason, to ensure that people wouldn't get stuck in that place between childhood and adulthood. It is a time when it is natural to think you have all the answers, but also a time when you lack the wisdom to be able to integrate those answers into the fabric of the world.

To counter all this and find a way back into ourselves, I feel we have to become centred again. Centred and at home in the world, so the fundamental underlying separation anxieties that haunt the modern soul can be relieved and released. This is so we can face fear and our primal selves without acting out and unleashing such destruction on the world. We can then move out of this collective dark night of the soul and back into balance and harmony with all of creation. Then we will be able to begin once again to become a part of the creation process inherent in nature and in that realise the joy that lies at the heart of life.

Because our connection to the earth in the modern world has been lost, it has meant that the part of us that connects us to nature and to ourselves – our Body Soul – is deeply wounded. This is our starting point and is reflected all around us in the destruction and pollution that is wrought on the natural world. It is also reflected in the sheer volume of new diseases, be they physical, mental or emotional, that are afflicting the modern soul.

To heal the problems 'out there' we must also heal them 'in here'. We must cleanse our inner toxins and come to terms with our demons. This will not only give us the clarity to focus on the ecological problems that we are presented with but also, more importantly, to engage in them a visceral, feeling way.

In my experience people only really 'act up' in life, i.e. behave in destructive ways, when they don't feel safe; when on a fundamental level they perceive themselves to be threatened. By connecting in a deep way to our Body Souls and the Mother, this constant underlying trauma and the neurosis that grows out of it can be relieved. Once this is done, we can then begin to change our belief systems about the world. We can alter our cosmological vision to one that reflects this feeling of connection and the trust that grows out of this.

If this happens, something magical and organic might then occur. We might view the world with new eyes and a new heart. We might, as most traditional cultures do, see the value in everything that surrounds us. And by seeing the value and beauty in all of this, we might want to base our whole societies around praising what we see. Our fundamental approach to life might then be one of immense gratitude for the endless gifts that are presented to us by nature.

This, in turn, will feed the desire to give back – with our offerings, with our ceremonies, with love and respect in our daily lives. It seems to me that too much of religion or spirituality seems to have a top-down approach – we are presented with a framework that provides a moral and social way of being in the world. This is often literally called guidance from above. However, we could instead focus more on a bottom-up approach, whereby our desire for worship comes from a place deep within us; a place of immense gratitude from our bodies for the things that give us life. This might alter the way we experience religion and spirituality.

Maybe then our belief systems and cosmologies won't be based on an inherent guilt for past actions or an intense fear that all this is going to be taken from us and we must in some way 'save the world'. Instead, they will grow out of the love that can only be truly felt when we know whatever happens we are safe, in the arms of something much greater than ourselves. We can become childlike again, in awe and wonder at the world. We can accept and embrace the mystery without endlessly trying to explain or dissect it. We can be playful, adventurous, joyous and wild, knowing that at last we have found our 'home' once more. And that, maybe, our real purpose in life is to celebrate that home – to dance, sing and praise it with the whole of our beings.

For this to happen though, we not only have to heal our relationship with nature and our Body Souls but also our relationship with the past. This involves healing the hurt of many generations of unresolved trauma that has been passed down, creating blocks in the system as a whole. It also involves, once these have been healed, connecting to the power and wisdom of those who have come before us in our bloodline. Thus, our attention now turns to our Ancestral Soul.

Chapter Ten

Ancestral Honouring

Every shamanic culture throughout history and across the world has spent a great deal of their time honouring and worshipping their ancestors. Why is this? Well, a first answer may be that our ancestors offer us a direct connection with the invisible world of spirit, as this is where they reside. Being related to us they have a natural concern for our wellbeing so this connection has the potential for being stronger than with other invisible beings. They are more likely to look out for us from the spirit world, as a distant relative might if we were ever to visit their new homeland. We are connected by blood to our ancestors, that magical substance that has its place in so many rituals.

They are our inroad to the invisible world, our closest connection. They act as mediators to that vast expanse of the unknown and will also help us to undertake that journey when the time comes for us to depart this world. This is why so many people report seeing loved ones who came to collect them when they have come back from near-death experiences, or those who are dying often see deceased relatives around them in the room just before they depart.

Most indigenous cultures, however, don't wait until death to explore the Otherworld. They know that the world of the living is fed by the invisible one and that keeping a connection between the two is essential to the survival and prosperity of both. The main responsibility for this would usually lie at the door of the shaman as they, as always, were in charge of ensuring a balance between the invisible and visible worlds. The ancestors were an essential component of this connection.

This connection also fulfils a practical function – the preserving and remembering of culture through thousands of

years and generations, something essential within oral traditions. The ancestors were always the link to the past and
preserving the ways of the past was of great importance. The
elders were leaders of the community as they not only had a
direct link to the past and how things had always been done, but
were closest to the ancestors, quite literally. They would then
petition the ancestors for help and their wisdom if any major
decision needed to be made that would affect or alter in any way
their culture or society

One of the reasons, the way I see it, for this focus on preservation of the past and the ancestral role within it, is that if you
trace your ancestors far enough back, they will go back to the
beginning of time. We all share common ancestors. Firstly a
common human ancestor, then going further back the animal
and plant life from which we have come from until eventually
reaching the primordial elements of the universe that miracu-
lously gave birth to life. Our oldest ancestor is what we might
call God, or the Divine, or the Great Mystery – whatever name
has been given to that ineffable creative source of life.

This all begins with our blood relatives, which puts our
connection to them into some kind of context and maybe shows
why shamanic cultures revered their ancestors in such a way. By
worshipping them we remind ourselves constantly of the
connection we have with all of life. And by preserving the past
we remain close to the ideal conditions that created life, and
hence are more likely to support it. We are part of the evolving
process and because we retain a constant connection to the
source, we do not seek to interfere too much in this process.

This, again, is a counter world view to the one of 'human
progress' that informs our cosmology at the moment, which
places the human not only at the pinnacle of creation, but also
firmly in the driving seat. In this viewpoint, it is up to us now,
driven by our technological inventions, to force evolution's hand
and somehow bend it to our will. I would suggest that this

dangerous world view originates initially from a disconnection with our ancestors that causes a disconnection from the past and thus with the creative source of life.

I was with a North American Indian elder once and someone asked the question: 'What is an ancestor?' He just pointed to the sky and then to the earth and said: 'Everything between heaven and earth.' This was the truth of his people, who recognised that everything in manifest creation is a relative of ours, no matter how distantly. From this perspective comes a much different relationship with our fellow beings, animate or inanimate, of the world.

But this ancestral focus isn't just about preserving the past. It is also, perhaps more importantly, about protecting the future. In many North American Indian tribes there would be a tradition that before you acted in a way that would have repercussions on or change the world in any way, you thought about how this would impact your descendants, seven generations in advance. This ensured that people or communities didn't act from a selfish place that would exploit or ruin things for those yet to come; that the spirit of life that had given birth to the human was preserved.

Just think how many of the world's problems would be solved overnight if modern society and our leaders adopted this simple philosophy; how much this would change our policies for dealing with our problems. It's really quite incredible to imagine and yet such a simple concept is seemingly impossible for us to grasp as a society. Again, I would say that this is a consequence of our disconnection from an ancestral way of honouring .

So how can we reconnect once more? Well to begin with, we have to focus on the healing of our ancestral line. This involves lifting off a lot of past traumas that weigh heavily on our Ancestral Soul and is what the first part of this section of the book is about. We will explore how these past burdens not only affect us individually, but also globally. In the second part we will then focus on different ways we can connect with our ancestors to bring forth what I like to call the 'ancestral gold': all those qualities and gifts that have lain dormant in our heritage. In this section we will learn that by 'feeding our ancestors' we can in turn be fed by them and how this can bring us ultimately the gift of spiritual confidence.

Because the old ways of interacting with spirit in the West have been lost, we've had to travel to or learn a lot from distant, exotic cultures. This is great and the indigenous people have been incredibly kind and generous in sharing their ceremonies and traditions with us. However, for us to fully embody these teachings in the modern world – and once again have pride and confidence in who we are and where we come from – I feel we must reconnect with our own ancestral way.

I wasn't born in the Amazon and though I can learn an incredible amount from the practices and teachings from that region, I have to connect it to the land where I am from if this thing is going to be fed down the line. This means to truly follow the old ways and acknowledge that our ancestors hold the key to a way of living that goes back to the source. To awaken our spirits, we must awaken the land, to awaken the land, we must awaken our ancestors.

Chapter Eleven

Ancestral Healing – Releasing Ghosts

We live in a time when there is much healing needed for the environment as our world is teetering precariously on the edge of ecological catastrophe. This we have explored in the previous section. Yet, as our world is polluted physically, so it is also polluted psychically. This is largely due to our mis-relationship with death, both literal and symbolic, which causes an unhealthy clinging on to life. This in turn creates a psychic environment that is haunted by the presence of ghosts from the past. These ghosts are both people who have been unable to continue their journey into the afterlife, but they are also stored traumas and memories that haven't been able to be resolved and thus released.

Shamanically speaking, everything has a life force or a spirit to it. It isn't just animate or inanimate physical objects that are included in this animistic world view, such as people, trees and rocks, but also less tangible things, such as ideas, memories, thoughts or words. Everything is alive and has its own unique presence in the world, even though this presence is often invisible. We cannot see or touch an idea, and yet by listening or perceiving in a certain way we may feel it and ascertain not only its quality, but also its place in the world.

As we explored in the previous section, ideas can take people over as much as being in love can. They can create the zeitgeist of the age and give birth to whole cultures or civilisations. This is especially true when the ideas have an emotional charge to them or appear to come from a transcended reality.

Memories also have a life force to them and they often contain the emotional essence of the original experience as opposed to what might have actually happened. In a way, memories are thought forms held in place by an emotional attachment, or vice versa, emotional energies held in place by a thought form. Thus, 'good' memories have the sheen of joy or love, often regardless of the original experience and 'bad' memories become surrounded by fear, grief, hurt or anger – again sometimes regardless of the original experience. They're subjective responses to reality as opposed to an accurate portrayal of it.

When we have a negative response to an experience in life – a parent leaves us when we are a child, for example, causing immense fear and pain from the perceived rejection or abandonment – if the emotional response isn't fully released at the time, this can then create a thought form or belief system around the experience. This is our subjective, felt response and has a reality to it whatever story our rational mind may build later around the experience. And this is the 'reality' that is stored as memory.

For example, the thought form or belief system experienced at the time could be, 'They don't love me because I am unlovable', or, 'People I rely on will always leave me', or simply, 'I'm never going to leave myself that vulnerable or reliant on anyone again as it only leads to intense pain.' When this happens the emotional experience gets locked in the psyche and often in the body as a traumatic memory, until it can be undone or resolved.

Shamanically speaking, this traumatic memory has a life force of its own and because of the nature of the thought form or the belief system; it has its own agenda and like everything in life, it wants to survive and prosper. So how can it prosper? Simply by recreating the conditions that gave birth to it – the fear and pain around rejection and abandonment. Thus, deep down belief systems around life can become self-fulfilling prophecies, which gradually create more and more energy or charge around the initial wound or trauma.

Psychologists have called these 'core wounds'. The trauma becomes our life; it takes us over and becomes the central plot of our drama. Yet without deep reflection into our past we may not even recognise that this is the case and simply put it down to bad luck or the unpleasant vagaries of fate. We will explore how these 'stories' or core wounds affect the individual in the final section of the book.

In this section the reason I have gone into what I have experienced as the literal, energetic reality of these memories is to highlight how they can live inside people and that they have their own life force. To take to this further, just because people may die, it doesn't mean that the memories die with them, they want to survive and will often actually stubbornly cling onto life. They are invisible after all and not subject to the same laws as the physical universe.

So what happens to these memories and the powerful energies if a person who was storing them dies, as they have to go somewhere? In my experience two things can happen. First, they can jump into the environment and get stored in the land. This is especially true in the case of collective traumas such as war when a lot of people are experiencing similar extreme trauma at the same time. Second, they can jump down the line into descendants and be stored in the Ancestral Soul. As the person will be kept alive in the memories of those left behind, so the person's memories can actually survive too and begin to prosper.

This happens on the invisible, magical level of reality where memories, ideas, and thought forms are actually contagious and can jump from person to person and culture to culture, defying the laws of time and space. The wound, or more importantly the story behind it, can then survive the physical death of the individual who experienced the trauma and live on through the bloodline as ancestral memory. Usually then, the life force of the trauma can generate its own reality and be added to, to create a core wound or story that constantly repeats itself and afflicts many generations.

Greek mythical tragedies often express this concept well, as the sins of the forebears would bring a curse down on a certain house that appeared to strike individuals randomly through incredible twists of fate. This is part of Oedipus' story. Alongside his own arrogance and belief that he can outwit the gods, at the heart of the story is the trauma surrounding the lies and abandonment of his birth – the resulting drama is all a consequence of this act. His daughter, Antigone, then goes on to suffer her own horrendous 'fate', fed by the power of the ancestral curse that has been placed on her family.

What these myths hint at, is that simple actions of lies and deceit can build and be added to over generations and end up having an accumulative effect, a bit like the proverbial energetic snowball. This also has parallels in the Eastern tradition of 'karma', whereby every action in the universe creates a reaction. However, the difference in perspective is that instead of an emphasis on personal past lives; the focus is on the power of the ancestral inheritance running through the bloodline. This is stored in what I would describe as the Ancestral Soul – the collective pool of ancestral memory.

So how does all this work in the context of shamanic healing? What can be done about these energetic snowballs once they have started gathering pace? Let's look at some simple examples to help illustrate this.

A while back an English woman walked off the street into a shop in which I was offering healing. She was in quite a broken down state as another in a long line of relationships had just finished for her in traumatic circumstances. This had been an ongoing pattern for her in her life and even though she had done a lot of healing on herself, exploring and reflecting on her past, she couldn't get to the heart of why this kept happening. Whenever she got into a settled relationship and began to relax into the security of it, it would suddenly end. Either the other person would just walk off and end it, without giving any reason or justification or she would feel compelled to do the same. Occasionally, circumstances would intervene and prevent them from being together.

Thinking that this pattern might have begun when she was younger through some kind of abandonment (real or perceived) I probed into her past a little. But she had already explored this with countless other healers and therapists and it had never yielded any results. So, I gave up and decided to let spirit take over and see what they could offer on the matter.

I then entered the trance state that I use to commune with the invisible world, letting go of any sense of time and space and allowing myself to be enveloped by the mysterious, otherness of the invisible world. Drumming, chanting and dancing to help myself lose myself. When I was fully ensconced and could feel the presence of my helping guardians deep inside me as they merged with my spirit, strengthening and protecting the fragility of my human self, I was guided to clear out some of the excessive grief that was hanging heavy on her soul, like the heavy, sticky black mess it usually takes the form of.

As I was doing this, I was suddenly taken off into the deep past where I could feel, sense and see her grandfather, trapped in some horrendous, hell-like place. The old adage, 'The past is a different country,' describes this well, as in the energetic reality of the universe the past is just a different place, slightly removed from the present, but still alive in it. It can be visited by shifting your attention to a different level of consciousness.

I was immediately drawn to go to this man, to somehow comfort him as he was in immense pain and suffering greatly. I could viscerally feel his suffering; it pierced this reality like an uncontainable howl across all of time. I was aware that he was imprisoned somewhere, and that outside were troops. The whole scene had the feeling and reminiscence of one of the world wars, I was sensing probably WWII. He was being tortured in this place and now was reliving that torture continuously.

At a loss as how to help or heal this man, I just held and comforted him, like I would do someone in the physical world, shielding him from the torment of the memory. As I did this, he gradually relaxed from the place of primal terror he was trapped in and eventually he began to grieve uncontrollably. I just held him there. As is usually the case in these circumstances, the role of the compassionate witness is the most helpful and potent of healing tools. This is both true of those dead in the spirit world and those alive, sitting opposite you, in this world.

Eventually, I felt his whole spirit relax and release, the energy was flowing out of the trauma like water from a cup and I was able to witness and hold this, seeing the energy disperse. I knew from experience he was trapped in the netherworld and that he would eventually need moving on to another world where he could continue his journey. This was my role as the healer to assist him in this.

Yet, I also knew that he wasn't yet ready and I had no idea how long this would take, or how this could happen. When someone has suffered that much trauma, it can be difficult for them to continue their journey anywhere. This is how trauma has a paralysing effect on people's spirits.

Then, out of nowhere I felt the presence of a woman I somehow knew to be his wife. She was also in a dark place herself, but not as dark. Though she needed healing she was clearly not in such pain. Instinctively, I knew that they were somehow separate from each other and that in death they had lost their connection. They were both lost, searching for the other one and not being able to continue their journey without them. It was intensely sad and moving and in that moment I knew why I was there – to help them find each other. I was to act as a bridge and reunite them, as the light from my being merged with spirit, was able to act as a beacon in the darkness to them both.

I reached out my hand to her and pulled her towards her husband and as I did this I felt the immense love and bittersweet joy of their reunion course through me. I was a conduit and it was a beautiful moment. And then they were gone, everything flowed organically as I watched them move on and join the rest of their ancestors deep in another world that it wasn't my place to explore or to fathom. With each other, they had the strength to journey on. I returned then to the rest of the healing.

After the healing I told the woman client what I had seen and what I had done for her grandfather and grandmother. She looked at me a little shocked and then told me their story. They had both been German Jews and during the Second World War had been sent to the same concentration camp together, but were then separated once they were there. Her grandfather hadn't survived and perished in the camp, but her grandmother did. She left Germany for England after the war and went on to live a long life. However, she had never got over the loss of her husband. She had never remarried and refused to forget him. The woman remembered her grandmother talking about her grandfather as if he were still alive years and years later when she was a young girl.

Theirs was a bond that couldn't be broken, but unfortunately the intense trauma of it also meant that it couldn't be healed, even in death. It needed an outside party, conjoined with spirit to help with this. And the energy or life force of this trauma, all its emotional power, had been passed down and was playing out in their granddaughter's life as a pattern of lost love. This was repeating again and again through her relationships, recreating in physical time an echo of that heartbreak which had led her to believe that somehow she must just be unlucky or fated not to find contentment in this area of her life.

She was amazed that it was this that had been affecting her life and yet when she thought about it, it became clear to her and I could see tangibly a whole weight had been lifted from her. It is amazing how clear this is. People often remark after healings how everyone close to them says how much lighter they look. Trauma, whether your own or that of an ancestor, is heavy. This was the healing she had been seeking for so long and the fact that the spirits had shown me all this without me knowing anything about her ancestry meant that she knew it was real.

This is another part of the magic that ensures all the invisible energetic work goes into a person's life and helps them to transform. For, when the spirits reveal information that I couldn't possibly know or guess, it shows that this stuff isn't just about the imagination or positive thinking. A person can then believe in it. Despite our seemingly cynical façade in the modern world, it really doesn't take much to send us back into our natural state of magical thinking – a state conducive to all healing and, I would say, to life.

The funny thing is that this woman coming to me wasn't as random as I might have imagined, as I had had to do a similar healing for my grandparents about five years previous. My grandfather had also died in WWII, three weeks before my father was born. He had been working as an engineer on the planes in the Battle of Britain, but had contracted appendicitis. However, he had ignored the intense pain his appendix was giving him as he was convinced that it was his duty to continue on the flying missions, that the war needed him. So he had not sought medical help. Eventually his appendix burst and as this was before the introduction of penicillin in hospitals, he died shortly afterwards.

My grandmother, although she did remarry briefly once, again had never got over the loss of her husband as they were still very much in love. I knew all this and also felt intuitively from my father a heavy, undistinguished grief he carried in his life, lurking beneath the surface of his optimistic, warm personality. This made sense to me years later when I started exploring healing work as I realised what intense grief he must have been born into. As a newborn baby, wide open to the world, he would have absorbed all of that sadness. Being very close to my father, I also knew I had inherited my fair share of this. We both shared a kind of poignant, poetically melancholic view of the world –

especially when recounting stories of life, or people's dreams being cut short, from film, literature and songs. This was our way of being able to explore this huge theme that was so present in our ancestry.

However, it took an experience in my real life to bring this into a sharp focus and healing to the ancestral wound. In my early 30s I was still drifting through life. I had been through a lot in my 20s in terms of getting well again from the sicknesses that had beset me and although I had found my cure through finding my path in shamanism, I was still somewhat lost. I was in a stage of thinking, 'Okay, I've found my path and healed myself, what can I do with this in the world?' What occupied a lot of my attention then and been such a central theme through my life was to find a partner, a soul mate to share my life with. I have always been a romantic. In a strange way, it seemed impossible to move forward without this as it occupied so much of my attention. But the more I looked, the more elusive this search became.

I had been seeing a German woman off and on for a couple of years, but for various reasons, including the fact that she lived in Berlin, I had been somehow ignoring the possibility that we could be together in any long-term situation. However, over a summer I suddenly woke up to the fact that this could be a real possibility, that in my search for something more I had been missing what was right in front of me. I was hit by the realisation that my search had taken me away from my real feelings.

This isn't unusual for me. Because I am often focussed on the bigger picture and am quite heady, I have a strong tendency to overlook what I am actually feeling, and often to miss the 'bleeding obvious' right in front of me! By this time though, she had gone off me due to my general lack of certainty and distanced herself completely. I had to win her back, which again suited my romantic nature!

She agreed to visit me in England in the autumn and through a weekend of honest and at times challenging exchanges, we eventually came back together. It was beautiful, exciting and fun and in a way surprised us both I think as we were both intensely strong willed and independent by nature. It was almost as if we had met our matches. She even agreed to move over to England so we could explore the possibility of somehow going forward together, in whatever way it might pan out. I didn't know where this was leading, neither of us did, but it seemed right in the moment, which was all that mattered. It was like the burden of having to find 'the one' had been finally lifted and I could actually just get on with my life. I was happy and my heart was open, the future seemed to be an open expanse of possibility.

Two weeks later, she was killed in an accident at work. The shock, grief and rage that followed took me on a deep journey that again took me to my edges and beyond, resulting in me not particularly wanting to be alive. This was the point where I experienced leaving my body consciously as I described in the previous section, which helped me to make peace with life.

The healing journey also took me into a waking dream where I met my grandfather in the spirit world and realised that he was still separate from my grandmother. Again, even in death, they were not able to be together and it was my role to help them reunite. It was only in my own grief though, that was I able to fully open up to what they had experienced in life and in a way appreciate and bring healing to their story.

My story of loss was a lot less tragic in a way. They were married and, with my father on the way, had three children that my grandfather would leave behind. Yet, the 'flavour' of the loss was an echo of this original wound and it made me determined to bring healing to this ancestral pain that I felt was running through my family.

For, the loss of my lover just compounded a pattern I felt had run through my life – that whenever the possibility of something beautiful opened up, a seemingly hammer-like blow would come down from the universe that would destroy it in its tracks. Part of this was my own story and the healing of such stories we will explore in the final section, but part of it came down through my ancestral lineage.

To emphasise the fate-like quality of this experience earlier, in the spring of that year, I had written a song that contained the verse:

The day I smelt the scent of autumn's breath,
Was the day I found out about my lover's death.
The news was rushed to me by the falling of the leaves,
Whispering you are free now, to chase your memories.

I had thought it strange at the time that I'd written specifically the word 'lover' relating to death as opposed to the more general 'love', but if I tried to change it, it didn't sound right. I even at the time played this song to this woman and we laughed at my propensity for writing poetically melancholic songs. She'd said to me: 'Why don't you try writing a happy one!' It was that autumn though that she died, as the song had predicted.

Several years later, when the grief had healed, I met a woman who I still believe is my soul mate. Although the relationship isn't always easy (which one ever is?), the quality of our connection is different from anything I had ever experienced before and one that I had yearned for all my life. Of course I had given up on all that romantic stuff by then, which is probably another reason why I found it. Yet, without the experience with that German woman and the deep healing that followed I am sure this would not have happened. I wouldn't have experienced that exquisite feeling of coming home that I now do when I surrender to my partner's embrace. It lifted the ancestral memory.

The other major impact this had on my life was to stop me drifting. It woke me up to the reality of how precious life really is. This meant that in the years that followed by channelling all that emotional energy inside of me and through a lot of determination and hard work, my healing practice took off and I fulfilled many dreams that had lain dormant in my soul. This continues to this day. Witnessing someone else's death, someone young like me, someone who was so fearless and full of life, finally woke me up in a visceral way to the real gift that life is.

The ancestral pain on this side of my family went back even further though, as is often the case. My grandmother's mother was one of five Irish sisters from Dublin, who had all married English soldiers posted there. During the Easter Uprising in 1917, the IRA knocked on all their doors and gave them 24 hours to leave the country, or face death. There was a kind of running joke in my family about my great aunt, one of the sisters who was quite an eccentric character, telling my father and aunt in a thick Irish accent: 'I hate the bloody Oirish! Kicked us out of Oirland they did, I hate the bloody Oirish!' When my aunt would say to her innocently, 'But you are Irish, aunty,' she would solemnly cross her chest, look up and say, 'God forgive me!'

The sisters had to start again, moving to and living a tough existence in the Gorbals, one of the poorest areas of Glasgow. When my grandmother met and fell in love with my grandfather (the one who would later die in the war) it caused another chasm. She was Irish Catholic and he was English Protestant. This time it was his family that completely disowned him when they married, never to have any contact with him again. Then, less than ten years later he died. So two generations running marrying the 'wrong' person had contributed to displacement and the breaking up of families.

I had never felt truly at home growing up in England and when I went travelling around the world in my 20s, I naturally gravitated towards and hung out with Irish people. We shared the same sense of humour I found. I also had a succession of Irish girlfriends. Around ten years ago I was involved in a project that was going to set up a shamanic community on the West Coast of

Ireland and we spent a bit of time looking at land over there. However, every time I went there I either got sick or my back would go. It was uncanny. But more than that, the level of grief I felt from the landscape was immense. Even though Ireland is a watery place, even more than England and I've always been prone to sensing sadness in the world, this grief I found overwhelming and unbearable. It was like I could feel my ancestors, but it wasn't a good feeling. Luckily, the project didn't come off.

Then, a couple of years ago I was invited to teach over in West Cork. I thought, having done a lot of ancestral healing work, my connection to the place would be different. However, it was the same. The intensity of grief was again overwhelming. I couldn't understand it because I thought my ancestors were from the other side of the country in Dublin. However, I was talking to my aunt about this who in her later life had done a lot of research on our family tree and had also got involved with Irish politics, campaigning for peace and reconciliation between Protestants and Catholics (an echo of the ancestral wound playing out in a positive way). She then told me that the family name was Horrigan. In Ireland you can trace where people come from originally through the surname, which was West Cork where I had been teaching. So I had been drawn back to the exact land of my ancestors.

At the end of that trip, I was sitting in the airport waiting for the plane home, when suddenly the emergency alarm went off. Cork airport is small and the security quickly gathered everyone together at one end of the departure lounge to shepherd us out of the building. But before this could happen we found out it was a false alarm. The whole (non) incident was over in ten minutes. However, in that time I was struck by a thunderbolt of intense fear and grief, seemingly triggered by that alarm. I couldn't understand it as everyone was calm, including the security staff who didn't seem concerned at all and yet inside I started panicking uncontrollably. As I then, driven by this fear, entered a strange half space, I found myself shot backwards through time and imagining what it must have really felt like to have to 24 hours to leave your country, your home, your loved ones, every-thing. Not only that, knowing that you could never, ever return again.

Although I had heard this story many times I had never really connected to the emotional power of it or imagined what that must have felt like. But, in that moment, as the alarm sounded its shrill panic above me, I could suddenly feel my family, leaving Ireland and not only the pain this had caused them, but the rupture in generations of ancestral connection to this land it had precipitated. I felt, beneath the ironic humour of my great aunt, the real bitterness and hatred this had created. I also sensed the strange, twisted self-loathing and shame, as what she was really saying when she said she hated the Irish was, 'I hate what I am.'

This seemed a familiar feeling inside of me. In that moment I felt all this flow through me and was struck by that familiar overwhelming sadness. By bringing awareness to it though, I could let it go; let it flow through me on behalf of all my ancestors. This happened for such a brief moment in time, but an eternity in timelessness as I stood there in that airport. I then got on the flight and flew back home to England.

The next time I travelled to West Cork to teach, the feeling of the land for me couldn't have been more different. I felt a lightness and joy and while treating people in healings, felt myself connect deeply with the ancestral spirits of that place. This enabled a feeling of deep healing within and also the coming together of both my English and Irish heritages; I felt immense pride and strength in both, instead of a split.

Also, this sense of displacement I had felt all my life, even though I had a settled upbringing, was gone. I felt at home in the world at last. All this ancestral healing I had gone through had been a long journey, but had brought peace to my Ancestral Soul.

These stories are just examples of the patterns of ancestral wounding that can run through generations and also the different ways they can be healed. We all have these patterns and it doesn't take much uncovering to be able to begin to see them. Usually they will be present in the stories that run in families, told and retold, though the real emotional power of the stories may be lost in the retelling – as they were with my great aunt. And the stories will go on repeating until the emotional charge or energetic sting can be taken out of them and released. This is just the law of nature as nature follows patterns.

As with the stories I have relayed, so often ancestral wounding is created by an interaction of personal lives coming into conflict with collective forces – for example, wars, social taboos or laws, struggles and uprisings that affect whole nations. The personal suffering of many people is then reflected and also has its cause in the actions and destinies of nations and people. So this level of healing also involves understanding the nature of the wound running through different states. To explore this further we will now look at how ancestral wounds and patterns can run through and affect whole societies.

Chapter Twelve

The Ancestral Wounding of Nations and Peoples

This is such a huge subject that it could take a whole book to explore in itself. Yet, it is important when we are exploring the Ancestral Soul to witness the powerful effects that the bloodline of our nation or community has had on us as individuals, or individuals within our ancestry. Shamanism has always emphasised the importance of the community as it based upon the study of indigenous cultures where the 'we' is far more important than the 'I'. Although we live in a much more individualistic age, collective cultural forces still have an incredible power over us. We have explored some of the ways this can happen in the previous section.

I would even suggest that as a culture, we're actually far less individualistic than we pride ourselves on being. That, by rejecting the notion of the collective and over-emphasising the individual, paradoxically it has become even more powerful over us. This is the simple psychological rule; whatever you reject goes into the unconscious (the invisible world) and becomes more powerful.

Thus, for example, we have the consistent outbreaks of nationalism that can take over a whole people, often in the most destructive of ways. Or culturally, the McDonald's effect, whereby cultures and the people within them lose their individual identity as it is consistently swallowed up by the drive for a homogenous identity. These collective forces have a greater power over us than is often recognised.

The 20th century was the most violent and bloody in the history of human kind. There have always been wars and killing, this wasn't the issue, but it was the sheer scale of the carnage and destruction that was wrought – industrial type killing for an industrial era. And with the whole world being drawn into the conflicts this extenuated its impact. I would venture that we are still feeling and dealing with the repercussions today, not just in the physical/political world, but also in the invisible/spiritual world.

However, the 20th century didn't just grow out of nowhere, in some ways it was an inevitable conclusion of the course the modern Eurocentric culture had set itself on, which in itself was due in some part to ancestral inheritances. Over the next couple of chapters, I will focus on and attempt to explore this in a two-fold way – the ancestral inheritances that led us to such an explosive and destructive century and the ancestral legacy these events have had, i.e. how this is affecting us today. This will illustrate how ancestral traumas can travel down the bloodline not only of individuals and families, but also of whole nations and peoples.

There is a lot of scientific research going into and backing up how ancestral trauma can be passed down the line and I am sure this will grow over time, as people begin to explore this subject more. This is beginning to filter down to the mainstream press in England. I am not a scientist, it's not my language though I appreciate it appeals to many. I present this all from what I have discovered myself working with thousands of clients in a shamanic way and from exploring myth and story – a language that is closer to my heart.

There is already a fascination with war that engages many writers and artists. The amount of stories we tell ourselves about such conflicts, how many books and films explore the subject are immense. I would suggest that this is due to an archaic need to keep our ancestors alive through retelling their stories. Also, in a lot of these stories, especially fictional ones, there can be an emphasis on redemption as the author seeks to put into context and make sense of the seemingly arbitrary horror that enters people's lives. This, I feel, in many ways is the author engaging in ancestral healing by sharing the emotional intensity of what has happened in the past and then finding the resolution for it.

The storyteller becomes what I call the 'compassionate witness' to these stories, alive as they are in the Ancestral Soul. Through the sharing of the stories, the writer can help release the emotional sting that has become trapped through trauma. The book *Atonement*, which was turned into a major film, is a compelling example of this.

In such stories, the reader or viewer is taken along and is often moved to release grief or is provoked to anger or fear on behalf of the protagonists, thus helping to cathart the emotional trauma. Indeed, as we have explored, one of the initial purposes of theatre as it was invented in Greek times was as a Dionysian ritual to release and cathart the pain held in the collective, often through the tragedies that had afflicted their ancestors. This is an ancient healing methodology that still goes on today, albeit unconsciously, through the actions of artists. Although the stories may be fiction, this does not discount from their emotional truth, which is stored in the collective or the Ancestral Soul as trapped energy. This is what the artist is releasing by tapping into these stories. The names may be made up, but the stories have a resonance of truth, which is the important thing.

When I was a history student, I spent a long time researching a dissertation on the First World War. In the Imperial War Museum in London there is a reading room that has thousands of first-hand accounts by ordinary soldiers of their experiences in the war. I used to spend hours in that room, being transported back to the trenches, reading of the horrors, but also the hopes and dreams of those men.

At times, I would be in tears and at others in sheer amazement at the bravery and resilience they had, to carry on and face what they were facing. I read original letters from those on the front line sent back home, hugely intimate insights into what a person was feeling. Then the letters would suddenly stop and it was clear this person had been killed. I would then feel tangibly how fragile existence is through the witnessing of these lives cut short.

I was particularly struck by the magnitude of the shock and the trauma that each one of these individuals had experienced and by the fact that there was really nowhere for this trauma to go to. Men could lose 20 of their closest friends, who had become like family to them, in an afternoon and yet still have to carry on fighting and just trying to survive. There was simply no time or space to process emotionally in any way what they were experiencing.

So where did all that grief, rage, pain, depression and feelings of absolute helplessness and futility at it all go to? Where could it go? Well, some broke down mentally, but the vast majority had to just carry on. Even after the conflict was over and the soldiers came home, there was still no place for the release of trauma. As a lot of them discovered, no one really wanted to hear about what had happened to them. In fact, no one could handle hearing about it. It was like a conspiracy of silence as if not speaking about the horrors of what these men had gone through would mean the pain of the war could be quickly forgotten.

Those returning also didn't even have the framework to put into any kind of context what they had experienced. How could they? One minute you're in a literal hell on earth witnessing and being part of the most grotesque and gratuitous mutilations of not just the human body but also of the spirit, the next you're back in so called 'civilisation', which frowns upon any outward show of uncontained emotion or loss of control. Is there any more of a double bind you could find yourself in? Horror and intense trauma followed by the emotional straightjacket of early 20th century European life?

So denial and uneasy silence reigned – the perfect psycho-logical ingredients for repression, followed by complete psychic and emotional collapse of the system. But this wasn't just individual repression; this was repression of entire societies and cultures.

There is only one place I believe that could store such a psychic powerhouse of unresolved trauma, and that's in the invisible world, in what I would call the Ancestral Soul. Ultimately though, this psychic energy has to break free from the repression at some point. When it does, this will then, in turn, cause the psychic collapse of the system and go on to affect the whole culture and society that has been involved in the repression.

This, I believe, is the situation we have found ourselves in since the end of that conflict, which has affected us in many ways in the modern world. Firstly, this is clear in the immediate aftermath of the war. Historians have long agreed that it was the botched and punishing armistice, which laid all the blame for the First World War at the hands of Germany, which set up the conditions that were rife for Hitler to exploit and led in a large way to the outbreak of WWII.

A prominent psychological response to repressed pain and trauma is to react with an over-aggressive assertion of will and power – to mask and somehow keep at bay the traumatic feelings of helplessness and grief that lurk beneath the surface. This is a particularly true response in the male psyche. Domination then becomes a survival imperative to keep the psyche from slipping back into the unacknowledged haunting depths of powerlessness.

To go through the barbaric meaninglessness of WWI would have been bad enough, but to then be faced with not only defeat, but also with the crippling consequences of starvation and economic catastrophe that followed, I believe sent the ancestral traumatic wounds in Germany ricocheting back up to the surface. All that emotional power of the repressed pain and wounds just needed exploitation; step in the master magician of consciousness that Hitler was.

On another, alternative level, at the same time that Hitler and his ideas were gaining traction there appeared another revolution across Europe, this time in consciousness. This was a time that the seeds that had been planted by Sigmund Freud and others with their invention of psychoanalysis began to bear fruit. Ideas such as the 'unconscious' entered the popular imagination and suddenly the invisible world had a place in modern, rationalistic society, albeit with a bit of rebranding and spoken about by predominantly white, Northern European intellectuals.

So why did these fringe ideas take a grip at this time (and again after the Second World War) leading to the point today where the unconscious and many other mythical and invisible concepts are taken for granted as real? Part of the answer, I believe, may be that after the chasm of WWI, millions of personal traumas were sent hurtling into the invisible world. There then automatically came the collective need to explore how and where trauma is actually stored.

As one section of the society was actively involved in the suppression of these traumas and the use of the emotional power for destructive purposes (the rise of fascism) at the same time another section was involved in their active exploration. And the more the earlier pioneers of psychoanalysis plundered the depths, the more they realised how connected we are, hence the invention of the term the 'collective unconscious' by Jung.

What these ideas enabled and initiated were the multitude of healing practices that are used to heal trauma now. Ideas that were dreamt up then about the nature of our psyches, we now take for granted. What this also enabled is the birth of the 'psychological age', which came at a time when we needed it the most as the amount of mental and emotional problems suddenly leapt from the fringes of society and into the mainstream as a whole generation had been so intimately affected.

This is the way of nature; whenever there is poison it automatically supplies a cure. Next to a stinging nettle grows the dock leaf, which soothes the pain from the being stung by the nettle. This is as it was with psychoanalysis growing out of the traumas of a war-ravaged people. The build-up to the First World War had taken place over a long time, from the end of the 19th century, as Europe fell into an inevitable path from its colonial, expansive, dominatory politics. The birth of psychoanalytic theory, and the huge confluence of ideas that came out of it, then tracked and coincided with the 20th century industrial-scale barbarism.

Bringing this into the present, the level of anxiety, mental and emotional disorders that are affecting and afflicting us as a society now are extraordinary. Every year new ones are added to the mix and huge swathes of the population in the Western world are taking medication to 'treat' these problems. Of course there are multitude causes and reasons for these disorders, but the one I wish to explore here is the ancestral legacy of repressed trauma, passed down and affecting the descendant of those who suffered greatly, but were unable to find healing or resolution to this suffering.

This is the situation I believe we find ourselves in now. The wars affected the whole world and previous to the 20th century we saw some of the worst aspects of colonial expansion and brutality over a 400-year period. Because of this, the level of trauma and displacement of people is huge. I believe you would be hard pressed to find someone whose ancestors haven't been affected in such a way by the world events that have created the modern societies we live in.

So many of the disorders today resemble the symptoms of Post Traumatic Stress Disorder – uncontrollable bouts of anxiety or depression, loss of meaning or ability to engage with life, feelings of being separate or a permanent sense of disassociation, not being able to engage in or form healthy bonds in relation-ships, addictions and other coping/distracting strategies, uncontrollable and destructive emotional outbursts. It seems to me that a lot of people are constantly exhibiting these symptoms of PTSD.

In a way we have created a society that actually causes a kind of constant, low-level PSTD with its constant over stimulation of our senses and vicarious ratcheting up of our emotions. Through our media we are fed images and scenes of violence and suffering, stimulating and replaying our trauma responses until they become buried under a protective film of numbness. No matter how good our intentions or what we do to try to make the world a better place, in the face of these stories and images, real or imagined, we are completely helpless. The problems presented to us from the world are just too big.

Thus, what some of our ancestors faced, the absolute powerlessness to affect change in the face of overwhelming and industrial type violence, is re-experienced again and again in the comfort of our front rooms. For the sensitive, this can be just too much.

As the poets of WWI told us, the romantic and heroic ideals of battle were lost the moment the machine gun cemented its annihilistic place in the muddy, bloody fields of history. To face death fighting a good battle throughout human history has always had its noble place. To face it crawling on your knees in the stench of defeat by an indestructible, intractable, mechanical force crushes the spirit. To face up to meaningless victory that brings with it no change or evolution, has the same effect.

Many people I see are facing this battle metaphorically within themselves on a daily basis. These are the people holding in their souls the most ancestral trauma.

But this 'story' of being defeated by an overwhelming force or having to fight to the death, goes back further in our ancestral history. It didn't begin and certainly didn't end in the 20th century. So, now comes the time to explore the deeper roots of this conflict and also ways that it can be resolved and healed.

Chapter Thirteen

An Ancient, Archetypal, Ancestral Myth

Ralph Metzner in his excellent book *The Well of Remembrance* traces the roots of our modern, dominant culture's origins back to Indo-Aryan tribes that came out of the Caspian Sea area. These were highly aggressive, patriarchal, warrior peoples who headed out across mainland Europe, the Middle East and Asia on horseback, taking over the more pastoral and matriarchal original inhabitants of these lands. Gradually these cultures merged, the warriors and pastoralists, creating great ancient empires such as the Greeks and Romans in the south of Europe and the Celts, Norse and Anglo Saxons of Northern Europe. In Asia they gave birth to Hindu civilisation and the Mogul empires.

Although the civilisations created were led by the patriarchal societies – what socio-anthropologists have called 'dominator' societies – they also retained many elements of the original people's earth-centred, goddess-worshipping culture. Thus, there was a fusion of shamanic, animistic ways with the sky-worshipping, thunder gods of the Indo-Aryans. Gradually though, the male sky gods took over more and more, firstly with Greek cosmology. Eventually the old Mother-centred shaman-istic ways were lost completely with the advent and domination of Christianity.

Whereas within Christianity everything earthy was rejected as being of the Devil, rationalistic science then took this one step further with the Newtonian viewpoint that nature was just dead matter, randomly pieced together. The whole life force was taken out of it. Thus the movement away from earth-honouring practices of our most ancient ancestors into aggressive, dominatory societies was finally complete. This is where we find ourselves today.[13]

The problem with a dominator culture's ideology is that it is founded on the need for constant expansion and aggression. These are the warrior aspects of the culture it is built around. When these warrior aspects are over emphasised, this creates two further important needs. First, to always have to protect and defend what you have built. Second, and more importantly, to have an enemy to fight against. Without an enemy the need for aggression and expansion becomes redundant. In a dominator society this has to be constantly fed. Thus, whole mythologies can be built around this need to have an enemy out there in order to feed the warrior impulse.

If you look at the main focus of Western societies, you can see this ancient archetypal myth being played out everywhere. You can see it in the expansion of empires that began in Europe then spread outwards, back into Asia but also to Africa and the Americas. You can see it in the mythology of capitalism that we subscribe to, whereby expansion and growth are worshipped as the only indicators of health for the society. You can see it in the US, as modern leaders of the Western world and their constant need for an enemy out there. This can be communism, terrorism or any other ism that might come next.

We saw it in religion, as Christianity went to war with the Devil, constantly seeking to destroy his influence wherever he reared his ugly head. As the crusaders or missionaries went to fight off and kill those who were unwittingly deemed to be possessed by him all over the globe. Conveniently, at the same time this opened up vast areas of territory for their people to control and dominate.

We can see it so clearly in all our films, those great containers of modern-day myths, as each popular blockbuster feeds off this ritual battle, the need for victory for the great and the good. These blockbusters often re-enact what might have been a literal ancestral memory as they build up to a climactic, near apocalyptic final battle. I see the image so clearly in The Lord of the Rings or Star Wars, as they feed a populist take on this epic archetypal theme and this continues with all the films that have come in their wake.

You can see it in modern spiritual traditions, which constantly emphasise the triumph of light over darkness or love over fear, which is essentially modern language for good over evil. Or, on the other side, the scientist, who wants the bright light of rationalism to triumph over the primitive darkness of superstition and will seek to intellectually destroy any proponents of what they view as regressive thinking. You can see it the medical profession as they go to 'war on cancer' or other diseases and how the drugs that are created seek to obliterate the offending chemicals or cells in the body. Many of these themes we explored in the first section of the book.

The important thing is that whoever is telling the story within this archetypal myth, presumes that they are on the side of good, fighting their enemies who embody all that is evil. For mainstream societies, the evil ones are the objectors to the relentless march of the modern world who stand in the way of its progress. For those outside the mainstream, it is the establishment that is committed to being greedy, feeding itself while destroying the majority. For the Nazis it was the Jews, for the communists it was the capitalists, for Islamic State militants it is Western society, for the West it is terrorism etc. It even affects relationships between the sexes in the modern world, as women have embodied more and more this warrior archetype to take back their power, battling against 'patriarchy'. It is at the heart of every 'revolution' whereby the oppressed rise up to power and then become the oppressors themselves. This plays out and will continue to play out ad infinitum.

There is no inherent problem within this story as such, for it is an archetypal myth which means that it taps into something that is fundamentally true about human experience of life. That often we define ourselves through opposition. However, the important issue is that it isn't the *only* story, nor is it the *only* truth. It is just one element of life that, with poetic irony, due to its inherent aggressive nature, has come to dominate. The myth or story of the warrior qualities of aggression and protection have now taken over. This creates imbalance and the need for other stories to come back to the fore, lest this story will end up destroying itself.

There are many other aspects and stories that are central to life. Nature has this aggressive instinct in abundance, as we explored in the previous section. However, it also has other stories. What, for example, is the story of the butterfly, dancing on the wind? Or, the sunflower, turning to open its petals to the sun? The human embracing a stranger, or the hummingbird finding sweet nectar?

The problem with the dominator myth of power over is that, paradoxically, it creates its opposite: the need to be hyper-vigilant and aware of someone or something that is going to threaten your existence, or take over your land, as you once did to them. This means that the fundamental bedrock of security can never be felt. When this fundamental need cannot be sated, underneath the exterior fighting lies an empty hole of powerlessness. The culture or society will then end up creating a story where the war can never be won. The need for conquest ultimately is there to ensure security and survival, but the security can never be felt, so essentially the battle can never be won. There can never be peace.

This is a big part of the world we have created right now, I feel. It is like this with the game of brinkmanship we are playing with survival as a species. Like the crazed Vietnam veteran played by Christopher Walken in the film The Deer Hunter, traumatised endlessly by the horror of war, the only way he can regain any control over his life is to literally play Russian roulette. When the central plot of your existence is a dance with death, the only place to feel safe is in the battle trying to defeat it.

Yet, death has never been defeated.

If we had nothing to occupy this need for perpetual battle, no enemy to defeat, we as a culture wouldn't feel safe. Paradoxically though, the battles we create are increasingly pitching us on the losing side, as they really only reflect this archetypal myth and the battle within ourselves, which has built up from thousands of years of ancestral inheritance. This is the myth or story that needs healing. As Metzner states, we have to reclaim the archetype of the warrior for positive purposes, so it can be reintegrated into the whole, lest it be used unconsciously to dominate us.

I undertook a ceremony with the medicine cactus San Pedro once, which gave me some insight into this. I had been working deep in the jungle with ayahuasca, often called the Mother due to the feminine nature of the teachings it imparts. San Pedro in contrast is known as Grandfather and the masculine element to its teaching can simply be observed by looking at it, as it stands tall, phallic shaped and proud! High up in the Andes of Peru I took this medicine and as the Grandfather took me deep into his embrace I began to travel back in time to some of my ancient origins.

This was before I had read and discovered about the Indo-Aryan tribes and their expansion across Europe, yet I had a strong vision of myself as a young warrior on horseback travelling across lands, dominating, raping and pillaging all the people that came in the way of the band I was with. I could feel the excitement and the glory, but at the same time I was aware in my modern sensibility of the brutality and heartlessness of my actions. I began to observe these actions gradually from a more and more detached place, as though I was watching a film. I felt no judgement for myself, even though I was witnessing myself being part of and undertaking cruel acts. Instead I had a sense, or rather the plant gave me a sense that these actions had brought me out of balance with life. This was what needed healing.

I then received the message: 'Make your peace with God.' I knew that this was an important message that I should heed. Luckily, the plant had already filled me with the sense of God being all around me before showing me this vision. In the flowers, in the trees, in the hummingbirds that flitted from flower to flower in their joyous flight of ecstasy, in the sun as it beat down on my back, in the clouds above as they would shift and change form to show me visions of animals and birds and great God-like beings and in the feeling of oneness with everything that reverberated through my veins. All of this held me in an embrace with everything, which enabled me to witness this vision dispassionately; the crimes that some part of me had perpetrated, which still hung heavy upon my soul.

I had always felt an inherent shame about being a man. This had been there for as long as I could remember and consequently in my adult life I had sought to hide the more obviously masculine elements of my personality and enhance and show more the feminine side. Maybe, I just felt the shame of an overly patriarchal society that was now coming in for so much criticism. A bit like the white man's burden of guilt for past colonial expansion, I just felt a man's guilt for being born a man. I don't think this is that uncommon, especially growing up now in a world where old gender roles have been going through so much transformation.

Yet the more I hid the aggressive masculine side of me, the more I could feel it haunting me from the edge of my awareness. It would play out at night in my dreams, which would be filled with violent, epic battles or the guilt dreams of having murdered someone and having to bury the body. Or, it would play out in my sexuality, which I hid, as if it was some kind of shameful thing, which would only increase the intense, frustrated desire I felt nearly constantly.

Being shown this vision I began then to understand the source of this shame. There was something unresolved in my soul that was an unresolved ancestral burden I had always felt as my own. I knew also in that moment that I could heal it, as my own. So, in the face of God, who I saw everywhere in the beautiful nature that surrounded me, I then faced up to this horrendous violence of the past, praying and asking simply for forgiveness. As I did so, I felt a huge burden lift off of me. It was really that simple, the burden was gone along with the passing clouds that animated that beautiful sky.

I then felt the plant speak to me, saying that the energy that had driven those acts from the past was mine as an ancestral inheritance – the pride, ambition, aggression, desire and willpower – qualities that might engender fear and respect in others. These were important qualities for me to use in my life as they would take me far. They should never be repressed or felt shame around.

However, the most important thing I had to be aware of was the intention behind using these qualities. They had to serve something that was for the good of others not just for myself and that ultimately fed and contributed to life. This would change the story from an overly destructive use of these urges to creative, life feeding ones. The warrior would once more come to serve rather than just conquer and as the San Pedro connected me to the solar masculine qualities of the sun, I realised that real service was only to one thing, to the spirit of all of life. I had to use this ancestral inheritance for the benefit of life on this amazing planet, in whatever small way I could.

Chapter Fourteen

Healing Ceremonies for the Ancestors

There are many ways we can bring healing to our ancestors through ceremonies and in this chapter we will explore some of these. The gift of shamanism is that as soon as you enter into the invisible world through altering your consciousness, you enter a place outside of time and space as we understand and experience them in the physical world. This means that there are no limits to what can be healed. When you fully enter the present moment, you enter infinity, as time and space are ultimately illusions that hold the manifest world together. This means also that you are able to direct your attention to any place or time that has existed or will exist.

There is a great moment in the film Aluna that illustrates this. A Mamo (spiritual leader) from the Kogi tribe is brought to a space observatory in the UK to meet a prominent astronomer. The Kogi claim to have an intimate knowledge of the make-up of the universe so the scientist shows the Mamo, who has never left his village before, a photograph of a part of the solar system that is impossible to view with the naked eye. He then asks the Mamo if he can tell him anything about the objects in the photograph. He immediately picks out one among many of the bright lights in the photograph and says this is an old star, but is dying. The scientist, baffled, confirms this to be astronomically accurate.[14] How did he know this? Because, as he explains, he has been there in his visions and communicated with the star itself.

It's not only space that it is possible to traverse in shamanic states, but also time and this is where we are able to go back to heal our ancestors. There is one ceremony that we undertake in the woods, which I would like to describe as an example of the healing that is possible. The first part of this ceremony involves drumming together as a group for a long time, to invoke power and energy from the spirit world to conjoin with us. This also has the effect of getting the everyday mind out of the way as the repetitive drum beat and movement gradually sends people into a deep trance. When the trance state is achieved, we then as a group set our intention to travel together to a specific place and time that has been pre-set. The time and place chosen usually is from one of the world wars of the past century as this is usually where the most healing is needed.

As you might imagine, these ceremonies can be extremely emotional and intense. Part of the role of the shaman is to act as psychopomp – the conductor to the Otherworld for the dead who can get trapped in this world. A lot of these ceremonies involve psychopomp work, but on a mass scale. One of the biggest tragedies of such large scale warfare isn't just the amount of death, but the lack of time to properly bury and honour the dead. Indigenous people would always have elaborate funerary rituals for the dead to ensure that their rebirth into the Otherworld would be a successful one. They did this because they understood that this passage, between life and death, is our most important initiation, something in many ways our lives have been building up to. They also understood that this was an extremely delicate time and all manner of things could go wrong that would mean the departing person doesn't make it and gets trapped in this world, as an invisible ghost.

Sometimes, the rituals would extend up to a year, when it was forbidden to utter the name or speak at all of the departed, in case this called their spirit back from its onward journey. In the UK and across Europe, burial chambers would be built to ensure that the person was connected to their ancestors in death so they were able to travel to the correct place in the Otherworld and rejoin the ancestral clan. In war, it is often impossible for even the simplest of rituals to be performed.

The other important element missing is the grieving that has to be done by those left behind, as they too are caught up in the immediate needs of survival that war brings. Grief is a separating agent for human beings. When we grieve fully, we not only acknowledge the loss, but also our helplessness to affect any other outcome in the situation. We have to face up to that power-lessness in the face of these natural forces, because when we do, it means we can fully surrender and let go. This is when grief takes over, because when we grieve fully it is impossible to maintain control.

If this doesn't happen, we can remain in denial of the finality of death and the past is inadvertently held onto. Whether this is conscious or unconscious it has the same affect. It is like all the natural emotion becomes frozen, which also freezes the past onto the present and destroys the possibility of new life. This creates ghosts.

Most initiation ceremonies and rituals are about acknowl-edging and releasing the past, whether it is through literal death or the many metaphorical or 'small' deaths we will face in our lives. This is then another way that horrors of war go on existing long after the conflict has ended. Which is why old battles will come back again and again through history. We are seeing this now with the troubles around Ukraine, as old wounds and allegiances from WWII are brought back up to the surface. But again the good news is that what was lacking at the time can be recreated, quite literally, through ceremonies in the present. We can bring the rituals and ceremonies that were missing at the time of the events, by bringing the time back to life.

In the healing ceremonies we do in the woods once everyone in the group has fully immersed themselves in the trance and become as one, we will travel psychically to the scene of the trauma. It is then that we meet the ghosts from the past, still often suffering and in immense pain. It can be very overwhelming when these lost souls come to you for help. Our energy, as individuals and a group, merge with spirit and acts like a light house or beacon for those lost and trapped in the half world between life and death.

There can then be a lot of unearthly sounding keening and mourning that fills the space as we witness those suffering and are able to cathart their pain. This is all expressed in the ceremony through haunting songs, through moaning, through tears or shouts of grief and horror; as through its expression the trapped energy is able to be released.

When you are healing the dead it is the same as healing the living, quite often the sheer power of the emotional energy needs releasing. The shaman's job is often to do this on behalf of the person needing healing, as they are unable to do it themselves. This doesn't change whether the person is alive in front of you or dead as a ghost who can only be perceived when you tune your perception in a particular way. It is incredibly moving work and in one ceremony it is possible to lift huge amounts of trapped trauma in one go.

Of course, one of the perennial questions that participants ask after the ceremony is, 'Did I just make all this up?' Or, 'Was it just my imagination?' One time we did one of these ceremonies we had travelled back to the date June 21st 1944, to Normandy in France. Of course this was in the midst of the D-Day landings and the subsequent advance of the troops and the battles this had brought.

After we returned from our travels and took our time to recover and somehow bring ourselves back from what we had witnessed, I invited people to share their experiences. One woman, B, shared that after she had undertaken the healing work, the whole scene had changed and she had a vision from a distance of a huge field of golden crops, swaying softly in the wind. At the same time the song 'Fields of Gold' had resounded in her mind. The beauty of this unexpected scene had moved her to tears. Because she was used to seeing fields of golden wheat and the song, she had presumed this was what it was. However, as someone else in the group quickly pointed out, the time we had travelled to was the wrong time of year for the wheat to be golden, being far too early. The strange thing was that I had briefly seen the same golden field as we returned. It seemed to surround everything with this incredible light. Not under-standing the vision we put it down to at best being a metaphor for a golden light of healing, and at worst, the fact that we'd probably not gone deep enough into trance to actually properly travel and were probably just making it up.

A couple of months later, the woman in the circle was working as a carer for an elderly French woman who now lived in the UK. As soon as she arrived in her house, she was immediately struck by a photograph on the living room wall, which showed the lady standing in front of a golden field. This was exactly like the vision she had seen in the ceremony and she was completely taken aback by it.

She asked the woman where this was taken and was again shocked to hear her say Normandy, as this was where the woman was originally from. Her curiosity invoked, she then asked her what time of year it was and the woman answered, June! It was a field of flowering mustard, which we hadn't thought about, that comes out at that time of year and grows all across Normandy. Despite her original doubt, B's vision had been vindicated. Spirit, in my experience, does this quite often; authenticates something we have seen in a vision in everyday life in these 'coincidental' circumstances, to help restore or keep our faith.

On another of these ceremonies I was taken in my vision into the heart of the Nazi command as they retreated in WWII. I was shown how they had appropriated the ancient magical symbols of Germanic and Norse mythology and how they had used them magically in a semi-conscious way. I witnessed them ritually using these, and how the 'spells' they had cast still hung heavy over Europe, especially France. That even though time moved on, the energy remained. I realised then that these needed countering and this was partly why spirit had guided me to undertake these ceremonies in the first place. I was guided by spirit and shown how to counteract the intent behind their magic, as I would on an individual client who had a negative curse placed on them by someone else, a jealous ex-lover or family member perhaps. This was an unexpected and powerful experience.

Later, I learnt about the magical warfare that did occur in the Second World War which Churchill, as an ordained Druid, was part of. Truth, as ever, is often a lot stranger than where the imagination could take us. Magical practitioners have been, and continue to be, a part of government since time immemorial. The well-documented use of psychic remote viewers by the CIA is an example of this, as is Ronald Reagan and many other seemingly 'rational' Western leaders being guided by astrologers. These ancient practices don't go away, they work too well! They're just usually hidden from sight, as they are counter to the current belief system of rational fundamentalism.

Or, cynically you could say, like the church beforehand, our leaders steal the magic for their own, while at the same time disavowing its reality, so that they have exclusive use of it. The important point though is that, as healers, we can counter the intent of how these practices have been used negatively and simply use them for healing. This will help to restore balance. But we may need qualities of the warrior explored in the previous chapter in ourselves to do this.

Another ceremony that involves healing the past and the Ancestral Soul is a very simple one. This is done for participants to heal their more personal ancestral line. The first step involves cooking up a meal that your ancestors may have eaten, say a hundred or so years ago. This will usually be something very simple. However, the most important ingredient is the intent you put into the food, which will be one of healing your ancestral lineage.

We then all gather in a circle to face outwards and present the food to the ancestors. Again, the drum and song are used to alter the perceptual consciousness of everyone and gradually the ancestors are invoked. After a while, the space literally fills with spirits, it is nearly always the most perceptible presences of all the ceremonies we do. This is usually due to the fact that our ancestral line has been forgotten so much in ritual that they are literally starving.

The food is both a symbolic offering and a literal one. So how does an invisible, dead person feed off the food? Simply, they feed off its essence, its aroma. Smell is the oldest of our senses. It is also the one that is associated with psychic phenomena as it connects us to the invisible world as, like breath, smell is invisible. Dogs have now been trained to smell illnesses such as cancer in people. In a shamanic healing I will often smell the energy of the sickness.

There has also been a lot of research into how smell connects us with the pineal gland which, is seen by many as the source of the 'Third Eye' of Eastern traditions, located in the centre of our forehead, which enables us to perceive reality in a multi-dimensional way. The pineal gland and the offertory system have also been associated with the storing of long-term memory in humans. By using the food we are actually calling back to the memories of our ancestors, the long-term memories stored in the Ancestral Soul, so they are able to find their way back into this reality.

The other reason we use food, is because in this world it is what sustains us. It is how we are kept alive, but also how we receive love and nurture, firstly in the womb through the placenta and after birth, in our mother's milk. In a primal way it is connected to the love we have received to make sure we survive. Mostly, our ancestors have been forgotten in our culture, thus they haven't been 'fed', they haven't been kept alive. So, this is an extremely important part of the ritual. We are feeding them once more, to sustain their existence in the Otherworld.

When the ancestors do arrive, it is then that we are able to do our work in the ceremony because, more often than not, they will need some healing and that is why we are there. Participants, again, can often find themselves overwhelmed at this point. So how do we help to heal them? The first step, as always, is to be the compassionate witness – to witness and re-experience their stories. This is often the most powerful place to be in any healing. To watch played out before you the story that couldn't for some reason be heard or told. The energy of it can spike and then be released. This is one of the reasons the death-bed confession is so common, as people know instinctively that if we take the burden of the secret or unresolved story to our grave we will be burdened by it and unable to move on.

Psychologists including James Pennebaker have done a lot of research on how keeping secrets can contribute to sickness, not just psychological, but actual physical ones.[15] Shamanically, the lifting and releasing of the burdens of secrets is not only possible with the living but with the dead also.

Another, extremely powerful healing tool is that of forgiveness. In fact I would say that forgiveness and reconciliation sit at the heart of what is needed in the modern world to stop us from repeating the past traumas that we appear to be stuck in. This has been practiced to great effect in places where there has been severe brutality resulting in unresolved social trauma, like South Africa with its truth and reconciliation trials.

As all spiritual masters or practitioners have told us, until we can forgive or be forgiven, we are holding onto and burdened by the past and the negative energy of whatever it was that happened. Again, the death-bed reconciliation, or asking for forgiveness, is another common theme that highlights the instinctual need for this.

However, it isn't always the case that this is possible and the dead need the opportunity to forgive or be forgiven as much as the living. The person in the ceremony can then act as the surrogate for this forgiving that needs to take place, either by sending their forgiveness to the ancestor as a representative of the family line, even if they don't know what it is for, or by allowing the ancestor to forgive, through them, the person they most needed to forgive. This is a very common theme in this ceremony. Again, you can perceive the weight being lifted in the space; it is tangible when this happens.

The shaman as a healer is often either the carrier of messages that have been lost or emotions that have become stuck. In this ceremony there is the opportunity for both and like a lot of ceremonies the trapped energy is released through the participants as they sing all the stories that are being relayed to them through the ancestral line.

What carries this and holds this, is the power of the group and the container of the ritual. If this was done alone, it might be easier to get lost or attached to a lot of that pain. But, through being in nature in a group, supported by spirit and held in a strong way by the experienced person leading the ceremony, we can bring much healing to that long line of people that stands in front of each person in the circle.

The power of ceremony and ritual is again the most effective I know for bringing healing, but this can also be done individually. The ancient art of pilgrimage has been used for thousands of years to bring healing or curing to individuals. There are many reasons why this may be effective, the main one being the symbolism or metaphor of the journey acted out literally. People when getting well are often said to be 'on the road to recovery', which hints at the power this archetypal metaphor has over us. Life is often seen to be a journey in itself. Also, when people find their purpose or meaning in life, something that illness can often precipitate the search for, they often say they have found their 'path'.

Healing in a shamanic way involves the focussing of intent on a goal – that goal often simply being of wellness. This is using the power of the mind to create and open up a reality conducive to our wellbeing. The steps we take towards that goal make up the healing journey. When this healing journey is acted out in the physical world, it can give greater meaning and depth to it. In healing we are always trying to translate what occurs in the invisible, energetic world, with the tangible world, as this is where we want it to manifest.

You could do the most spectacular energetic work on the invisible level, removing blockages and demons, healing long lines of ancestors, but that doesn't necessarily mean the healing will always manifest in the physical world. Some of why this might not happen could be around belief systems which we will explore in the final section. To assist this in happening here though, we need to build a bridge between the invisible and the visible world. Ritual is just that bridge.

The Body Soul, or unconscious, has to know that healing has occurred, by experiencing it. Thus, when we act an inner process, or energetic reality, out in the physical world it goes deeper into our bones and has much more of a possibility to manifest in that physical world. This is the power of ritual, or what they used to call in the old days 'sympathetic magic', which nearly all magic is based upon. With healing, as with most things in life, it's the journey that is more important than the destination. Hence, the power of pilgrimage.

What greater gift then, could you give to your ancestors than to go on a healing pilgrimage for them? Holding your intention before you set out to bring all the healing you can for the long line of people behind you. Often, this might mean travelling back to the land of your forebears as it did for me when going back to Ireland. This also happened for me in a more spontaneous way one time, which I would like to share.

In the early days of my shamanic training, we once had to be shown in a vision a place in Britain or Ireland and to be given a symbol in this place by our spirit helpers. When we came back from the vision, we had to find that place on a real map. We were then told we were to undertake a pilgrimage to that place to find in real life the symbol we had been shown. For some people this was a daunting prospect as it involved travelling huge distances. I was left disappointed though as I love travelling and wanted to have been given a place furthest away from where I lived, but instead had been shown somewhere just 25 miles away, in the same county.

I decided, to make it more exciting, to do the pilgrimage in the traditional way and to walk it and to not take a tent and sleep out under the stars. Also, I resolved not to take a map and to find my way following the sun and my instinct. I was lucky as the route to Arundel, the place I had been shown, from Brighton, where I was living, covered much of the South Downs Way, an ancient pilgrimage path in itself. I thought how hard could it be? The answer, in reality, was quite hard.

It took me two days and nights to walk those miles and after getting lost quite a few times and spending one of the nights alone in what I later discovered were renowned haunted woods, I arrived tired but exhilarated in Arundel. I then just had the simple task of finding the symbol.

The symbol I had been shown was of a snake twisting around what looked like a cross. Logically I thought the first place to look would be the castle that stood high on the hill in the town. I was fairly confident of success, given the historic nature of the town. It was also full of antique shops if my search of the castle proved fruitless. But, at the same time, I felt the pressure of having to prove in reality my vision. I also knew that we had to report back to the group our findings, which added another layer. I have always been quite competitive by nature and didn't want to be the only one not to succeed. At the same time I was trying to remember that this was a spiritual undertaking and competiveness, or the idea of success or failure, really shouldn't come into it! This didn't stop me not wanting to fail though.

However, after an exhausting search through the castle and then the antique shops I started getting a little despondent. The now three days of walking were catching up with me and I was also aware that I had to leave that evening and was running out of time.

Eventually, I flopped down in the gardens of the castle, completely out of ideas. As is usual with me, I was a little slow on the uptake, as only then did I get the inspiration to ask the spirit helper who had shown me the symbol in the first place in my vision where to look for it. Why I hadn't thought of this before I don't know, I probably got too caught up in the desire to find it for myself. Once more I was astounded at my slowness in grasping this whole shamanic stuff, I often still am!

So, I then recalled the vision, sitting on that ancient lawn, and asked the guide where this symbol was. Instantly the answer came back: 'In the cathedral.' Now this surprised me, as the idea of a symbol of a snake curling around a cross, which had a quite strong pagan flavour to it, in a Christian place of worship, didn't seem very likely. I remember arguing then with the guide about this, but she wouldn't be moved. In retrospect, what I must have looked like to passing strangers, as someone who had been walking and sleeping rough for three days having an animated debate (albeit silently) with an invisible being in the middle of a tourist attraction, I don't know, but I was really too tired and fed up by this stage to care!

Reluctantly then, and without much expectation, I heeded the guidance and set off for the cathedral. Upon arriving and going in through the doors though my spirit was immediately lifted as it really was a beautiful building. Walking around, I was struck by this beauty and in that moment realised that it didn't really matter whether I found the symbol or not. The most important thing was the journey itself and the many gifts it had already brought me as I had already faced a lot of challenges and fears and learnt a lot. Of course, as is so often the way; that was when something happened.

I suddenly noticed out of the corner of my eye a small, gold plaque on the wall with a symbol of a snake coiling around a cross. I couldn't believe my eyes and took the proverbial double take. On closer inspection, however, I noticed that the cross combined with an anchor and the curled snake was in fact rope coiled around it.

Yet, it had the same tapered ends and the whole symbol looked virtually the same as the one I had been shown, I had just presumed it was a snake when I saw it in my vision. I then looked at the engraving, the plaque was dated 15th April 1912 and was dedicated to all those who had lost their lives on the Titanic, which had sunk on that day.

My mind whirled and in that exhausted state I kind of staggered back at the shock of seeing the symbol here, but then also realising the significance of what I was seeing, as not only had the Titanic sank that day, but it had also been the day my grandmother had been born. This brought memories of her flooding into my mind. I had always been very close to Nan. She was the only blood relative of my grandparents that I had any kind of relationship with or knew. However, she had died on Christmas day about five years previous and because I was away in Australia at the time I hadn't been able to get back for the funeral. I'd always regretted that decision as I felt I hadn't been able to say goodbye properly.

But, as I sat down on a pew in that magnificent cathedral, taking it all in and thinking about Nan, already in an altered space through the tiredness and the exhilaration of finding the symbol, I suddenly felt the presence of her behind me. As I looked up, I saw her, standing at my side, as real as life. I gazed speechlessly into her eyes as she just stood there radiating the most exquisite light and smiling the most beautiful smile I have ever seen. Then, as quick as she had arrived, she turned and glided down the aisle, gradually fading away into the altar.

It was an incredibly moving experience as I finally felt I had the opportunity to say goodbye. I also felt intuitively that she had too been waiting for this before being able to continue her journey and had been partly guiding the whole episode of this pilgrimage. I realised it had taken the whole journey to get me to that point of surrender as I wept in that cathedral and grieved for her in a way that was full of both sadness and immense joy and wonder as to how she had brought me here; the perfect way to say goodbye.

Chapter Fifteen

Spiritual Confidence through Ancestral Connections

So far I have been focussing on ancestral healing as an important first stage in reconnecting with our ancestral kin. I would say, because of the loss of this connection and the many unresolved traumas from our past, this is a necessary first step. However, this is only one side of the story. The second is the releasing of what I like to call the 'ancestral gold'. This is all those buried qualities and potentials that have lain dormant in the Ancestral Soul; gifts that can enhance our lives immeasurably. In this chapter I would like then to focus on how to release and embody these, and how this can affect our lives individually and affect society.

The first point to note is the issue of spiritual confidence or authority. This is something I feel we often lack in the West due to the fact that a lot of our traditions have been lost. This cutting off from our spiritual heritage, the spiritual heritage of our land, left a huge hole. Religion may have filled this temporarily. However, religion doesn't teach spiritual authority. It teaches rather the opposite in fact, to give away our authority to the priest, church or anyone who is interpreting a book and who is therefore perceived as being closer to God.

Animistic traditions are different in that each person has their own unique connection to the divine, something that has to be sought out and individually experienced, rather than explained by a book or another. The diversity of these connections is celebrated as simply reflecting the diversity in nature.

The ending of our pagan traditions happened brutally with the genocidal witch hunts that swept across Europe and North America between the 15th and 18th centuries. Anyone who did practice their own medicine, had their own connection, or whose spiritual practice was outside of the church's control or remit, was persecuted, tortured and executed. This would have been enough to persuade all but the most resilient of souls that spiritual authority was not something it was wise to claim for yourself.

This is another huge part of our ancestral legacy and even though the shackles of religion were thrown off in the late 19th and 20th centuries through the rise of scientific rationalism, our relationship with dogma and who holds control over what is considered the truth about 'reality' continues. In many ways we have simply moved from an age of religious fundamentalism into the reactive one we now live in of secular fundamentalism.

What remains is a tendency towards subservience when it comes to claiming our spiritual authority, i.e. our own personal relationship with our souls and with the spirit of all of life. It is deeply ironic that we call the part of the world we live in the 'free West' as we are constantly being told how to think, how to act and what to believe by our schools, governments, parents, experts, media, society in general or anyone in a position of authority. What we're fundamentally not taught is to trust our own instincts, intuitions or experiences.

This ultimately means that when people do start to open up spiritually and begin to question the lazy assumptions or sheep-like passivity of general society, other cultures whose spiritual traditions were not so brutally wiped out can become incredibly alluring. They often offer a way out of the modern, Western dogma. This happened a lot particularly in the 1960s when traditions from the East were brought back by intrepid travellers. These exotic and often ancient practices, which promised personal enlightenment or salvation, were understandably incredibly attractive. It has continued to this day in the shamanic world, with many people offering the wisdom of other cultures that is often then appropriated as our own.

However, because of the ancestral legacy of giving away our authority, very often after the initial liberation that people feel having left their own culture's limitation behind, the same pattern creeps back in. What happens then is the authority is then given away to the exotic new/ancient tradition or the people from that culture. Both of these are put on a pedestal of spiritual greatness, one that we in the West couldn't hope to ever reach. This is what many have labelled 'the enlightenment trap' – the forever seeking of the elusive goal of enlightenment. But it is also the ancestral wound. What we are trying to heal, the way I see it, is the hole that has been left by the rupture from our traditions, our natural ways of being in the world.

In early 2000 I did a reconciliation ceremony in Australia with a small tribe of Aboriginals. I had been particularly in awe of the Aboriginal culture as learning about them for the first time in Robert Lawlor's excellent book *Voices of the First Day* had introduced me to the concepts of shamanism, alongside being inspired by the ancient spirits of the land; alive and vibrant as they are in the outback of Australia.

The purpose of the ceremony was for a group of English people to apologise on behalf of our ancestors for the terrible acts of genocide, theft and destruction of land that had been carried out in the name of our people. This was supported by a lot of other Europeans and North Americans. Individuals then got up and spoke in a heartfelt way, taking responsibility for saying sorry on behalf of our nation. After they had spoken, there was a silence. The small tribe then seemed a little uneasy in the ceremony, as if they felt that something was expected of them.

Then, after a long while the youngest of the tribal members, a man probably in his early 20s, got up and spoke. Firstly, he thanked everyone for their words and went on to explain that they were an incredibly shy people and were not used to standing up and talking in front of so many people, especially when they were meant to be replying on behalf of a whole continent.

There was disappointment in the air, as if we as a people doing the apologising, needed something in response from them, a blessing or acknowledgement of some sort. Or even some sort of wisdom or teaching. The level of spiritual hunger (so often prevalent when Westerners meet with indigenous people) then became tangible as people began to call out for the tribe to share their wisdom with us. The apology and reason for us being there seemingly forgotten.

Responding to this instinctively, the young man then got up again and this time he spoke passionately:

'We have nothing to show or teach you here!' he said. 'We are a humble people. We learn from our ancestors, they teach us about our land. If you wanna learn to be in harmony with your land and yourselves, go back and speak with your ancestors. They will show you the way. Go speak with your ancestors!'

Even though I was disappointed at the time, as I, like everyone else wanted, some kind of teaching from this ancient people, I have never forgotten his words. For what they revealed then, what the teaching really was, which I only fully understand now is that the route to getting ourselves back in harmony with ourselves and our land is through our ancestors. This is the way we can refind our spiritual authority and through that our spiritual confidence.

At another ceremony, the Shuar medicine person I talked about earlier said that over the 20 years he had been coming to Europe to share his traditions, the two biggest things he had noticed that we lacked and made us sick as a people, were 'love' and 'confidence'. This, I feel, is largely due to the disconnection we have with the earth, as explored in the first section of the book, but also our disconnection with our ancestors. Both are intimately connected for it is our ancestors' bones that are buried within the land, as are their stories, their triumphs and failures, their loves and hatreds, their blood and their tears. All this makes up the land as much as the chemical components in the soil; for it makes up the spirit of it. It is this spirit that we can wake up by reconnecting with our lineages.

As we give birth to a new spirituality from the wreckage of a thousand years of religious domination and persecution, this connection to our heritage is incredibly important. If we are going to build lasting traditions, the spirit of the land must be a part of this. This is what will sustain any transformation we are going through as a species right now.

Indeed, humankind's religion and spirituality initially was brought forth through an honouring of the spirits of the place that gave them life and sustained them. This was what precipitated them wanting to begin worshipping in the first place. It was always a highly practical endeavour as well; to use the powers of ceremony, magic and ritual to ensure success in hunting, the growth of crops, the birth of children, the death of the old ones and the removal of sickness. In short, anything that helped with the survival of the people, but not just human people, also those other relations that the humans shared the planet with: the tree people, the bird people, the animal people, *all* the people. As a North American elder I did some ceremony with used to say, 'All our prayers and ceremonies are for the continuation of all of life.'

The 'genius of the place', as Celtic traditions would call it, has at its heart an interaction between the ancestral spirits of the land, both human and non-human, and the human beings that honour that place through their prayers and ceremonies. Our connection to our immediate ancestors is the first point of contact to this. This is why honouring and celebrating them is so important.

However, because there has been so much displacement of peoples, questions then naturally arise about those who are not originally from the place they are living in. You might ask: 'What if my ancestors are from the other side of the world? Do my ancestors travel with me or have I left them behind?'

These are complex questions with no neat, easy answers.

In my experience, however, the displacement of people in this world is also reflected in a displacement of ancestral spirits in the Otherworld. Many times when I am healing an ancestral line of someone, beyond any traumas or emotional energy that has been blocked, I find what is needed is for me is to help find a 'home' for the ancestral spirits in the Otherworld.

Indigenous cultures would have a place in their environment that was the 'home of the ancestral kin', similar to the 'navel of the earth' we explored in the first section. This would be somewhere that the community could gather to send their prayers to their ancestors and also do their ceremonies to feed them. The effect of this in the invisible world was to secure a home in the Otherworld for the Ancestral Soul, as what is real in this world is reflected in the Otherworld.

The burial mounds of Britain were an example of this and were immensely sacred places. According to Metzner in the aforementioned *Well of Remembrance*, this grew out of the original European culture's practice of burying their dead beneath their houses. So not only were their lives literally built upon those who come before them, but they also kept their ancestors close to ensure that connection in the continuation of life.

As this place of honouring the ancestral line has been lost in our communities, forgotten about or built upon, so this is reflected in a displacement of our ancestral kin in the invisible world. Graveyards have often performed this role, which is why headstones would be put up to mark the barrier between the worlds. If you are lucky to have many relatives buried in the same cemetery then this is indeed a place of ancestral worship, which is part of the reason why there was a taboo about building on cemeteries as doing so uproots and disturbs the dead in the

Otherworld. This disturbing of the dead is of course another reason why our ancestors are restless and in need of healing. This is possible, as the shaman is able to assist the dead to find a place in the invisible world to come to rest again, as I have been guided to do in many of the healings I have undertaken.

In terms of the questions above and helping the living connect to the land if it is not the land of your bloodline, this can be done in many ways. I would suggest that ancestors do travel, especially if you consciously remember them, as this brings them back to life wherever you are. However, it is important to also honour and respect the ancestral spirits of the land you have arrived on, to build up a relationship between your ancestral kin and those of the land.

You may feel an amazing kinship with this land and its people, or you may feel like a complete outsider. Either way, I would suggest it's useful to request that the ancestral spirits of the land adopt you, that they welcome you. If this request is done in a heartfelt way then, as in all adoption cases, the bonds can be as strong, if not stronger, than familial ties as the water of kinship can indeed be thicker than blood. But, as with all relationships, this has to be worked at consciously.

I was working with a South African man once who had married an English woman and was now living in England. Although a lot of his ancestors were from Britain, Ireland and other parts of Europe, he had never felt at home here, or in some way accepted by the culture. I suggested a simple ritual whereby he take some offerings to a place he deemed sacred in nature and to introduce himself to the ancestral spirits of this land. In this ritual he was to take them offerings and to tell them his story and the story of his people, but also to ask permission from them to be here to make his home, petitioning them to welcome him here.

He did this in a heartfelt and respectful way and came back a couple of months later saying he felt completely different about being here, but also more at peace and at home in himself. He now, years later, assists me in some of the training I do in the woods and one of his deepest passions is about making shamanism relevant to the land here and bringing back to life our ancient traditions.

The simplest way you can ensure that you have a strong connection to your ancestors wherever you reside is to build them an 'ancestral spirit house' – literally create a home for them in this world where you can send prayers, give offerings and connect with your lineage. Having this in your home or outdoor space if possible will begin the process of 'housing' your Ancestral Soul. This can bring a sense of peace to the past and also ensure continuity into the future. It can also ensure that the ancestral gold, all those latent gifts of your people, can travel down the line and into you. These gifts could be artistic, creative, practical, intellectual, emotional, psychic, archetypal or virtually anything.

It is amazing how many times a special 'gift', if not used then actually becomes a burden. This is because a negative energy of something being unfulfilled gets built up around it, often leading to grief or frustration, which is what then gets passed down to the descendants. For the recipient down the line, this might then feed a kind of insatiable longing or hunger in their lives that can seemingly never be fulfilled. Or there can be underlying feelings of failure, no matter what the descendant achieves in their own life, because the sense of 'failure' actually began a few genera-tions back. When this is healed the 'talent' can be revealed in a full way. As the inspiration for the gift usually comes from the invisible world anyway, this is another blessing of ancestral healing in this way, as it connects us more fully to this source. Another way of looking it, is that it connects us to our 'power'.

Thus, when I am retrieving ancestral gifts from the past, I am actually retrieving power. This power may have been lost through suppression or my ancestors may have experienced it being forcibly removed from them through a disconnection with their land. Or through the devastation of their culture and the shaming of their traditions. This has happened to many peoples across the globe in the last five centuries or so. By healing this consciously, releasing the trauma of powerlessness and shame, we can then reclaim that power and our rightful connection to it.

There are two further potential 'traps' it might be wise to avoid in doing this though, which we will now explore.

Chapter Sixteen

Avoiding Fantasy and Healing the 'Scapegoat'

A lot of the modern shamanic renaissance of the past 40 to 50 years has come out of the United States and hence has been highly influenced by Native American spirituality. This is so much so that shamanism and Native American spirituality can become synonymous to some people, even though the word comes from a European/Asian (Siberian) tradition.

The fact that in the US there are still living traditions, albeit sometimes having been suppressed and influenced heavily by the dominant culture, means this would have influenced people there who were attempting to bring back these old ways. Many of them would have trained with native peoples. However, I would also say that the ancestral spirits of the land there would have influenced hugely the way people think and feel and dream, and thus the 'medicine' they then share with others.

This is part of the hybrid that we now have that makes up modern shamanism: ancestral spirits of European settlers mixing with the land spirits of indigenous peoples, not just in the US, but wherever pioneers and seekers of ancient traditions have gone and brought back teachings, to create a modern/ancient phenomenon we call 'shamanism'.

As ancient prophecies like the Cree one have suggested, this is probably what is needed at this time, people coming together to create a new 'Rainbow Tribe'. However, I would suggest that in order for this to happen we have to have a strong connection with our past and ancestral kin to get a strong enough identity and the spiritual confidence to be able to be a part of this coming together and to integrate it properly. Also this can guard against cultural appropriation, which is a big issue now, whereby people steal another's culture and pass it off as their own. To do this means reclaiming our spiritual authority that was lost through the onslaught of politically motivated religion and cosmology.

A lot of people in the West are doing this through researching and recreating our ancient traditions. This is great and there is a lot of scholarly work going into it. However, sometimes this can also lead to modern day myths being invented and proliferated. The past is as exotic and foreign a country as somewhere the other side of the world and because, like all shamanic cultures, the ancient cultures of Europe were oral traditions it means we have little first-hand knowledge of them.

When people talk of the Celts or other ancient peoples in terms of evidence of how they lived, what they believed and thought, we only have the writings of contemporary Romans observing them and some texts of ancient myths and poems that were recorded later by Christian scribes. We also have archaeological evidence and theories. Yet we don't have anything 'from the horse's mouth' so to speak, which means that there are a lot of gaps in our knowledge.

Thus we are always looking at them through a lens of another person's perception. As people don't necessarily like gaps, these can be filled in by quite a few stories that are presented as facts about ancient cultures, but which have later been found out to be completely invented by authors.

Another one of the perennial problems we have in modern shamanism the way I see it is that some of the founding texts that helped ignite widescale interest in the subject have also later been found out to have been made up. Carlos Castaneda began this in the 1960s when he presented his stories of the 'teaching of Don Juan' as anthropological 'fact'. This has since been disproved by many sources. Looking back, the sheer fantastical nature of the stories in a less heady time I'm sure would have alerted people sooner. Yet, these stories still sell well and the concepts introduced in the books have even been taught by a lot of shamanic teachers as part of their training programmes.

There is an often unacknowledged dark side to this as Castaneda, it has been reported, developed an abusive, cult-like set-up around him with many disciples, mostly woman, who allegedly had to sleep with him as part of their initiation. In some ways equally as damagingly, as with a lot of cults, initiates had to cut off all contact with their families, creating much trauma in those being left behind.[16] This brutal cutting off from the past that a supposed 'warrior' has to do in order to find 'freedom' is something well advocated in the books and has influenced a lot of people and a lot of teachings. It makes me wonder though just how much ancestral trauma has been created by this cutting off from the past that at some point will need healing.

The less dark, but perhaps equally insidious, side of the influence of such books is that they created a fantasy around what a shaman or medicine man was supposed to be. What we don't take into account was this fantasy was the creation of one man's heightened and at times twisted imagination, albeit fed by anthropological research. People since have rationalised this by saying whether the stories were true is irrelevant as it brought the idea of shamanism and other states of consciousness to millions. However, I would say this was a misguided idea for, as Terence McKenna notes, the books have nothing at all to do with healing, and healing is central to the shaman's role.

Also, if the books had been presented as fiction then that would have been different, as fiction can often come closer to the 'truth' than rational analysis. However, in shamanism everything as we've already noted is about intent. A big part of the intention behind these books was to deceive. To present something as truth when it is fiction is simply a lie and as most actual traditions practice, a 'warrior' is only as good as their word. If they lie, they have broken a central tenet of their existence.

Castaneda's books weren't the first to present as spiritual truth traditions that had simply been made up, albeit through research and knowledge of some living traditions. What he set in motion has been followed by many people. It is remarkable how many books written by modern day teachers are presented as truth, but have their home in fantasy. They always follow the same narrative whereby the author is somehow a 'special one' chosen by an exotic teacher or tribe from an ancient forgotten tradition, who have been waiting to impart their wisdom, so the author can share it with the rest of the world. This need for validation that may drive people to make up such stories is part of the wound caused by having been cut off from a living tradition.

The problem is that when you discover that what you have been presented with as 'truth' is actually pure fantasy, it can have quite a devastating effect on your whole spiritual path and can lead to deep disillusionment. I have experienced this myself and met students of teachers who have done the same. Although this disillusionment is an important part of any path, as it can assist what Buddhists call 'killing your teacher', which is an important stage of gaining one's own spiritual authority, when you discover you have been lied to, this process can be unnecessarily harsh and can tempt people to want to throw the baby out with the bathwater.

It also makes me think a lot about the question of integrity, which when you are working with people's souls, feels of fundamental importance. It is, after all, ultimately an abuse of power through an abuse of trust and this is something that has been carried out too much in the past in the name of spirituality through organised religion. There have been too many lies presented as ultimate truths, which means it is already an ancestral wound. Also, how can this work begin to be taken seriously in a world where cynicism at any form of magical thinking is commonplace, if it doesn't adhere to basic principles of truth telling?

The antidote to all this I feel is that of ancestral honouring, for it is through this we can find our way back to our ancient kin and this will also bring us into connection with the land. To bring the old ways back to life we simply have to listen to the land as this was how these old societies created their culture in the first place, by listening and responding to what was already inherent in their environments. This will bring us spiritual confidence.

Also, if we start this work by connecting to and healing our immediate relatives we will eventually find that connection back to those from long ago who practiced these ways. If we can learn to communicate well with our relatives already in the spirit world, we can then learn to communicate with the ancient ones. This is not to dismiss real scholarly research that goes into the past traditions, but to complement it. Because our immediate family might need a lot of healing, this can be another reason people want to ignore them and go back to a seemingly more glamorous or spiritually powerful time which again, seems like another form of spiritual bypassing.

I see many people for healings and something I often hear is: 'I feel like I was born into the wrong family.' This is then often accompanied by: 'I feel like an alien or like I'm from another planet, I don't feel at home here.' Usually these are people who are carrying a lot of ancestral pain on behalf of their family, which is a huge burden to them. This ancestral pain can be actually coming between the person and their family. The reason for this is that no one wants to be reminded of pain or negative energy, so it is therefore natural and human to reject anything or anyone who is carrying it. But the energy has to go somewhere. It has usually been stored up in the Ancestral Soul for quite a long time, so usually one or two members will take it on unconsciously. They will then be subtly and unconsciously rejected by the rest of the family until it can be healed.

This is a common theme when it comes to ancestral healing and connects in with the archetype of the scapegoat, which is very strong in the West. The scapegoat, as esteemed astrologer

Liz Greene explores in *The Dark of the Soul: Psychopathology in the Horoscope* originates from a tradition from the Old Testament, whereby every year two goats would be sacrificed to appease God on behalf of the community. The first goat would have its throat slit and the blood would be the sacrifice and payment. With the second one, the priest would whisper all the sins, all the broken taboos that the people of the village had carried out in the previous year onto the goat, projecting magically the negative energy of those sins onto it. The goat would then be driven out of the village and never allowed to return. Thus, symbolically, the village would be cleansed of this energy. Hence the name, 'scape' – from the same root as 'escape' – 'goat'.

Liz Greene suggests that this is an important archetype in human society and that many people play the role of the scapegoat now in families, in that they carry the 'sickness' of the family and are then rejected by it.[17] Again, traditionally the shaman would do this, as one technique of shamanic healing is to literally take on the sickness of the person you are curing and then to go to vomit it out in a safe place away from the sick person.

However, they would do this consciously whereas a lot of the time now it is done on the unconscious level. This scapegoat archetype is incredibly strong in the West due to the fact the main mythology of the past two thousand years, Christianity, is built upon it. Jesus is the ultimate scapegoat, sacrificed while carrying the sins of the world. Hence, a lot of Christian focus is on transcending the world, as it is impossible to feel at home here when you relate so strongly to this image of the scapegoat as they are the perennial outsider. You will always feel that longing to go somewhere else that is home. As Liz Greene points out, many modern-day healers of any kind hold and relate to this archetype a little too strongly.

In my experience, the decision to carry the burdens stored in the Ancestral Soul is usually taken on the invisible level before birth. Thus, although those who have chosen to carry this may have had seemingly nice, settled childhoods, (equally often they may have had the exact opposite) these people will always have felt somewhat of an outsider or subtly rejected by the world, hence the feelings of not being from the 'right' family or of being an 'alien'. They will also more than likely be natural healers, as this is part of the reason why they may have come here at this time, to help heal the ancestral wounding.

All the shamanic healing methods we've been exploring in this section can help hugely with this and help the person release those feelings of being rejected and begin to become at peace with being here in the world. The most important connection in my opinion that needs to be made is between a person and their ancestors, as this can begin the process of healing what until now has been unconscious and invisible.

In doing this it is like people can suddenly gain the perspective on their life and the pain they have experienced and place it into some kind of context that isn't so personal and doesn't make them feel 'mad' or unstable because of always having felt like an outsider. Until we can feel safe and at home here in the world, there will always be a tendency towards destructive behaviour or patterning. Healing the Body Soul helps us to orientate and feel secure in space whilst healing the Ancestral Soul helps us to orientate and feel safe in time. Both are intimately connected and necessary before we can begin to ascend into different realities.

Another side of the birth of psychoanalysis and its popularity over the past hundred years or so, that we haven't already explored, is the fact that it has meant that a lot of emphasis on people's 'problems' or mental difficulties has gone into establishing a causal factor in childhood. Early experiences are seen as holding the key to patterns that adversely affect the person later in life, and indeed this is often the case as we will explore in the last section of this book.

The approach to mental illness seems to be caught between this diagnosis and the even more popular biochemical model. However, such an emphasis on childhood has meant that a lot of attention and intention has gone into exploring difficult relationships and traumatic early memoires. For some people this has been relevant and has worked, yet for others they cannot relate to this as they feel that their upbringing was relatively trauma free. Yet, they are still in pain later in life.

The potentially dangerous side to this method is that there can actually be too much seeking of trauma and this in itself can become a self-fulfilling prophesy. This happened when a lot of childhood sexual abuse memories were suddenly 'recovered' in therapy that went on to destroy families and later were found not to be true. If we go looking hard enough we will always 'discover' (or create) a story around our pain.

This is human nature. I have experienced this myself when I was involved once in heavily psychologically influenced process work. I was guided (later I realised more encouraged) in this session to recover such a memory and although a part of me experienced it as true at the time, as the only thing that could explain the dark feelings I had always had around my sexuality, another much larger part felt something inauthentic and grabbing at answers within me.

Looking back from the perspective I have now, I could have been recovering an old ancestral memory or even just something in the collective. Childhood sexual abuse is one of those big taboos that looms huge in the collective unconscious, something that is beginning to come out now through very real experiences and suffering.

When you're in a lot of pain and mental anguish, as I was at the time, you want something 'big' to pin that pain upon. We grow up to be taught that the universe works along reasonable and rational lines, i.e. A+B=C and everything has a causal relationship to it. Thus, this pain must have a tangible reason that can be traced back to a specific event in the physical universe. This simply may not be the case, as the cause could lie in the invisible world, across time and space and indeed peoples.

Another side of this emphasis on childhood experiences is that parents often don't come out of it very well, which can precipitate the splitting up of families. Sometimes this is a necessary process and it can feel a little like opening Pandora's Box when we begin to delve into our past and the less-than-healthy relationships that may have been present in our childhood. Most people expend a lot of psychic energy keeping a firm lid on such a box.

However, there can also be an equal tendency, when that box is opened, to want to always go back to it, to get more and more out of it, to discover more and more what was wrong and how we have been wounded. This can lead to feeding off that energy, which can be as equally strong a distraction or avoidance. I have worked a lot with therapists and one thing I have noticed is that sometimes, unless the person is going through a 'process', i.e. digging up something from the past, it can feel to them like they are not really 'doing the work'. It took me quite a while to realise that this can be just another mask.

I am deeply psychological as a person, as might be blindingly obvious through reading this book! I am also fairly good at translating that psychological insight into a language and structure. In short, I'm good at talking about it. This makes me quite heady as a person which can be both a blessing and a curse. I was in a ceremony with the plant medicine ayahuasca in the jungle in Peru once in which this ability to track my processes and find meaning and reason behind reality was finally switched off.

It was the third ceremony of a group of six intensive ones, so gradually my defences and protections were being worn down by the plant spirit. In this session, as the plant spirit began its work I was again surrounded by mysterious beings manifesting physically and as before they were strange. There was a woman, although there was nothing human about her, who was dressed in a safari outfit and she kept grabbing hold of my hair and pulling my head back, almost as if she was trying to distract me from something. I knew by then not to bother to resist these beings. However, I was then beset by the darkest of feelings I have perhaps ever felt, that had a deep sexual flavour to it. It was like all the dark emotions or times I had experienced in my life were condensed into that one moment and I knew it was something I was going to have to face. I began to feel intensely nauseous and knew instinctively that I was going to have to release this darkness somehow. My mind began to scramble to get a hold on it, where was it from? Was it my childhood or past? Was it ancestral? Was it someone else's?

But the more my mind tried to do this, the more the woman would pull my head up as if to say stop looking and eventually, for the first time in my life, my mind stopped working completely. I went to a place beyond thought; there was only silence and the experience of that sickness inside of me. I began to vomit it out, yet the more I heaved the stronger it seemed to get. I then began to moan, a guttural and unearthly sound that seemed to move through me rather than being of my creation. I lost all self-consciousness and I lost all control as my body heaved and wretched into the bucket by my side.

The only thing I had any awareness of, in the faint dimness of space, was the shaman who was holding the ceremony as he began to laugh in a light, playful way. And the more I heaved and writhed around in what I was experiencing as unimaginable pain, the more he laughed. Funnily enough, in that moment I found his laughter immensely reassuring. I knew then deep down in my awareness that I was safe, that this darkness that I had been carrying for so long could be released, I didn't have to protect others from it, for he was clearly completely unafraid of it.

After a while, on one of my many heaves into the bucket, I felt something tangibly come out of me, a presence from my right shoulder. As it did I suddenly came back to some kind of awareness and a single thought come into my head, the first one for a long time, which said simply: 'Oh, it's gone.' That was that, I felt a thousand times lighter and knew that whatever it was, it had been there for a long, long time.

I still had to do some physical cleansing though and later when it was coming out the other end and I was sitting in quite a lot of pain on something resembling a toilet with no roof on, being bitten by industrial type mosquitoes, I suddenly thought to myself: 'Why the hell I have come the other side of the world to do this to myself?' The complete lack of any kind of glamour that I may have read about in this situation suddenly struck me as absurd and I burst out into laughter. As I did this, my heart instantaneously opened and I felt an immense love surrounding me. I knew then, the healing was complete.

I have never known what it was inside of me that needed to come out that night and have never even bothered looking. I know it was released and that in no small way it changed my life. When I got back from that trip, I immediately had to face very difficult personal challenges that before I went I know would have knocked me completely sideways, as they were the culmination of many years of intense difficulties.

However, although it had not been easy, I found I was different and therefore able to respond completely differently to these challenges. Something had been removed from my soul that had been blighting me for most of my life, and the lightness that came in its place opened me up to infinite more possibilities.

Sometimes we need to know what is afflicting us, sometimes we don't and it's discerning the difference that is important. It is after all, in the end, just energy. Too much raking up of the past can separate us from those who brought us up. This then has the effect of cutting us from our ancestors as it is our parents who hold the first and most important link to our ancestral line.

Whatever they have or haven't done in our lives it is essential that we can accept and forgive. For, in the face of anything that might have happened, they gave us the ultimate gift – life. In rejecting them and our family, we are ultimately rejecting life itself.

Another final antidote to slipping into fantasy as we bring back these old traditions into the modern world is to ensure that at the centre of our practice is a connection to the land, as this is where the ancestral memories are really stored, not in any book. Because the problem with books, as with this one, is that it is only ever the author's interpretation of reality. The truth lies in the land and our connection to it, as does our spiritual authority, because the earth is the only real authority here.

It can also ensure that we stay literally 'down to earth' when bringing back these potentially expansive and mind-blowing traditions. That is something that has united all the indigenous people I've had the pleasure of learning from, their down to earthiness and lack of pretension or affectation. They spend most of the time laughing and gently mocking us Westerners, especially when we are trying to be so earnestly 'spiritual'. It highlights for me a deep inner confidence and wisdom. I remember standing outside a sweat lodge with a Native American elder once, and as everyone prepared to enter and fell into a reverential silence, he suddenly quipped, 'Let's go play Indian!'

I would say it's now time to go play with our ancestors, to renew the ancient sacred traditions that were once widespread across the earth, to help fully wake up the spirit of the land in the modern world. For, as we do so, we release the ancestral gold, awaken our own spirits and join that sacred dance that is the continuation of life.

Chapter Seventeen

Integrating the Ancestral Soul

The journey into the Ancestral Soul is a journey into remembrance. As Odin, a strong figure in Northern European shamanic tradition, discovers, it is through drinking from the Well of Remembrance that we discover who we really are. For eventually, if we drink deeply enough, we can travel back through our ancestral line to the beginning of time, when this mysterious thing called life began.

Beginning with our immediate ancestors, we have a real connection to this origin, not just of the human species, but of existence itself. We then discover what all religions, spiritual systems and mystics have been telling us since time immemorial, that we are all one, there is no separation and that this is the ultimate truth. However, by connecting with our ancestors, at the same time we also celebrate our diversity. We are all one and yet we all have a unique heritage, a long line of people and different traditions from which we arise.

In the past 2,000 years or more there has been a spread of monotheistic religions that have attempted to unite all people under a single God. This continues in the modern secular world. It can be seen in our obsession that all people need to embrace democracy as a system of governance or through the corporate takeover of the world that attempts to make everyone's experience of reality the same, so they can become the perfect market for consumption. Even on the internet, where a few social media sites are subtly ensuring that people are melting into that pot of conformity of what it is to be human. They influence how you should look, how you should behave and how you should present that image of yourself to the world.

There are people who actively wish to ensure that we are all grouped together as a single entity – from the shadowy realms of a One World Government, to the overt religious warriors battling to create a world where everyone believes in the same god and worships in the same way.

Even subtly this can be the case in the spiritual realms. Some spiritual leaders proclaim that we should act in a certain way. For example, saying that to be spiritual means to embrace loving compassion and kindness, ignoring the warrior values of fierce nobility, or that we should all become vegetarian to show we are spiritual, ignoring that the hunt is a deep part of indigenous culture's practice and spirituality as it brings them into a meaningful relationship with death and the natural world.

Even the word 'shamanism', invented by academics, is an attempt to unify thousands of different (many contrasting) traditions under a singular umbrella that can become easy palatable to us in the West who still struggle holding concepts of contradiction. This means people can then turn shamanism into a quasi-religion with certain rules and structures that have to be adhered to. On a certain level this book could be attempting to do the same thing, which is why the structures and what it is saying should be taken very lightly. To try to counter this I would just say if it is practically useful to think of things in this way, then great, if it isn't then great as well!

Communism, capitalism, Buddhism, Christianity, Islam, shamanism, socialism, fascism, atheism, belief in science, humanism, all these things on a certain level try to play this game. The effect of imposing these systems of thought on human life ultimately is to destroy diversity. However, if we were to truly take our lead from nature, then we would see that diversity is the key to life. Indeed, this human story of trying to create singular organisms is even being reflected in the natural world as species are dying out and going extinct at an alarming rate. The dream we are creating is being mirrored back to us.

I believe that the problem here is again that all these systems are imposed in a top-down manner and that spirituality originally evolved in the opposite way. Spirituality grew organically from people's interaction with each other and the environment that they were a part of and as a means to express gratitude to that nature for its endless providing. It also grew out of the need for social cohesion, to bring people back together after the inevitable conflict that would descend. If you get a group of humans anywhere and put them together for long enough they are inevitable going to fall out. Thus, spirituality – focusing the community on a bigger picture or higher ideal – helps with this, as does ceremony as a balance restorer.

Each tradition then has a sacred and unique relationship between the community and the land of which it is a part. It grows in this way, and I believe that uniqueness is something to be celebrated. It is also unique to the time and will gradually evolve as the world around the people changes. It can never be fixed. Though based upon certain structures, it is alive and vibrant, which then acts as a natural built-in protection against stasis. Put simply, traditions reflect nature, constantly changing and evolving, but at the same time adhering to certain fundamental principles.

The land I come from is green and full of water. The songs that come out of this land tend to reflect this as they can be melancholic and mournful, but also full of joy and ecstasy. They also can be quite rebellious, not wanting to fit into certain boxes, again reflecting the weather here which will always confound expectations!

This is a very brief and simplistic overview and yet a tradition that grew out of the dry, hot and sparse desert, i.e. Christianity, with its emphasis on asceticism, I feel, doesn't work here that well. In the desert, denial of the senses could have grown quite naturally out of the relative lack of life that surrounds people in the environment. It is a place of fire and air, masculine elements that emphasise a detachment from the body. The land in Britain is much more of earth and water, feminine elements that emphasise and celebrate the opposite, an enjoyment of the sensual body, but also the emotional connections that go alongside this.

In the desert the skies are huge, heaven in all its majesty can be witnessed and beheld. The power of the weather also holds the fragile balance between life and death. This would have been a similar experience on the sparse Asian steppes where the Indo-Aryan people originated from, before setting forth to conquer Europe, the Middle East and Asia. These warrior herding tribes with their powerful sky gods of thunder and war over-ran the original pastoral inhabitants of Europe, whose emphasis was on worshipping earth deities.

In the forest, which most of Northern Europe would have been covered by up until the modern age, the sky is not so relevant or even present. It would have had far less power than the land spirits that surrounded the people. This is about a natural interaction with the land.

I love being in the mountains, the air there is clear and I can see for miles. The insights are astounding as I am literally touching those heavens. Yet, again, it is a different experience from being in dense woodland. Mountain life emphasises the masculine element of air and can again lead to traditions that have asceticism at their heart.

Although we have mountains in Britain, they are rarer, which in a way highlights their sacredness. But if spirituality grows out of people's daily interactions of the land they live on, as I believe it does, traditions that grow out of interactions with the desert, mountains or vast plains will always sit a little uncomfortably here in my view. It is like we are trying to fit a square peg into a round hole.

This is not to say that there won't be similarities or truths that can be gained from any tradition, or that traditions from different lands can't influence people in a positive way. I think the lack of big skies in Britain affects our thinking as a collective in a limiting way often, as it can lead to a distrust of new ideas and can make us quite parochial at times. Thus, big sky vision can be a blessing to us. However, if this comes at a cost to, or ignores, the nature of the nature that we grow out of then this can lead to an incongruence of ideas that go against a person's natural instincts.

Because the modern world has such a mishmash of cultures and peoples living together, this whole notion becomes much more complicated. However, for me, it is about honouring all our influences and finding ways to integrate and make peace with them all. Thus, if I am from a European heritage living in the Midwest of the US, I have the opportunity to integrate my ancestral influences, which may be heavily influenced by forest dwelling people and their love of mischievous woodland spirits, with the land spirits from the land where I now reside, which may be fiercer and more visionary.

Thus, I can honour both, as I will contain both in my being. Whole ceremonies can be created around this and, eventually, as has happened throughout human history, which is full of migratory peoples, new mythologies and ways of viewing the world will emerge that take into account both influences. These will be flexible and able to evolve through that magical interface between the land, the time and the people.

Working with our ancestors is the antidote to singularism, as it is the antidote to fundamentalism, something the world is now constantly being affected by. However, it does so in a way that honours both the past and the present. It is a way that we can bring back the diversity of our traditions and more importantly celebrate this diversity. Also, it holds the key to integrating the various ways people have been influenced by their surroundings to worship the divine spark that is at the heart of life.

Monotheism, and its modern secular counterpart of rational fundamentalism, has in many ways grown out of and has a parallel in the way we began to interact with the land thousands of years ago through farming. Gradually these farming methods have become more and more about the intensive cultivation of very few crops.

So, our traditional hunter gathering lifestyle, whereby diversity and adaptability would be key, has been replaced by the desire for predictability and repetition. This can also be seen in our interpretation and relationship with the spiritual, which has gradually been reduced to a set of instructions that, if followed, will guarantee you a place in heaven, or enlightenment, depending on your goal. In many ways, it has become a results business, which reflects the way we have interacted with the land: 'You will reap what you sow'.

In the modern world the desire for repetition has become something of a neurotic epidemic, as our dominant culture of capitalism seeks not only to make every city centre in the world the same, but also turn us all into the perfect, model consumers. Alternative cultures that do organically spring up, such as happened in the 1960s, are then swallowed by the dominant culture's ideals and sold back to us as neat, well packaged, 'lifestyle choices'.

You can see this most clearly in the way we are sold the idea of freedom. Alongside sex, this is one of the most overused marketing tools – every new gadget implies the same message, that we're somehow getting closer to this ideal of total freedom. Democracy has this as its fundamental guiding principle and yet continually creates the opposite – you are only free if you fit into, and obey, the rules of an increasingly narrow criteria of reality. If not, you are labelled mentally unstable or maladjusted, but don't worry there are drugs that can fix this imbalance and get you back on track!

Each of the great religions or philosophies that have come to dominate human thought and belief, from Christianity through to Hinduism, Judaism to Islam, Buddhism to capitalism and communism to secularism, began life as a cult. That is, they emerged out of specific time, with a specific set of circumstances (political, ecological, social and economic). I would say also, at their heart, they reflected the interaction and relationship with the natural world (even if that relationship was covered by the veneer of industrial revolution) that the people of the time had. They emerged out of the very human need to place meaning on the world and then to worship that meaning.

The point is they were never meant to hold a completely universal truth, although they may be based on one. That is where we have been tricked or, rather, we have tricked ourselves in our search for absolutes. I believe the time has come to go back to the myriad different ways we, as human beings, have found to worship and celebrate the invisible force that runs through all of life.

Connecting with our Body Soul, and then our Ancestral Soul can assist us in doing this. Then our inspiration can come from the subtle interplay between place and time, and there is no need to impose this order on anyone else. New traditions will organically spring to life and they will be suited to the circumstances, suitable to the present, which is the only time that really exists anyway.

Many different ancient traditions, separated by time and space, have prophesied that the age we are now living through is one of destruction, preceding an age of renewal that will grow out of it. Things are coming apart. This can in a way be glimpsed all around us, and a lot of this I have covered so far in this book. So, if the meaning of this time is things coming apart, how can we work with this? Well, one way could be to separate the different traditions we come from in order to bring us back together as a tribe of humanity.

When you celebrate the differences that make us human, the different clans that make up the different tribes and the different tribes that make up the human family, and then the different species that make up the wider nature; when we can celebrate and honour the differences, so *then* can we honour the fact we are all one. Many people try to do it the other way around and try to honour that we are all one before defining themselves as individual and separate. This ultimately leads to a lot of unhealthy merging and, ironically, behaviour as though we're all one, but if only if everyone believes what the trendsetters believe, for example that being a vegetarian is the only way to express a love of nature or to be spiritual!

By honouring our Ancestral Soul, we can then celebrate and have a world once more full of diversity. This diversity, which comes out of the first two souls we have explored and our connection with the earth and all of life, will hopefully then be heart-led, as opposed to head-driven. This leads us on to the third part of our book. For, in a world of diversity, it can then be possible to be a true individual. There is space enough in the collective and ancestral belief systems to enable you, and me, as individuals to prosper and to thrive. Thus comes our connection to our Dreaming Soul.

Chapter Eighteen

Life is but a Dream

The spirit of life as it runs through everything is cultivated and directed by the dreaming part of us. From there, it can create a multiverse of possibilities; such is the magic of life. Shamanic cultures for millennia have understood this to be true and have interacted with this creative principle in a living, breathing way throughout their lives. This is the essence of magic; something can be manifested in the physical world through the power of our 'imagining' it into being.

On a practical level, we have the aforementioned analogy of the architect who dreams up the vision of the building that is then created in reality. This is an obvious example of thought preceding manifestation. Yet this principal is at work in much more subtle ways. As all the mystical traditions have taught us, consciousness makes up reality. It is the material from which our world is made. People tell me that quantum physics is now saying a similar thing and that on the sub-atomic level, the normal 'laws of physics' do not prove to be valid. I don't know enough about this system of thought to comment, but it does seem that the deeper people look, the more mystical reality seems to become.

So if consciousness is the 'prima materia', it is through the part of us that dreams, this part of our soul, that we access the fundamental basis of reality. In doing this, we have the opportunity to become the architects of our reality. In this section of the book we are going to explore how this can happen, for the positive and negative, and how we can begin to master this aspect of ourselves, not just for our own benefit, but for the benefit of our communities as well as the wider world. In this way we can explore how to re-dream the reality we are inhabiting, beginning on an individual level, and then helping to restore harmony and balance to the world.

The starting point of all of this is an ability to access our own 'dreaming'. So what does this mean? As I have mentioned before shamanic cultures hold as a tenet that nothing happens in manifest reality before it has been dreamt first. The Aboriginal culture in Australia, one of the oldest on earth, express this perspective beautifully through their concept of the 'Dreamtime'. This was a time in the mythical past, whereby the earth was born and given form through the dreaming of their ancestors – beings that literally through their thoughts, actions and intentions manifested the physical environment.

The stories of this time that the Aborigines continue to tell connect them to this birth of reality, but also act as essential practical aids in their ongoing relationship with their environments. Thus, a story about the dreaming of a water spring will also have coded within it important instructions on how to access the spring in the vast expanse of outback, so that there is never the need for any maps or other external aids. All the information is held within the individual and the tribe.

The stories will also have as an essential part of them instructions on the how to respect the spirit of the place, in order that the delicate harmony of nature is forever held in place, and not influenced or affected by clumsy human actions. Thus, one story contains not only a living, breathing history that connects people to their landscape, but also the practical information needed to survive and the moral/spiritual code needed to prosper as individuals and a society.

What cultures like this understand, I feel, is that the part of us that connects us to story, myth and creativity, the imaginal part of our beings, is actually limitless and can therefore contain much more information than other more rational sides of our being. Not only this, but this part can also hold sometimes apparently contradictory or opposing thought forms in a unified whole. Or, to put it better, it can retain the unified whole while also dealing with the seemingly separate needs of the immediate functionality. For example, my immediate need for water for survival does not contradict, but rather enhances the mystical foundation of reality and at the same time connects me in time and place to my history, my environment and to the dawn of creation itself. That's quite a package when just going for a drink!

The necessity for moral codes of living, such that religions and other philosophies have set up, does not then become disconnected from the everyday. It is not something that needs endless study and discipline in order to get to the heart of the mystery, buried by thousands of years of occult knowledge. Rather, it is as simple as following in the footsteps of your ancestors and listening to the stories that connect you to everything.

I was in a ceremony recently with the Wixaritari (Huichol), the aforementioned tribe from central Mexico who have resisted interference from 500 years of Spanish colonisation and held onto their traditions. The trainee Marakame (shaman), a friend of mine called Rodrigo, put it beautifully when he said that people tell you that the indigenous people's wisdom has been hidden for millennia and that their sacred ways are secret, which he said simply isn't true. People want to tell you that because they don't want to face up to the truth; that indigenous spirituality and culture simply is about living in harmony with their environments, it really is as straightforward as that. He also said that if we took the time to truly listen to and observe nature, we too would begin to practice these ways quite naturally.

The Wixaritari connect to their Dreamtime through the use of the peyote cactus that grows at the foot of their sacred mountain in the desert at the end of their pilgrimage point the Wirrikuta. This place is seen as the birthplace of the earth, and through communing with the plant that grows here they are able to access the knowledge and healing that will keep them in harmony with the world as it was created, as it was meant to be. The cactus as a teacher plant is psychoactive and takes us quite naturally into that place beyond the rational and into the imaginal realms. It connects us with the Dreamtime.

As mentioned before, the Wixaritari have no other medicine that they use. For any illness they connect with the peyote and, more importantly, the Blue Deer, who is seen to be the spirit of the plant. Like most shamanic cultures they see the cause of sickness being of a psycho-spiritual nature. And like most indigenous people who have managed to keep their traditions pure, they live incredibly long and healthy lives. It is not unusual for members of their community who are nearly a hundred to go on the arduous 500km pilgrimage and as friends have reported to me, be the first ones up the top of the mountain, leaving a few Westerners a third of their age trailing in their wake!

One of the problems in the past that has been experienced when accessing this knowledge directly, is that it goes against mainstream society's need to dictate and control people's perception of reality and therefore shepherd them into ways of being that conform to these 'rules'. For example, if most sickness is indeed of a psycho-spiritual nature, which can be cured by accessing the inner knowledge that we all have within us, what does that mean for the huge pharmaceutical industry that props up many Western economies?

Or, before that, if you were able to access your ancestors and the creative source of life, God, or whatever name you wish to call it, by simply following your ancestors' stories and going 'walkabout' in the outback, what would this mean for the huge conglomerate of money, power and control that was and is the Church? Both would be rendered fairly superfluous, which organisations or institutions that are used to a lot of power and influence don't find particularly easy. They tend to cling to power as much as they possibly can, whatever the consequences.

Thus, there is of course a strong agenda against setting free our imaginal realms innate within our society. This can be seen in the reaction to any psycho-active substance, be it in plant or drug form, that can threaten to unleash the power of the imagination. Not only this, it can also be seen in the way indigenous people, beginning with those who practiced in our own Western lands, who practiced their own form of communion with the divine, have been and continue to be persecuted and forcibly pressurised to convert to the mainstream ideology of religion or, now more subtly, science.

Because we have lived with this way for quite a few generations now, it has become something of a habit. This affects us not just on a society basis, but also on an individual one. We have become adept in many ways at controlling our levels of perception. It is like a form of brainwashing that has sunk deep into our being. Anything that threatens our perceptions of reality is likely then at best to be treated with suspicion and, at worse, extreme hostility. This can lead to us either ignoring what our wider perceptions are telling us or outright trying to destroy their influence. All this can be happening on the unconscious level, or subtle realms of reality that can get in the way of healing as we explored in the first section. In short, our own minds can trip us up a hell of a lot.

It can even get to the ridiculous levels that someone can have a very real, visceral psychic experience, but because of the overriding belief system that this stuff isn't 'real', then completely dismiss it. This happens continually. I remember being in the woods on a burial ceremony with my partner once and she was bemoaning the fact that she never 'sees' spirits like other people. We were above ground around a fire supporting those under the earth and periodically through the evening would go around the graves and drum to help those below to dream. On one such of these occasions as we were drumming my partner, who was in one section of the woods on her own, suddenly ran back to the fire. When we got back we asked her what was wrong as she looked ashen and in shock. She said: 'There's a man over there standing by the tree, he just suddenly appeared and was as real as you or me.' After a little investigation we just laughed as it was clear she had seen a spirit who had manifested physically.

The spirits had heard her moan and decided to play a little trick on her, something in my experience they are very apt to do! Interestingly, all day she had been making a model out of the clay that came from the graves being dug up, which had turned into the head of a male figure and before everyone had gone into their grave she had placed it in the tree that later the man appeared leaning on. That was the same night that the aforementioned C had her 'miracle' cure in the ceremony. Life really is mysterious sometimes and trying to explain it will often only actually diminish rather than enhance it. That certainly was a strange night in so many ways.

Alternatively, the other side of the coin is that because the imaginal part of our being is something we are not fully used to employing, when people do open up to these realms there can be the tendency to slip into fantasy. A lot of this will involve projecting unconscious desires upon the invisible worlds, then experiencing them as real. Part of this tendency we explored in the previous section, with books that are just fantasy stories that have been made up. It is something that in my experience, when working with spirit, we have to guard against constantly.

The amount of times I've been around people who have said: 'Spirit told me to buy that super expensive crystal,' or to do this that and the other. It does make me wonder whether the invisible ones are that interested in how we spend our money or whether it might be just sometimes that we want something for ourselves. Discernment takes a long time to master and can only be learnt through experience, and through tripping up a lot and making a lot of mistakes. It seems as a society we are stuck between excessive cynicism and extreme flights of fantasy.

However, access to the levels of consciousness we are describing begins with and comes through something so natural to us that we are engaged with it every day – our imagination. There is no real mystery or profound secret. All there is the realisation that we should take this vast, mysterious aspect of our being seriously and instead of dismissing it, we should actually work to engage and explore it. The next time someone says to you, or you say to yourself: 'It's just your imagination,' ask them or yourself to actually define what the imagination is, where it exists, and how it is possible to measure it. Then ask for evidence of anyone who has measured its outer limits and where they found its ending was. I'd sure like to visit that place!

The imagination is the doorway to dreaming levels of reality. There are different levels and this clearly takes a lot of training in order to fully master it. When we fully go through the doorway of the imagination, it feels less and less like the imagination we are used to perceiving with and more like what the shamanic cultures have been telling us – that it is possible to access different worlds, as real as this one, but that exist in the realms of spirit. We are able to perceive these worlds not just with something that relates to our mental faculties, but also with our whole bodies and beings. We are able to touch, smell and feel these different worlds as viscerally as we do this world.

In those moments we enter the Dreamtime and, as at night time, we forget which is so-called dream and which is so-called reality – we forget we are dreaming. Or rather, we wake up to the fact that actually we are always dreaming, even in so-called everyday reality; that what we are experiencing in this altered state is just another aspect of a vast continuum of what we call consciousness, or life. Herein lies the magic. So to what purpose might we wish to engage and hone these faculties of our being? Let us now explore this in more detail.

Chapter Nineteen

Personal Stories that Make Up
our Dreaming

Reality, through the shamanic lens, is made up of patterns of energy. These patterns of energy are held together and then create form through the narrative of story. Story is central to the web of existence as it defines reality, which we perceive as a series of electrical impulses, and makes it into something that can be navigated and made sense of. It is the way we dream.

As we explored in the first section of the book, the story or myth of an age binds cultures and societies together. This can be religious/spiritual story or scientific/rational, it doesn't matter as either can have a profound effect on the people of the culture by defining and limiting the way people think and subsequently behave. These belief systems set the boundaries and parameters of what is collectively then agreed upon as 'reality'.

We have a tendency in the modern world to get very attached to our stories or belief systems, which can be seen in a near obsession of trying forcing them on other cultures as if they were the only ones that could exist – from Christian missionaries or Islamic fundamentalists through to equally zealous proponents of democracy. Thus, any idea or story that challenges the prevailing belief system is often met by extreme reactions as one belief system seeks to destroy another. The number of people who have died fighting for what they believe in throughout history is extraordinary.

It is like this faculty of our being has become increasingly limited, which has created an urge towards fundamentalism and obsession. Yet, at the same time we seem to instinctively under-stand the power of our stories to literally hold together our experience of reality, hence such urgent need to defend them.

We're aware of their power on an unconscious level, which is why we can go to such extremes when gripped by the fervour of an idea (any revolution of the modern period is a testament to this). Yet, at the same time, we deny rationally that our belief systems could ever have an effect on something as objective as the reality outside us. This mixture between denial of, and being possessed by, beliefs is a potent and dangerous combination. For, as with any repression, it creates highly irrational behaviour in humans.

I remember listening to a Native American storyteller once and as he shared the creation myths of his people he would always add the caveat at the end of the story with a playful, self-deprecating smile: 'At least, that was the way it was told to me.' This seemed to me a very clever way of ensuring that the story wasn't received as any kind of fundamental truth. We seem to have lost that flexibility with our minds and with our stories.

This inflexibility and urge towards fundamentalism has also affected us in our personal stories – the threads that make up the meaning of who we actually are. Like stories that hold cultures together, our personal stories can exhibit an equal amount of power over how we define ourselves. Through this definition, they can then exert huge control over reality, or rather our perception of the reality we inhabit. So what might make up our personal stories, how do they come into being and how might they be transformed? These are the questions that we will explore in this chapter.

When I undertake a healing on someone, one of the first things I will do is psychically travel into their energy body – another name of which has been called the 'Dreaming Body'. In this invisible, energetic counterpart to the physical body the currency instead of being flesh and bone, becomes story. It is like entering a matrix or web of ideas and thought forms, which if read in a certain way unveils itself as a narrative. This is part of the skill of the healer or shaman, to be able to interpret this tangled mesh of energy as something coherent that is creating the reality of the person; the way they are 'dreaming'.

The energy that thought forms have on the invisible level, especially when charged up by the power of emotional intensity, create who we are, they create our personal stories. So how might this work? Trauma can be a great example of the dynamics of this interchange. Let's look at an example.

A child is fairly happy and adapted to her environment, but then at the age of three her parents suddenly go through a protracted and bitter separation. What was once a safe, held environment becomes one that is full of tension, conflict and break down. The story of the childhood has taken a sudden and unwelcome turn for the worse. How might the child respond to this? Well the likelihood would be that this didn't come out of the blue to the child, as when we are younger we are particularly open to the psychic environment of our surroundings. Thus, any conflict between the parents, no matter how latent, will have been felt for a while even if this conflict was only coming from one of them and was being internalised.

As children we read energy much better than understanding what people are saying or how they are trying to act. This is because we are so much nearer to the invisible, spirit world, we have only just left it and our brains haven't been so conditioned into ignoring most of the perceptual information we are receiving. So the break up or break down could have been felt as being in the air for a while. However, the actual occurrence of it in the physical world could still be met with shock and fear as a world that had been relatively predictable up to then becomes highly volatile. At the same time the child is more than likely to act as the psychic sponge for all the emotional energy and pain that she is surrounded by from one or both of the parents.

So, this child goes from having to deal with the normal perceptual conditions of growing up and integrating the vast expanse of information received on a daily basis, to having to deal with this invasion of crisis. This, understandably, could create a lot of fear, but also of a whole load of heavy emotional burdens. What does the child then do with all this excessive emotion, when the conditions of security that enable healthy expression of emotion are themselves being torn down? Usually, they internalise it.

The thought form that assists or seals this internalisation could be, 'Life is not safe,' as the onslaught of change and the emotional blast that comes from it could strike at any time. Another story that can come out of this could be, 'Those I love and rely on cannot be trusted.' Or, another one could be, 'I can only rely on myself to survive in this world.' There could be a myriad others that encompass self-blame and even guilt for somehow causing the situation. Because the girl is only three, the separation from her own internal world and that of her parents is highly porous. She will also tend to come to quite black-and-white, simplistic conclusions as she is not yet aware of the complex intricacies of the adult world. Because she is only three, these stories will be forgotten and yet remain active and potent in the unconscious. They will be made with her whole being as opposed to any rational response to the situation.

These initial core stories can then be built upon with a whole variety of creative extrapolations. For example, when this child grows up still holding onto the energetic burden of this unreleased emotional charge, there can be the intuitive sense that something lurks within which, as life isn't safe, could actually erupt at any time. This is all the unresolved emotional trauma. The story then grows from, 'Life is not safe and I can't trust those I love,' through to, 'I can't fully trust what is inside of me,' or simply, 'I can't trust myself.' It is very hard to trust ourselves when we are loaded with unresolved trauma.

This then begins a journey of separation between herself and this now woman, which will then manifest in several seemingly fateful experiences that reinforce this perception – that life, people or her deeper feelings can't be trusted. This embeds the pattern, making the story stronger and adding to the now considerable load of unresolved internal feelings of rage, grief and fear that are the quite natural responses to being hit by life's unexpected blows.

In fact, from a shamanic perspective, the 'story' actually energetically attracts situations in life that will help to keep it going. This can be simply through the unconscious actions of the woman who because of this core lack of trust in others will push away those people who do offer to support her, as they might threaten the edifice of this story and thus release all these unresolved feelings that she has now spent most of her life keeping down. Instead, she will go after those elusive souls that will always let her down, thus keeping the story safe and the emotions held in. This is a simple example of the self-preservation and attempting to keep safe – even if it is in pain – that trauma creates.

At some point though, maybe years later, this separation from herself that this story has precipitated will eventually reach a crisis point. The woman, no more energised by youth, will reach a crisis of meaning. 'Who am I?' might then be the legitimate, but haunting question she asks. Or even: 'I have lost myself and can't feel a thing anymore.'

The catalyst for this might be a physical illness, an event in her life, a psychological breakdown, or simply some kind of existential crisis. However this happens, this will be when the healing journey can actually begin. And this journey will involve the woman having to at some stage confront the story she has unconsciously told herself her whole life and the intense feelings that got buried beneath this belief system, now magnified by 40-odd years of existence.

This is a simple and relatively straightforward example of how these stories can get created then locked in the energetic or dreaming body of a person. The interesting thing is that when you undertake shamanic healing on someone, you can see the whole of this playing out before your eyes, or rather within your vision. You don't even have to know anything about a person; their energy body will tell you it all.

The amount of times I have shocked a person with the level of detail and insight into their internal worlds is countless. But as I say to them, it's not really me that sees this stuff, it's the spirits that show me. It is a subtle but important distinction as it's not as if I walk around all the time picking up all this information about people, it's only when I consciously interact with the spirits that I get it, and they choose what to show me.

Again, the practical side of this, beyond the healing that can be done, is that it by showing the person things that you couldn't possibly know about them, you can stimulate their belief system in that what is happening must be real. That it's possible to see deeper into reality than the surface and all this shamanic stuff, crazy as it often seems, must have something to it. As we explored in the first section of the book, when you have a person's belief on your side, it can be a potent tool in healing.

Yet, showing this stuff is real is only a part of it, as it is also possible not just to diagnose the story that is inhibiting a person's growth and soul experience of life, but also to bring healing to it. As explored, the story is only a thought form charged up by emotion and both are only energy. They can therefore be transformed, healed and then removed. This will often involve on the invisible level separating the emotional power from the thought form, making it benign. Once this is done the thought form can naturally disperse or too be removed.

Our night dreams, when our conscious awareness is no longer exerting its control over the personality, can often reveal to us the stories we are telling ourselves about life and ourselves. Especially repetitive ones, as this can often be the soul's way of trying to resolve or disperse the trapped psychic energy from the core belief systems.

The power of these belief systems over us before they have been healed can be immense. They are what traditionally have been known as spells. These 'spells', though they often have their roots in another's perception of us, are much more likely in the modern world to be placed over ourselves, than used against others, as would be the traditional way to view sickness in shamanic cultures. For example, the idea that someone is casting a negative 'curse' on the person. Nowadays this type of psychic warfare, although common on the unconscious level, is actually happening much more in our own inner worlds – we curse ourselves constantly with the negative belief systems we hold about ourselves.

In fact, in most healing cases I see, the sickness on an invisible level essentially involves the clash between a person's belief system about who they think they are or what life is and something powerfully organic that is trying to rise to the surface, which contradicts this. The friction created keeps the sickness locked into the system. By removing or resolving the conflict, the whole system is able to relax and the body can then get on with the natural process of healing itself.

A common and difficult belief system may simply be that I don't deserve to be well. The root of this then needs careful unravelling in order to get to the trauma whereby this unnatural belief system was created. To explore how we can get to the heart of some of these wounding stories and transmute them into healing ones, let us look at a framework that can assist us.

Chapter Twenty

Cycles of Sickness and Healing with the Wheel of Life

North Americans have something in their culture they call the Medicine Wheel. This is an ancient method of transposing their cosmology upon the physical landscape they inhabit. Most ancient cultures have had a similar system. The most prevalent the world over, like the Medicine Wheel, involves a recognition of the four directions, east, south, west and north, set within a circle as being the bedrock of a people's cosmology, orientating their Body Soul in space.

Each direction not only has a physical reality, but also brings a certain quality that can relate to a person's physical environment and to their experience of internal reality. In the same way that the Aboriginal stories hold practical information and also the dreaming of their ancestors, the wheel that the four directions creates inhabits and transcends earthly life simultaneously. Thus, spiritual truths do not become divorced from their natural environments.

In Western traditions particularly, the four directions are associated with the four elements: fire, water, air and earth. These are seen as the bedrock of reality. Creation is seen as a constant interaction between these four archetypal powers that gave birth to life and continue to hold it in balance. As outer reality is an exact reflection of inner reality, these four elements also hold the key to keeping the invisible reality we inhabit in balance.

Thus, the Wheel of Life can be used as a map that aligns us with the outer cosmos at the same time as aligning us with our internal landscapes. There are infinite ways of utilising this map, far beyond the scope of this book and there are many books dedicated to just this one subject. However, the one I wish to explore here is the way it can reveal to us cycles of sickness, and then consequently how these can be transformed into a cycle of healing.

There are also many different wheels that people use, each with a different element in each direction. Some it is claimed are ancient but, like a lot of so called ancient traditions, many have been shown to have been invented in very recent times.

The one I use is the same as that used by astrology and other divinatory systems popular in Europe for many years. Although not seen to be distinctly shamanic, I know that my ancestors from this land have used this wheel as a cosmological system for at least a couple of millennia. It has not been invented recently and thus has some legs to it. However, people do use others with successful results so I am not fixed that this wheel is in any way more truthful than any others, it just works for me.

In the east is the element of fire, the rising sun that initiates all new beginnings, the power of our passion and spirits to give

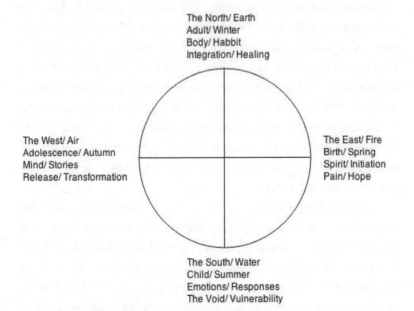

The North/ Earth
Adult/ Winter
Body/ Habbit
Integration/ Healing

The West/ Air
Adolescence/ Autumn
Mind/ Stories
Release/ Transformation

The East/ Fire
Birth/ Spring
Spirit/ Initiation
Pain/ Hope

The South/ Water
Child/ Summer
Emotions/ Responses
The Void/ Vulnerability

The Wheel of Life

birth to something in life; the spark of life. It is the time of spring when nature is full of the energy of growth. In the south is the element of water, the place of the child and all our emotional vulnerabilities, where we feel life from and drink from its well, it is the time of summer when the earth is abundant with her beauty. In the west is the element of air, the place of death and letting go as the leaves do in the autumn, as we prepare to go into the dark, it is the time of adolescence moving into adulthood when we begin to know our own minds and how we define our worlds with our thoughts. In the north is the element of earth, a time of winter, nature stripping itself back to its core, a place of eldership and maturity, where our spirits are manifested, integrated and grounded in earthly reality.

This is a very brief description of an immensely deep and endlessly fascinating cycle. However, for now, we will focus how this map of reality can describe cycles of sickness and subsequent healing.

To initiate a cycle of sickness, the element of fire in the east comes into our lives in its destructive form. This can be in the form of a sudden shock, an emotional trauma or a physical accident. It could be the death of a loved one, the end of a relationship, the loss of fortune or a physically traumatic event in our lives. Whatever form it takes, we are suddenly introduced to the destructive power that gives birth to sickness. In a way we are introduced to the spirit of sickness itself. It is a little like Pandora in the myth when she opened the box that let out all the Furies and 'evil' into the world.

After the initial shock of this meeting with the fire and the destructive side of nature, there then comes a strong emotional reaction, which is when we move around to the south and the element of water. This reaction could be grief, at the loss of whatever it is that has been destroyed by the fire, it could be an intense, paralysing fear or just simply the overwhelming sense of too much emotion flooding up to the surface. Or, conversely, we could choose to stay in the fire and try to fight whatever it is that is threatening to destroy us, thus embodying anger. In this scenario, the spirit of the water is one of illusion, as the more vulnerable feelings that have been provoked are denied and repressed.

In the south we are at our most vulnerable because it is the place of the child – the one who is caught between two worlds, that of being of spirit, the fire from where we have come from, and being human, what we are here to become. The child is then trying to integrate these sometimes conflicting worlds. It is where we truly feel life from, whatever age we are and how we connect to that sense of vulnerability and the innocence that creates it. In the cycle of sickness that innocence is lost and in its wake we learn of the more painful feelings of being human. It is where the void that we explored in the first section can lie.

Then comes the west and the element of air. This is when the mind and thought gets involved. The first two elements deal with stimulus and reaction in this cycle. Now comes reflection and attempted understanding. However, because of the nature of this cycle, we are often still in reactionary mode when it comes to the aspect of thought. Thus, the initial thought might be simply, 'That hurts!' or 'That's painful'.

But this can then lead to lot of questioning, for example: 'Why did this happen to me?' 'What have I done that to deserve this?' 'What am I being punished for?' At some point these initial thoughts, fed by the pain of the fire and the intense emotional charge of our reaction, then coalesce into a story. This is when the initial trauma has the potential of either being let go of and healed or, as this is the cycle of sickness, what often happens is that it becomes a pattern of thought that holds the wounding in place.

So the story might be: 'I did something wrong and now am being punished.' This can then lead to: 'I deserve to suffer.' This is such a strong story in the collective for the past couple of thousand years in a lot of traditions. Or, as we have explored a lot, it could be: 'Life is painful, which I don't like, therefore I will not allow myself to be vulnerable again.' With that scenario my heart closes down and I close off to all the feelings that provoke vulnerability, including the positive ones such as love.

Or, there could be a darker thought/belief system: 'I have suffered and been hurt so now others should experience the same.' Then an unconscious revenge motif takes hold, leading to aggressive/destructive behaviour acted out on others. This is the classic scenario: 'I hurt those who come closest to me, or just anyone who gets in my way.' It is more likely to occur when the person has stayed in the fire of the east and responded to the initial wounding by fighting it, denying the vulnerability of the south completely. This also is a strong unconscious story in the collective and drives a lot of dominatory and predatory behaviour. This is the fire driving the show and seeking to destroy constantly – a masculine (but not necessarily male) response to trauma.

These patterns of thought or belief systems then begin to organically create habitual patterns of behaviour and this is where we travel to the north of the wheel and the element of earth. It is here that the wounding then becomes cemented into everyday lives through the habitual patterns of behaviour that it has created, which in turn changes our physical environments.

It is in the north that the sickness reaches deep into our lives and our bodies, which then carry the weight of unresolved past traumas. This is when the physical environment is changed by our habits, i.e. the ones that are trying to keep us safe, and the emotional traumas of the south become compulsions. This could simply manifest in a way that I begin to control my environment, trying desperately to shield myself from the shock of the fire catching me off guard again. There then comes the desperate compulsion to make life somehow safe, which feeds into and is behind so much pain and sickness in the modern world. It is this fear of pain and subsequent attempt to insulate ourselves from it that drives huge marketing campaigns and manipulates us into buying endless amounts of stuff, to somehow become safe.

As we explored in the first section of the book, we are quite addicted as a people. Indeed the whole of capitalism, the modern story we have used to organise ourselves into a society, is based upon the need to keep people addicted. Without consumption in an endless arc of expansion, capitalism falls apart. It has the effect of keeping people addicted, keeping them in fear and desire, but also keeping them traumatised. As all the unresolved emotional energy from the south is manipulated to keep the compulsive need for stuff alive in us. This keeps us in the place of the wounded child, who just needs deep down to somehow feel safe.

Our traumas have been huge, as we explored in the last section of the book, through ancestral wounding – the fire when it has come into life has been through the extremes of wars that engaged the majority of people on the planet in some way. After each war the rise of consumerism has taken on another leap of huge proportions. On a nationwide level, the belief has been that the richer or more well off the inhabitants, the less likely there will be the need for war. Prosperity is equated with safety and security. Yet, if the emotional traumas of the south aren't addressed directly, all prosperity creates is a need for more prosperity to ward off the unconscious trauma that is being held onto, feeding belief systems that limit the individual from truly ever feeling safe and secure. These in themselves become self-fulfilling prophecies.

Thus, we have people who by any definition of mental wellness are quite sick as they are compelled to hoard fortunes so vast that they couldn't even get near to spending them in several lifetimes and then are driven to actually accumulate more. This isn't well-adjusted human behaviour and is about as far from rational response to existence as you could possibly get.

The indigenous people of North America could see it when the white man came over and was driven insane by the lust for power that gold or oil rushes would bring. It is part of our insanity that would actually threaten the survival of our species in this endless quest for more.

Put simply, it is mental illness on a grand scale. The real mental illness that affects our society and not the type that is being expressed by those sensitive enough (and stuck in the south of the wheel) to perceive that the way we are carrying on isn't what it means to be human and who are expressing this through their inability to adjust to such an insane world. This is the intensely negative side of the element of earth in the north in this cycle of sickness.

Back to the individual level, the patterns cemented in the north could mean that I avoid situations that will challenge my story – i.e. something that will show to me that life, although containing pain, can be full of security and love. It can be trusted, as can I. Or, it is possible to experience pain and *not* take it personally, not build a story around it that will perpetuate it. For this to fully happen we then need to move around the Wheel of Life through the cycle of healing, which is the counterbalance to the cycle of sickness.

The cycle of healing begins with us having to go back to the east and into the fire again, back into the initial wound that has created so much sickness in our lives. This is when we begin the process of initiating ourselves consciously. Most healing is a journey and what stops most people from starting this journey is the instinctive understanding that in order to fully heal something then they might have to re-experience what it was that actually hurt in the first space. They might have to go through some of the pain again – like a physical wound needs to be exposed to the air in order to heal itself organically.

In the Greek myth, when Pandora opens the box that lets out evil into the world in the shape of the Furies, at the bottom of the box what is left is Elpis – the spirit of hope. This intimates that beneath all pain or sickness in life lies hope and it is this sometimes most elusive of qualities that is at the heart of all healing. So when we do return to the east, to the initial wound, it is then essential that we go with some sense of hope. This is often the role of the healer, as we explored in the first section of the book, to provide the framework where hope can prosper and is also the purpose of ceremony, to be the container of hope.

Again, the Wixaritari ceremony with the sacrament peyote is a beautiful example of this. The ceremony begins at night, with the purpose to sing up the sun in the east again in the morning, to ensure that life can once again prosper. The Marakame will sing five songs throughout the night to ensure that this happens. Each time he sings, he brings another layer of healing to each person present in the ceremony.

As is normal, the night will begin with a lot of discordance in the circle of people taking part, as each person will face their own darkness or demons of control. They could be jealousies, judgements, fear, anger or grief; anything that can stop us from connecting with our true selves.

There may be purging, there may be weeping or just the quiet intensity of people facing up to what normally goes unacknowledged or ignored in their minds or souls. All the time the Marakame is singing and clearing these energies, working alongside and channelling the spirit of the plant, giving each person the opportunity to once again be renewed and healed. When you do a series of these ceremonies over successive evenings, gradually all the blocks melt away as the group comes back into unity – the way humans are meant to live – and each person begins to connect once again with their own inner light.

Thus, as the sun rises once more, so we are reconnected to the spirit of hope it brings within ourselves. For someone in the midst of pain, the simple fact that the sun will rise once again, and they can be a part of that, can be the most amazingly healing thing.

Many times life will initiate the person who needs healing back into the fire itself, as there is a magic that seems to operate on the soul level where nature, including our inner nature, is constantly attempting to right itself. This may come in the form of a shock or another trauma that wakes us up out of the slumber that we have been inhabiting in our lives. This trauma will often mirror in some way the initial wound that set the course of our lives in a certain direction in the first place.

Again, here the most important thing is our ability to see this as an opportunity to begin a healing journey. Although we may be only semi-consciously aware of this, it may be just that the pain is so much that we're finally driven to seek some kind of help or change in our lives because the alternative is too unbearable to cope with.

As a healer I often have to stand with the person in this fire, to help initiate their healing journey. I will stand with them witnessing and honouring all of the white heat of their piercing pain, all the wounding they have spent most of their life either running from, hiding or being consumed by. At the same time, it is my role to assist in the transmutation of that pain into hope, or simply into energy that propels that person onwards in life and deeper into themselves.

Once we've unearthed, acknowledged and honoured the wounding, we then have to travel to the south and begin to explore and witness all of the vulnerability that this pain has left in its wake. If the beginning of the cycle of healing in the east involved the ripping off of the plasters or bandages that had covered the wound, but were now suffocating it and making it rot from within, this part of the cycle involves really feeling the sensitivity to hurt that this wound initiated.

It is here we must nurture and heal the inner child. Often this child has been one carrying the full emotional burden of the wounding, and as many psychologists or therapists will tell you, it is often this wounded child that is running the show in terms of the person's life.

How can we bring healing to the south and the waters of vulnerability? Here we must learn to fully grieve, as grief is the separating agent that when fully released disconnects us from the past. The water washes away everything. As the physical waters of our planet are so polluted, so are our internal landscapes as resentments, bitterness, guilt or just the unreleased burdens of grief and the past weigh us down. We explored how this works on the ancestral level in the past section. This then keeps us locked in a place of helplessness as, rather than protecting us against vulnerability, denial and repression actually keep us constantly locked in that prison. We never leave the trauma behind and instead react from this place, creating then more trauma.

Again, forgiveness is such a potent tool here, the need to forgive anyone who may have been part of causing the pain we suffered, whether it is a logical connection or not. Or even simply forgiving life itself. Real forgiveness is a journey and usually something that cannot be done overnight. I can say I forgive someone, as many people do, because it makes me feel temporarily better about myself as it must mean I'm a good person and not one to hold grudges, or simply that I'm above all that and no one can really hurt me anyway. However, we may need to go a bit deeper than that. In my experience people can often try to leap to forgiveness too early, and make the simple mistake of not fully honouring and expressing in some way, the reasons why they *can't* forgive the person. These feelings of anger, bitterness, rage, deep sadness in the place of the south need to be honoured first, given a voice to, so that acceptance can be found and then forgiveness.

A simple way to do this, is to imagine the person you feel you might have a problem forgiving, see them in front of you, and then out loud, talk and express yourself from your gut not your head, what your true feelings are and why you *can't* forgive them. Don't censor yourself (we spend too much of our life doing this) and try to reach deep into your being for those parts of you that you've spent quite a while sitting on. If you fully let go you might surprise yourself.

Then, when all that stuff has burnt itself out or washed itself away and you feel much calmer or more at ease, *then* forgive them. At the same time reach into yourself where you feel intuitively is right and give them back some energy of theirs you have been holding onto.

From the shamanic perspective, the belief is that if we cannot forgive someone, we are actually holding onto part of their soul. This is a lose-lose situation as we have a part of their vital life force from their personal soul, which drains them, probably as some kind of unconscious act of revenge. But at the same time it doesn't sit well with our energy and instead is a burden.

Hence when people do truly forgive someone they often feel a lot lighter. If you do the above exercise with integrity you will feel the same. It also means that after we die we aren't able to travel onwards as there is unresolved business with the parts of souls being held on to, hence again the common death-bed forgiveness ritual.

Another essential part of this forgiveness process that can be overlooked, is the importance of forgiving ourselves. This might seem an unusual thing, especially if we have been the victim of others' actions, yet it is almost as if we know intuitively that on a soul level, we are actively co-creating this thing called reality, even if we are blissfully unaware of it. When we begin this healing cycle in the east, it is essential that we take full responsibility for everything that has happened to us in our lives. This is the way we can take back power, especially if we have been the victim of other people's destructive actions or abuse. We have to claim back our soul. This taking responsibility, however, isn't done in a self-blame way. In fact in the south we are attempting to move through and cleanse away all blame. Instead it is done as a fire act of the warrior.

Thus, when we get around to the south it is time to forgive ourselves deeply, so we can fully move on with our lives and free up enormous amounts of trapped psychic energy in our souls. This energy simply translates to love. The journey of the south is to find the love amidst the pain, for love is the ultimate release. It is also to transmute all this emotional energy into something that can enhance our lives, as opposed to burdening them. When we do this healing we become naturally child-like again and often realise that it is our vulnerability that is our greatest power.

So what to do with all this energy once we have gone through this process and it has come back to us in the form of power? Then, we move around to the west and the element of air, for it is time to recreate a new story for our lives. A healing story, as opposed to the wounding story that has been directing the show. To change our life, we have to change our belief systems.

At this point we can get involved magically in our healing and can use the power of the mind to make real change. It is the time in a healing journey when suddenly the opportunity comes to broaden all expected ideas we have of ourselves.

The stories we tell ourselves about ourselves and about life, as explored before, are like spells. When we have gone deep into the pain of the wound in the east and south, we suddenly realise that the things we have been running from or hiding don't have that much power, only what we've given to them. We realise that to be vulnerable, although taking us through a kind of death, a death of the controlling facets of the ego, doesn't mean the end and can actually give birth to a lot more life.

This has the effect of breaking the magic of the spell a little, for the spell or the curse keeps us asleep and unable to face up to ourselves. Now we have the opportunity to recast a new spell; a thought pattern that will enhance our experience of life as opposed to taking away from it.

A lot of pain caused when we are sick is when a story someone has told themselves about themselves or about life is too limiting and comes into conflict with the actual reality they are experiencing. This is something I see again and again. In many ways this creates the soul crisis that manifest in the form of sickness in the first place. A common one of these stories is that if I am 'nice' and 'kind' life will be 'nice' and 'kind' to me back. This is a deeply embedded story that comes from the reward/punishment strategy that most people are brought up with.

I see many people whose whole life has been based on this philosophy, either consciously or unconsciously, and yet their experiences of others have been anything but nice or kind. In fact, they have usually been to the contrary as people with this story embedded in their psyche tend to attract others who could have the opposite story, i.e. 'If I am selfish and go after what I want the most, life will reward me.'

This is simply nature's way of balancing itself and has nothing to do with what is 'morally' right. Yet we play this game with life constantly, making these unconscious deals and strategies to get what we want. This is one of the ways we attempt to control our reality.

So much of the time people get into spirituality, or go on a healing journey, with this semi-conscious expectation at the root their decision – that if I do this, if I give myself over to it, my life will be become so much better and endless happiness will be mine. There's a whole industry devoted to selling this illusion to people with the at times blatant refrain: change your life in this way and that elusive thing called happiness will be forever yours.

Whole religions have been built upon that promise, not in this lifetime but in the afterlife, which has driven people to extraordinary lengths to fulfil this destiny, even to the point of blowing themselves up and taking many people with them, to get into their heaven. The only difference with the 'new' spirituality is that this reward incentive is now offered in this lifetime, you don't have to wait until you die as things have moved on and everyone's got a bit more impatient now! We want to have our cake and eat it, quite literally.

Yet how does nature really respond to such bargaining? Usually by ignoring it and carrying on the way it always has, keeping the delicate balance in place so life can prosper. This is because such bargaining comes from a place of insecurity and fear and not from a place of love and confidence. It is from the place of wounding that sees us as somehow cut off from the source of love and creation in the first place and therefore having to bargain to win back its affection.

Unconditional love, in my experience, is at the heart of life, which means that all our reward seeking prostrations are ultimately pointless, because love is all there is and it is ours whatever we do and whoever we are.

Everything else, all the moral codes and ways of behaving, are put in place by society and have their purpose, which is to assist in the smooth functioning of such a society. They are there to ensure that it doesn't collapse under the weight of everyone just behaving how they want and looking out only for themselves. When you take away such moral precepts you get to the place we pretty much are now in the secular west, where morality is secondary to other more important considerations such as the permutations of the fluctuating market. It's interesting though how we've created a system of living that is again at the mercy of a detached and arbitrary controlling mechanism, i.e. the market. This would suggest that although we've thrown off the surface story of religion, the deeper and more real narrative – that we are at the mercy of a rewarding/punishing controller – is still alive and prospering. God is now the economic market and instead of living in the sky on a cloud, he lives in tall buildings in the centre of every major city. This is the way with these stories we tell ourselves, the characters, costumes and sets may change, but the central plot remains essentially the same.

Healthy systems of governance, both personal and political, are useful adjuncts to spirituality. We need the moral framework to hold us in place and time and to help us grow under a safe, protective embrace of community, or to help us prosper as individuals knowing what we hold true.

However, if these moral frameworks are manipulated politically to control people and keep them weak and repressed, it is then that the 'bargaining with God' can take on unhealthy proportions. It is also when the top-down rules of being begin to clash with organic needs and drives inside of individuals and cultures. It is essential to remember in those times that the 'word of God' is usually in fact the word of man. This 'God' can be out there or the internal law giver inside of our own psyche. That word of God can be written down in a book to cement it as a belief system, or it can be written in an individual consciousness, which can be equally powerful as a belief system.

When it comes to healing, I feel we need to cut through the illusion that we will be rewarded by 'God', wherever he/she resides, for obeying our belief systems. Instead we need to look at these belief systems and how much life is actually challenging us to transcend their limitations. This is not about throwing the baby out with the bath water as most revolutions are based upon. It is not about having no moral framework or guidelines to live by and within. Rather it is to find ones that fit better with the actual reality we inhabit.

As a healer, it is often my role to assist others in rooting out their limiting ideas and replacing them with ones that serve the greater needs of their souls. Spiritually, we may then get to the point where our story is simply one to serve the spirit of life as it resides within and comes through us.

So if my underlying story or belief system is that in order to feel accepted and worthy of life I have to win the praise and love of a distant, all-powerful figure, how might I respond to this in my life? Well, it could be one of two ways. Either I subvert my needs and desires in forever trying to please this arbitrary force and become passive and powerless in my life. Or, I get frustrated with this approach, and instead try and overthrow that God and instead become it. I think Nietzsche articulated this second desire perfectly in his most famous of statements:

> God is dead. God remains dead. And we have killed him. How shall we comfort ourselves, the murderers of all murderers? What was holiest and mightiest of all that the world has yet owned has bled to death under our knives: who will wipe this blood off us? What water is there for us to clean ourselves? What festivals of atonement, what sacred games shall we have to invent? Is not the greatness of this deed too great for us? Must we ourselves not become gods simply to appear worthy of it?[18]

Probably, if my belief system is strong enough, I will waver between the two poles of passive submission and active attempts of overthrow. I will act this out in my life with any figure that I perceive as being in a position of authority. The problem with both these approaches is that they create a constant state of internal tension as I continually battle for control of my soul over this all powerful figure.

So what is the antidote to this? Simply, it is to change the belief system into something more harmonious with my existence. And what might this be? That there is no arbitrary, powerful figure in the universe separate from me. The judge and internal critic (negative manifestations of the element of air in the west) are manifestations of my own limiting belief systems that themselves come out of wounding. In the past, maybe I was judged too harshly and my self-worth as a person became intrinsically tied up with trying to live up to a false image of what it meant to be a 'good'/'successful'/'useful'/'loved' human being.

The healing then is to realise that God, or the spirit of life, is actually inside me and all I have to do is to unveil my soul and give of myself, to become like the butterfly dancing on the wind, to feel in touch with that love. That my life is really an offering to the spirit of all of life and that in hiding parts of it away, I am denying not just myself, but I am also negating life.

Nelson Mandela, on leaving prison, read out a quote from Marianne Williamson that offered the perfect antidote to the prevailing, limiting belief system we are talking about.

> Our deepest fear is not that we are inadequate. Our deepest fear is that we are powerful beyond measure. It is our light, not our darkness, that most frightens us. We ask ourselves, who am I to be brilliant, gorgeous, talented, fabulous? Actually, who are you not to be? You are a child of God. Your playing small doesn't serve the world. There's nothing enlightened about shrinking so that other people won't feel insecure around you. We are all meant to shine, as children do. We were born to make manifest the glory of God that is within us. It's not just in some of us; it's in everyone. And as we let our own light shine, we unconsciously give other people permission to do the same. As we're liberated from our own fear, our presence automatically liberates others.[19]

Once we shine, we have no need to be seen to shine. The air, the place of our belief systems, sits opposite the fire, thus the new healing spells we weave around us with our belief systems have to be inspired by that fire. We live by myths, it is our mythologies, whether conscious or unconscious that inspire our lives. Thus, it is in mythic terms that we can counter the negative systems of thought and replace them with positive ones. We will explore this a lot more in the next chapter, when we focus on the hero/heroine's quest.

For, now, once we have changed our belief systems and

weaved a new healing story; it doesn't stop there. This is when a lot of healing can fall down, as people begin to believe that through working this out, the problem has been solved. Instead, what is needed now is for us to move around to the north and to the element of the earth.

We must now integrate this new way of living into our lives. We must ground all this healing and make it real in the physical world. Often this means we must take all this information and new way of viewing reality and actually change our habitual responses to life. This can seem like the really hard part, a little like turning an oil tanker mid-course as, deep down, we are creatures of routine and habit.

Structures of thought lead to structures of habit, which create the very worlds we inhabit. We are but animals and like the deer who follows the same patterns of movement across the land, making her forever vulnerable to the predator, so we are vulnerable in our habits to the predatory nature of our negative thought patterns. Yet so we are also liberated by the freedom of our thoughts to ingrain within us habitual patterns of celebration and growth. The paradox and important point here is that the thoughts, flying seemingly free like an eagle, must at some point sweep down to earth to survive, lest they forever circle upwards into nothingness.

To look at how the two are connected we can again go back to an ancient culture connected to the earth, the Aboriginal people of Australia and their 'song lines'. These songs as we have already explored had coded into them the stories of the creation of the earth from the ancestral dreamers alongside practical information that mapped their landscape to ensure the survival of the people. They carved into the landscape the stories that held the society together, both culturally and practically. Every time these songs were sung, through their repetition, the land would be dreamt back to life, as it had been on that very first day of its creation.

What, I feel, indigenous people understand and what we have lost, is that reality is not as fixed as it presents itself to be. Instead, it is more like the proverbial blank canvas that the artist has to face every time he starts a new creation. The canvas, paint and brushes are ever present and yet the world which will be created will be different every time.

Thus, there are basics and fundamentals, but the real depth, colour and meaning are painted on. This is the role of the artist in the modern world, but in most indigenous societies this is the role of the human. We are here to help dream the world into being. In fact, for most indigenous societies I would suggest this is the main purpose of their lives, the mystery or truth at the heart of life that we seek so much. We are here to be dreamers. And with that of course, comes responsibility, to preserve as much as possible the integrity of the creation.

This means that when something is out of balance in the physical world, when sickness enters the story, it is time to redream the world how it is supposed to be. This will always involve not only psychic effort, as we have to do in the west of the wheel, but real physical action too. The physical world can be changed by a mixture of intent, thought and action. Shamanically speaking, as explored before, ritual is the bridge here, between the invisible world of thought and the visible manifest world.

An example of this once more is Wixaritari people of Mexico. Their sacred, pilgrimage site of Wirrikuta, the birthplace of their world where their sacrament peyote grows, is now highly threatened by the Mexican government giving mining concessions to a Canadian company. In order to counteract this they have been told by their elders do undertake a 'Renovation' of their land. This is an ancient ritual that hasn't been done for several generations, but is stored in their ancestral memory. It involves pilgrimages to their five most sacred points of their landscape, which sit in the five directions of east, south, west, north and centre, taking offerings to feed once again the spirits of their land.

The way they see it is that this ritual when it was last done several hundred years ago has helped them maintain the harmony between themselves and the land, but the power that it generated has now run down and needs charging up again. This is why they are having problems in the outer world. To our Western eyes this way of dealing with the outer problem threatening their world may seem at best fanciful and at worst downright deluded. However, they firmly believe that it will have the positive effect needed. It wouldn't be the first time either that such magical thinking has actually worked.

In the early 2000s I worked for Friends of the Earth as a campaign researcher for a while and came across a story where one of the main oil companies had been given rights to drill for oil in the Amazon. All preliminary tests had indicated that the area was indeed full of oil and they were waiting for six months before beginning drilling. During that time, led by their shamans, the local tribes people conducted continuous ceremonies, rituals and offerings to the spirit of the oil to ask it to temporarily divert its course away from their land. Incredibly, six months later when the company began its drilling they could no longer find the oil! Eventually, they decided not to take it further and gave up their concession.

The Wixaritari people are not only undertaking their ritual pilgrimage, they are canny enough to resist this desecration of their lands on all levels and have taken their fight to the UN and also the home of the company itself. They are activating many different avenues in order to change the story and help to preserve and recharge their sacred ways of life. At the moment it is working in small ways as they have a temporary injunction against any drilling. They are also aware enough, that in order to really change the bigger picture, they have to engage with and assist us in the West to change the way we dream, because it is largely our nightmare that is creating the destruction of world as know it.

Thus, they are bringing their medicine and teachings to help us to heal our pain so we will not have to act it out on the world. Also, it is to assist us in waking up the spirits of our land so it can be charged up and therefore empower and charge us up again. They are taking this Renovation further out and around the world.

I have witnessed in ceremony with a Marakame, Don Santos, from their people, how I perceive this is being done. This ceremony was undertaken in Devon and during one of the songs he was singing in the middle of the night to renew the sun, I saw in my vision the spirits of the animals of the land there that had died out being sung back to life. I heard his call being sent out and their response. I had seen this in a lesser way in visions before and had the feeling that those beings that have died out are ready to come back, yet it was clear we had to find a way to do this and I didn't know how it might be possible. In this ceremony in Devon I saw how it was possible, if we learnt the right songs and were able to hold the integrity of the right ceremonies. The beings might come back in different forms, but their spirit shall live again.

The indigenous people can teach us this, as it has been passed down through their ancestral wisdom stretching back to the beginning of time. We just need to attune our hearts and minds to be able to listen again and to be shown the way.

So how might this work on an individual level? One of the problems with healing pain on a long-term basis is that it's so seductive. Fear, which as we explored is the grandparent of a lot of sickness, mixed with desire in our bodies creates a form of pleasure. This is something that it easy to become addicted to.

As a culture, it is the stress chemical cortisol beneath these energies that we are most addicted to, which feeds our general unease and lack of ability to find peace as a people. To wean our bodies off these addictions, we are going to have to change our habits. The north of the wheel, the earth, sits opposite the emotional vulnerability of the south. To begin this change in habitual responses to life we have to honour all the feelings that can get trapped in the body. The sadness, the anger, the joy, the surprise, the excitement and the fear – these are all gifts of our natures.

At a fundamental level, I feel we must realise that real power in the world really comes only once we have mastered our own souls as they are contained here in this lifetime in our physical bodies. That freedom comes from containment and responsibility more than from expansion. Our gift is our lives; it is our bodies and the means to experience reality through them. In many tribes, you only become human later on in life when you have earned this title through a lifetime of initiations. We are born of spirit and we will return to that. Yet, to learn to fully become human, that is the gold we are being offered here. To transcend limitation, you must know intimately that limitation, or else you are transcending nothing.

This means that when all the energetic work has been done in a healing, there usually comes later a test in life. This often happens when a similar if less extreme scenario to the one that created the initial wounding that we have been healing somehow randomly happens in our life. In this situation, the initial wound may again be stirred, yet this is the breakthrough opportunity. It is the time when we can fully claim our healing by responding in a different way in life, a pivotal moment when we can take our power back.

Thus, if my wound was around abandonment and the lack of love and security I felt on a fundamental level that this constantly provoked in me, after I have been on a healing journey for a while, healing and releasing the past pain, changing the story I had become attached to, then someone close to me might suddenly leave. Or, I might suddenly be impelled to leave them. And instead of sinking into a well of depression or despair, or covering feelings of loss and sadness with distraction, this gives me the opportunity to fully stand in the feelings, to go through the mini 'death' and at the same time to remain sure within myself that life continues and I am on the right path. That this is just another episode in the rich tapestry of my existence. In that moment I might then fully reclaim a part of my soul that had been lost in the initial trauma. Then, the healing is complete as it has fully integrated into my body.

Approaching sickness and healing as a cycle provides us with a map. To take this further, let us now look at how we can integrate our healing stories in a deeper way through the age old heroic quest which complements the cycle of healing beautifully.

Chapter Twenty-One

The Heroic Quest

Who am I? Where do I come from and why am I here? Three questions are outlined by Lewis Mehl-Madrona in his excellent book *Coyote Medicine* as being central to a North American indigenous world view concerning health.[19] Their belief is that if you can answer these three questions authentically you will have wellbeing of spirit and therefore good health. In order to be able to answer these questions, as all stories of old tell us, we often have to go on a journey or a quest.

This journey to ourselves, both inner and outer, is at the root of most spiritual traditions. And it is this journey that can help to fully connect us and help us to realise our Dreaming Soul – the part of us that is unique and holds the key to who we really are. It is also at the root of most healing journeys.

So, why this need to find ourselves? Where do we get lost along the way? Well, as we have explored throughout this book so far, there are many ways to get off track. There are many places to lose ourselves, even in our own souls as they connect to the earth and our ancestors. This is probably the way it is meant to be. For we only really value something when we have struggled for it. To give birth to life involves immense pain and courage. For us to give birth to ourselves it is the same thing. We don't come here fully formed. It is like we are given a torn, barely decipherable map and a vague set of instructions and then sent out of the door and into life. This is the adventure that sits at the heart of existence.

However, even setting out on that adventure can be as daunting a prospect that we ever might face. This is compounded in the modern world by the excess of trauma that we have been exploring in the book so far.

In the 1960s US psychologist Martin Seligman carried out a series of quite cruel experiments on dogs, which resulted in a theory called 'learned helplessness', which he then associated with people suffering from depression. In the experiments, there were three sets of dogs tied up in a harness. The first group were left alone while group two and three were given random, painful electric shocks. The second group could stop these by pulling a lever, but the third group had no control at all over the pain.

The three groups were then released and while the first two groups recovered quickly, the third group started exhibiting similar symptoms to human depression. They were all then placed in a small cage where the shocks continued through the floor. However, they could escape the shocks simply by jumping over a small partition. While the first two groups of dogs did escape, the third group just lay on the floor, whining but enduring the pain. They had lost the ability to help themselves through the trauma, hence the theory of learned helplessness.[21]

Experiencing seemingly arbitrary pain and suffering has a profound effect on the spirit in that it crushes it. If you want to control a people, and I think colonial powers learnt this one well, traumatise them with random abuse, then challenge and take away their sense of meaning or purpose. They will then usually destroy and control themselves through addictions and other mental and emotional diseases of the spirit.

In a universe without meaning, such as the modern paradigm has created, then a lot of pain and suffering, other than the obvious self-created examples, appear arbitrary. There can be no meaning to the pain because ultimately there is no meaning to life.

Added to this is our belief that life is a series of random events happening to us, it's just nature dishing out unexpected shocks now and then. We can have no control it, which is compounded in the way the media feeds back to stories to us of endless suffering, which we have little control over. This all creates an almost perfect model of learned helplessness. There's little surprise then that so much depression and mental/emotional disturbances are eating away at the modern spirit.

In many ways, our starting point in the modern world can be almost like one of those dogs in the third group. I know this is how it felt like to me when I was in the midst of my healing journey, battling that seemingly random pain that the universe was meting out to me. This is also why our society can be so passive in terms of healing and spirituality, and it's getting more so. We expect that magic pill that will suddenly take away all our pain and heartache, not realising that actual healing takes a long-term commitment and can actually in the beginning stimulate more pain as we have to challenge and change all the learned and limiting beliefs that we have been holding onto.

The quest to find oneself or to find meaning in life, far from being a symptom of a bored or over indulged people – as it is has often been presented – is actually then an essential tool of empowerment and healing. Without it we are a merely stooges in an ongoing drama, like Shakespeare's most tragic characters, being buffeted by the uncaring winds of fate. We have to reclaim our power and know what we can affect it for positive change. This process is like the myths have told us, a battle for our very soul. What more important a quest in the modern world could there be?

There have been many mythologists and psychologists who have charted the narrative that myths lay out to us as metaphors for inner exploration, from Carl Jung to Joseph Campbell. The Hero's Journey was first marked out by Joseph Campbell, which he noted was a universal theme that runs through all cultures. I won't attempt to examine the ancient myths here as that has already been done far better than I could manage. Instead I wish to look at the themes and relate them to a healing/shamanic journey.

Setting out on that quest becomes the first major challenge we have to face. To actually start the journey means going against the atrophy and passivity that sits at the root of our culture right now. It also involves the prospect of truly facing up to ourselves. In order to know ourselves we have to release false images of who we want to be, or who were told we should be.

We must drop the masks that attempt to protect our real identity not just from others, but also from ourselves. This can be painful. It involves going deep into the unknown, so we need a fair bit of bravery to begin this voyage. Sometimes that bravery may take the form of anger as the poet Dylan Thomas expresses in one of his most famous poems.

> Do not go gentle into that good night,
> Old age should burn and rage at close of day;
> Rage, rage against the dying of the light.[22]

For this journey is a death, whatever the age. The old self must be sacrificed and left behind in order to give birth to the new, as yet unformed person.

Sometimes it may be just that we are impelled to go on this journey, with no understanding or analysis of what we're actually getting ourselves into. As Bob Dylan expresses in one of my favourite pieces of writing, which has guided me through my life:

> If I'd thought about it I never would've done it, I guess I
> would've let it slide
> If I'd lived my life by what others were thinkin', the heart
> inside me would've died
> But I was just too stubborn to ever be governed by enforced
> insanity
> Someone had to reach for the risin' star, I guess it was up to
> me.[23]

Sometimes, like the Fool at the beginning of the major arcana in

Tarot, we just have to step off the edge of the cliff, not knowing whether we are going to crash down to the rocks below and die a horrible death, or soar like an eagle, flying towards our dreams. This is the naivety and trust we must somehow embody to begin, as without it life itself wouldn't have begun. Life is a full-contact sport and no one gets out alive.

Culturally, this is again interesting as one of the symptoms that comes up again and again in mental disorders or social maladjustment diagnosis, is impulsive behaviour. Like the young boys who are being drugged and labelled ADHD for not being able to contain themselves physically in square rooms with abstract information being force-fed down their gullets, this level of spontaneity is being pathologised. This has the convenient side effect of keeping us passive.

This is having a particularly brutal effect on the male psyche, though it is not limited to it. In the UK three quarters of all suicides are men and it is now the biggest killer of men under the age of 50, with 12 men a day taking their own lives.[24] These are shocking statistics and there are myriad causes, including the lack of role models or traditional roles in society and the conditioning of emotional suppression and inability to ask for help that a lot of men feel.

However, what is also clear is that the old male roles and qualities that were once thought virtuous – bravery, fierceness, honour, pride, impulsiveness – are being at best marginalised and at worst manipulated into serving the status quo and therefore seen as negative. There are many foot soldiers, but not many warriors left.

Yet, as it is the male seed that begins the process of life, so it is these male qualities that begin the impetus for new life, in this form of the journey. That doesn't mean it is exclusive to men, far from it, but it is the inner male in us all that initiates the challenge – like lightning sweeps down from the heavens to recharge the earth.

And as the male seed seeks the female egg, so after the initial thrust outwards, we are then led by the feminine in this voyage. Thus, as mythologists have noted, after the initial high that accompanies the start of this journey, the breaking free from old ways of being and paradigms, often comes the descent into the Underworld, which can then precipitate a 'dark night of the soul'. This is when the journey or quest gets very interesting and I would like to explore this further.

Chapter Twenty-Two

My Own Quest

I will share now an outline and more details of my own story to illustrate this, simply because it's the one I know most intimately. After I had my initial spontaneous 'opening' experience at the age of 14 described in the introduction of this book, I then had a long period of unspecified illnesses, which would culminate in me ending up in A&E with a variety of symptoms. Eventually, I ended up in hospital to have my tonsils out as the flaring of these symptoms was put down to repeated bouts of acute tonsillitis.

Although this didn't feel exactly correct, as I would be struck down by this unspecified terror that would cause my temperature to rise and me to being convinced I was dying before being rushed in to A&E, it was enough of a reason to calm my spirit at the time. Around the same time, I injured my knee in a football game and had another operation. This injury would later spell the end of my dream of a career in football.

Years later, I had a healing from my best friend Andy and he travelled in his vision back to this time in my life. When he came out of the trance, he told me that he had met with one of my spirit 'guardians' who had told Andy that he (the guardian) had been responsible for causing the injury at that time. He had said that I was getting too obsessed with becoming a footballer and that this was taking me away from my real path.

This was quite a difficult thing for me to hear coming out of this healing, that I had been stopped by spirit from fulfilling my dream. To ensure I got the message, the guardian had said to tell me to look at a photograph I had from when I was signed on for my club on schoolboy terms when they were playing against Manchester United. He said that if I looked closely enough I would see him in the picture.

This sounded a little unbelievable to say the least, yet of course the first thing I did was to study the photograph when I got back in. It didn't take me any time to see him though, as there in the distant crowd scene behind my left shoulder, seemingly floating in mid-air within the rest of the crowd, with a head twice the size of everyone else, was a figure, almost a cliché of what an indigenous warrior looks like! He has long, black hair tied back and an all-consuming presence. I have shown this picture to many people to verify I wasn't just somehow seeing what I wanted to and they have all seen the same thing, that guide behind my shoulder.

I thought it was an incredibly brave thing of Andy to do, to risk telling me exactly what the spirit had said to him and not keeping quiet just in case, as in normal reality one might expect, the spirit wasn't in the picture. However, I am immensely glad he did, because it makes things a lot easier to believe in guardian spirits when you can see them with your own eyes! It seems that I was being well guided even then, even though I had no idea of this fact. This is another theme in spiritual/healing journeys, that there is always some kind of guide for us, though we may not be able to always perceive their presence. This is part of the trust, to allow ourselves to be truly led.

A few years later, when I was at university, I had an experience when I took half a tablet of the drug ecstasy and ended up again in A&E. I remember being on the dance floor at the beginning of the night and being filled with the most beautiful, ecstatic love, not only for everyone in my life but also for the entire world. It was like I was transported briefly back to the place I had experienced at 14, not to the same intensity, but again I was being shown a glimpse into another world. Soon after though, in a microcosm in one night of what I had experienced in my early teens, I then began to experience the overarching terror that something was wrong and the preceding sensations of a fit. It was then an ambulance was called.

They kept me in A&E for most of the night and had me wired up to all kinds of machines, and then, as day was breaking and the effects of the drug were wearing off, they suddenly broke the news to me that there was something not right with my heart and they were transferring me to the main hospital.

I will never forget that feeling as I was strapped into the back of the ambulance that was used to transport me, the terror that I was about to die. There had been a lot in the media at the time about ecstasy-related deaths and with my already fragile state of mind, I was absolutely convinced that I had somehow finally met with my destiny, what the years previous had initiated into me through the many fears they created. Worst still, I thought I had caused it myself.

After a while of being in the hospital, however, I was dismissed by a doctor on the grounds that my heart was bound to be irregular due to the drug. It was a strange, but scary experience, yet as I walked out I did not expect it to affect me too much.

However, it did affect me as shortly afterwards I experienced a period of insomnia that then led to the onslaught of psycho-logical symptoms, most of which I described in the first part of the book. It was then that the convulsive fits got really bad. This began a time of intense introversion as the symptoms robbed me of most of my personality and left a shell of a person. It was a period when I was most passive in what I was experiencing as I had no context to explain what was happening. Mostly I just thought I was going mad and, because of an intense shame I felt, I didn't tell one person what I was going through and kept it all locked inside.

I began to self-medicate and would drink alcohol with the sole purpose of blacking out as it felt like this was the only way to escape the enemy that was my own mind. It became a compulsion, to destroy what was inside of me. Of course, when I did manage this blacking out, the after-effects of having lost control so much and not knowing what I had done would add to the pain.

One time I awoke in my house, not knowing how I had got back there and went outside and saw that my car, which I had driven out the previous evening, had a huge dent in the back of it. I was terrified as I had no idea how I could have driven it back, having blacked out completely. I wondered what the hell I could have done. Luckily I found out later, I had tried to get into the car to drive it, but a friend had wrestled me out of the seat. Instead they had driven me home, but had reversed into a lamp-post upon setting out. I was lucky that someone was watching out for me then.

During this time, which lasted about three years, I constantly shifted between anxiety-driven compulsions, psychotic symptoms that divorced me from reality, convulsive fits and deep depressions. Alcohol became a temporary solace. Without it I couldn't sleep and developed insomnia that would last for weeks on end. However, its after-effects would always increase the anxiety. This was my first descent into the Underworld and the dark night of my soul.

Finally, somewhat randomly, I saw an advert in a newspaper for a book about night terrors or some such thing I'd never heard of. However, for some reason I ordered the book and when it came it was actually all about anxiety/mental disorders. There wasn't so much known about them in those days as this was more than 20 years ago when even depression wasn't considered such a problem as it is today.

The book, however, was something of a self-help manual, which described symptoms in detail as well as ways to combat them. I had never even heard of an 'anxiety disorder' or 'panic attacks' or OCD before, yet this book laid out clearly some of what I had been suffering for the previous three years.

I was completely astounded. Something magical then happened as a combination of reading about these symptoms and realising that I wasn't fully going mad. Alongside other changes in my life, including getting a job as a gardener, which was very grounding for me, this meant that spontaneously the symptoms started to disappear.

I have since witnessed this many times in others, in that getting a 'diagnosis' can calm the spirit and mind enough for spontaneous healing to occur. It is somehow like the mystery and unknown, which is the terrifying part of any healing journey, is taken out of it. This gives the opportunity for the body and spirit to heal themselves, as the mind relaxes its grip through the safety of 'understanding'.

For a couple of years I then lived in a kind of extended moment of bliss as I felt I had been given my life back, which was an exquisite gift. I started to appreciate the little things in life, like being able to read and watch films again without being beset by a haunting mind that made these simple pleasures impossible to endure when I was sick. I felt like I was somehow back in the world, but also floating above it, as the everyday concerns that affected a lot of people wouldn't seem to touch me. Compared to what I had been through, they didn't matter or mean that much. Coming through it all alone actually instilled in me an inner confidence as well, as I had never shared with one person what had happened, although they knew something was wrong.

I then started travelling, which was also something that deeply fulfilled my soul. It was a beautiful respite from my journey in the Underworld, and a time of a great flowering of my spirit. Through going to India, where the gods are still alive and tangible in the air that you breathe, I suddenly became awoken to different concepts of reality offered by a spiritual perspective. All these mystical ideas of freedom of the spirit and exploration, I naively thought had begun in the 1960s with the cultural explorations of that time that had spoken to my soul, I now discovered were thousands of years old, rooted in ancient cultures. My conscious spiritual quest began in earnest as I read all that I could find on old traditions.

This island-like respite couldn't last forever though and this quest was about to open another door into the Underworld. Having read a lot about spiritual matters I was eager to experience something that could open up the doorways I was reading about. I then heard from a work colleague at the time about a meditation retreat happening outside Sydney, which was the city I was living in then. This was quite an intensive ten-day retreat of no speaking and meditating for up to 12 hours a day. Having never practiced meditation before, for some reason I naively thought this would be a good idea as, by immersing myself in it, I could learn it all at once.

However, it wasn't a good idea.

The problem for me was that, as someone who I later met described the process, it was like deep psychic surgery and I had nothing to prepare myself for it. At the same time I had only relatively recently come out of a period of quite intensive trauma, and even though most of the symptoms had dissipated, I was to find out the underlying causes were still very much alive in me. In those darkened rooms for those endless hours, suddenly all the inner conflict and violence that had afflicted me in my previous dark night came surging up to the surface. And I had no way of dealing with this.

Many times I would run out of that meditation space and throw myself on the earth. The people supporting the retreat would try to bring me back in, but I just wanted to stay there, all night sometimes, even though there were snakes and all kinds of poisonous insects around. I felt so much safer being close to the earth. I now know why, but at the time it was purely instinct that took me to embrace the ground. I needed holding and to feel safe in my trauma, yet at the time I didn't know the Mother could do this as I hadn't yet discovered shamanism. Eventually, those running the retreat would persuade me to go back in to the meditation hall. Yet there was something inside of me that I just couldn't face.

I left the retreat early, not being able to face my demons, but also not feeling supported in doing so. There was something that just seemed inhuman about the whole experience as the few times I managed to talk to someone there about my struggles and the conversation would lead onto life in general, they would stop themselves as the 'rules' of silence were being broken.

At night they would play videos of the guru from India who created the whole structure of this particular type of meditation. He would say things like: 'If you do not master this technique of meditation then all the lifetimes of suffering you have experienced, you will carry around with you.' Or: 'This is the *only* way to break your karmic ties.' I have since thought that in the wide open and vulnerable state that the course puts you in, this is tantamount to brainwashing and can actually cause people to believe in and act out this kind of 'curse'. I know that was how it worked out for me.

It is a very real danger, as culturally India is very different with a very different set of experiences and wounds to those in the West. I have met many people since who have equally bad experiences coming out of such retreats. Intensive 'psychic surgery' like this without the containment of ceremony and the holding of humans that have experienced similar wounds, isn't always the best combination for the psychologically vulnerable I feel. To be fair, I have also met many who have had positive experiences, but they definitely aren't for everyone.

When I left there, I left with my demons once again in full voice and feeling like they had possession again of my soul. It was my second descent into the Underworld. In many ways this time was so much more painful as I was consciously aware that what was afflicting me wasn't real and I was just experiencing symptoms of a 'disorder'. Yet this knowledge did nothing to alleviate them, as it had done before. It just made matters worse and made me feel even more helpless in the face of their onslaught.

In this round I tried everything to help myself, including different diets and on instructions from a book on treating OCD with Cognitive Behavioural Therapy. I locked myself in a hut for 12 days straight listening to recordings of myself repeating the worst my thoughts could throw at me for ten hours solid, to try to somehow immunise myself to their power. Needless to say, none of these attempts to try to force myself to heal worked.

At the worst of times, I would be walking along the road and at the same time I could see and feel a split off part of myself crawling up the walls, or falling off of buildings. I couldn't separate between myself in my body and other parts of me outside of my body, sending my thoughts and sensations reeling into madness. I was hallucinating constantly and in ways that felt threatening to my survival. This obviously led to a lot of paranoia. It was like the thread that held reality together was gradually fraying and I was just waiting for it to snap completely and cast me off into the abyss.

More than a couple of times I flirted with suicide. I remember one time standing on the edge of a balcony at a party, apart from everyone else, willing myself to throw myself off. Like most people, it was the thought of hurting others that brought me back. I was told that later that night, I ran straight into the middle of a busy three-lane highway, but semi-miraculously avoided the traffic. I don't remember as again I had blacked out through self-medication.

I lost a lot of weight as I became physically sick with parasites as well and looking back at photographs of me at that time being all skin and bone and with a haunted expression, someone once said half-jokingly I looked like I'd just left a concentration camp! They hadn't known what I had been going through. It took a long time to recover my soul on this second descent, about five or six years.

Eventually, after travelling across the outback of Australia and feeling deeply touched by the land there, hearing the whisperings of an ancient culture in the wind and on the landscape, I discovered shamanism and began that journey back to myself. Again, I had a context for what I was going through, though this time a deeper one, connected with a deeper meaning. Rather than just a set of symptoms and a disorder, I now knew that I was going through what many people had since time began. I was on the path to becoming a 'wounded healer'. At least then, I had some purpose. That's not to say that the symptoms suddenly dropped off as they had before. This time I had to heal myself consciously, and to do this always takes time and a lot of effort.

About three years into my shamanic training, having brought deep healing to myself, I left the desert in Mexico having been on retreat for a month there. It was then that the symptoms of the soul sickness I had been battling with on and off for 15 years came back for the third and final time. This is often the way in a healing journey/heroic quest, when we have found the path back and are upon it, life can again throw that final test. It is here that it is often easy to lose all hope.

Again, I was struck by a profound and overwhelming sense of meaningless, as if the filter that I perceived the world through had been tipped back into one of darkness and nihilism. Nothing made sense anymore as I experienced again that complete disconnect from the world. I wrote a song at the time, and one verse seemed to capture this sense of existential pain and helplessness the best:

Frozen in circle, born and born again,
When will you come my way, and say this is the end?

I was waiting and willing that end, and at the same time was terrified of walking through the doorway, thus I became stuck in the nowhere land of soul loss. I was about to break through though.

One night on the road in Mexico with a girlfriend, I had a strange dream. We were travelling near the Guatemalan border in the heavily patrolled state of Chiapas. I had always wanted to travel to Guatemala for two reasons. The first being that it was the country I had done my history dissertation on about the 1956 CIA-backed coup that got rid of a democratically elected government and precipitated 40 years of state-sponsored bloodshed and terror. I had always felt a deep compassion for the people's struggle there.

The second being that it was the home of the town of Santiago on Lake Atitlan that Martin Prechtel had written about in his books about Mayan culture. Something in these books had touched my soul and I wanted to do some kind of pilgrimage there.[25] The problem we had was that we were in a hire car, which meant we couldn't cross the border.

In this dream, however, I was travelling with Osama Bin Laden (most hunted public enemy number one at the time) and we were trying to smuggle some cannabis across a border somewhere. Back in the real world I actually had a small bag of marijuana that we were driving round with. This had been given to me by someone in the previous town who I'd helped out with something. I'm not sure why I accepted the gift as I didn't really smoke it, especially when my head was in a difficult space as it had been as it didn't agree with me. Yet, for some unknown reason I had taken the small bag. Consequently it had remained unopened, but I hadn't got around to giving it away yet.

Because Chiapas, the state we were travelling through, had previously had an armed uprising and was still a hotbed of the resistant indigenous revolutionary group, the Zapatistas, there were a lot of army checkpoints we had to travel through on the road. We'd been through a few that day and each time I'd remembered the contraband we were carrying. This was probably what inspired a part of the dream.

In the dream, however, as we were trying to smuggle the cannabis across we were caught by the armed guards and locked up. This felt really unlucky as we had got so close to getting across before being pulled back, but there I was locked up. I was not sure in the dream why I was travelling with Bin Laden, yet this feeling of being locked up was very familiar at the time. That sense of powerlessness and imprisonment was exactly what I was going through at the time, as once again my soul sickness was rearing its head. Probably Bin Laden represented a denizen of the Underworld I was traversing.

Then, in the dream, I suddenly had an idea, one that would help me escape. I thought to myself, what if I put an invisible spell on the bag of cannabis they had confiscated from me and then ask to be shown the bag as evidence of why I was being locked up? So I concentrated hard, focusing all my magical intent (something often a lot easier in the Dreamtime) and put the spell on the bag. I then called out to the guard, 'Hey that bag you caught me with, I deny carrying it. I've been wrongly imprisoned. Show it to me, so I know why I've been locked up.'

The guard looked at me strangely as if I was crazy, but then agreed. He unlocked the prison door and then took me to a room and started looking through a huge see-through bag, which contained all the small bags of confiscated materials, each one neatly labelled. As he was doing this, I saw my offending item slowly disappearing and sure enough, after searching and searching he couldn't find what he was looking for. He called out to his superiors and they had a brief discussion before turning to me and saying: 'We can't hold you any longer, you're free to go.' I walked out and across the border.

I awoke with that ecstatic feeling of having somehow not only escaped imprisonment, but also having gone across a symbolic blocked crossing. I also woke determined that the dream was a portent that we would able to cross over the border into Guatemala. After quite a long argument with my travelling companion who, quite understandably, thought I was completely crazy and that it was a waste of time even trying, we started out on the two-hour drive to the border. The nearer we got to the border, the more it was playing on my mind, to finally get rid of the bag I was carrying of cannabis. But there never seemed the right time without looking completely suspicious.

Eventually, just around the corner from the border, I stopped and got out to gift the plant back to the earth. However, just as I was doing this, my partner said to me: 'What are you doing?' I told her, but then she looked at me with a strange will in her eyes and said: 'Keep it.'

This astounded me as she didn't smoke at all and I said this to her, to which she simply replied: 'No, but I like the adventure!' There wasn't much I could say to argue with that, considering I was dragging us on a seemingly pointless mission to the border.

So I kept it and we carried on towards the border, now not only trying to get across illegally with a hire car, but also with a plant that governments in their infinite wisdom have declared illegal. 'Oh, well,' I thought (not that I was thinking that much, there was something else impelling me now), 'in for a penny, in for a pound.'

We got to the border and managed to get across the first couple of checkpoints easily, even having our passports stamped with a Guatemalan visa. However, just before the final passing point, which had a chain lying across the road and a guard with a machine gun, there was a window and as we drove towards the crossing, someone flagged us down. They immediately then collected our documents.

My partner was dealing with it as she could speak Spanish fluently, yet it didn't take much to work out that it wasn't going well for us. The last comment I heard from the attendant was, 'Stupido!' as he shoved our paperwork back in my partner's hand and sent her away.

And that was that. We had to turn around and go back, having got so agonisingly close. My partner, understandably then let rip on me at being so stupid that I thought we'd get over and not listening to her. As we sat there in that no-man's land just a few metres from the border, all I could say was, 'Can't we just drive across and see what happens?' But I knew this was a weak fantasy that I was clinging onto. She then stormed out of the car, slamming the door loudly.

I just sat there, gazing at this border, which suddenly took on this huge significance. It seemed in that moment to represent all the blockages in my life and a place I would get to no matter what I seemed to do – trapped between not being able to go forward and not being able to face going back. Trapped in that no-man's land, that had haunted me for so much of my adult life – not in my body, but not out, not alive and not dead, not sane, yet not fully, raving mad. All the time just trapped.

I also felt, crazy as it might seem, that this was another slap in the face in me trusting my dreams. And this felt even more important, as a huge part of the reason I was in Mexico was on trust that the shamanic path, the invisible world accessed through the Dreamtime, could help me fully heal, to cure the disease of my spirit. Ever since leaving the desert a month previous, I had been as bad as I had ever been. In that heightened sense of reality I was experiencing, being blocked at that border was now taking on a huge significance in the battle that had been waging in my soul for so many years.

Then the car door suddenly opened and my partner was there, all pumped up and excited. 'Come on let's go,' she said. 'He's gone on a break.' She meant the guard with the machine gun. I looked at her, not quite able to take it in. Then I realised she was serious. She was willing me to walk my talk, stand by what I had said and drive across! Yet, we still would have to pass within a couple of feet of the window of the office that had turned us back, as it faced onto the border crossing. And God knows where the guy with the machine gun had gone, as he could just have been in that office taking a break. But I knew I couldn't back down now, I had brought us this far, I had to take the risk.

Then I remembered the dream and suddenly I knew what I had to do. I grabbed the packet of marijuana from the back, jumped out of the car and found the nearest tree, then I knelt down and offered the plant back to the earth. Giving thanks for my dream, offering the plant back to the Mother, I prayed that we would safely get across. I then got back in the car and focussed all my intent on making the car and us inside it invisible.

I also instinctively knew that when you are going to do something illegal and want to be hidden, the best thing to do is be as obvious as possible; to hide in plain sight. So I started the car and drove towards the border as slow as was possible to drive and then continued at that speed as we slowly crossed, my head passing within a couple of feet of the customs window that had turned us away. Not that we could have been that inconspicuous anyway seeing as we were travelling in a bright red VW Beetle! I knew that, however compelled I was to do so, I couldn't turn and peak to see if they were watching us, but had to just face forward, concentrating on being invisible.

Even when we were across, as I expected any moment all hell to break loose and gunfire to rip into our back window (I knew that in countries like this they don't mess around), I held my nerve and continued to drive at that speed for the next hundred metres or so. That drive seemed to take forever until finally we rounded a bend and I put my foot down. We'd made it and suddenly I let rip, as all the tension slipped away, screaming in delight and frightening the life out of my partner!

That night as we rested in an indigenous town high up in the mountains I felt something had shifted deep in my soul, something had moved through and I knew I was on the road to healing, strange one as it was. This was a symbolic crossing. But the story wasn't about to end there.

The next day we began the journey to Lake Atitlan. As we were travelling down the mountain, I was driving again and had some fire in my belly from the previous day's adventure, so was going quite fast. As I was careering around those tight bends, with sheer drops below, I suddenly had the random thought in my mind, 'I wonder what I would do if my brakes failed?' This had happened to me once years previously in Australia, so it wasn't such an unknown prospect. Then, I hadn't been able to stop and had gone straight into the back of a car. So as I had this thought going down the mountain, I mentally went through a check list of what I would do, which was to slam it in gear without the clutch and pull the handbrake. Not that it would have particularly helped at the speed I was going, so almost straight after I had the thought and gone through this I forgot about it and carried on.

Then we rounded another bend and, suddenly there appeared on the road a workman waving a flag desperately at us. They were digging half of the road up and he was signalling at us to stop. Luckily I just managed to halt just in time with a screech of the brakes. He looked at us pointedly and I resolved then to slow down a bit. After a short while waiting, he signalled for us to carry on and I started again driving towards another of the many hair-pin bends we had faced. And then, just as I came to slow at the bend, the brakes completely went. Again, I had that heart wrenching feeling of putting my foot down and it going completely to the floor with nothing happening.

By the luck of the gods though (or something else) I had only managed to pick up speed to about 20mph and had already gone through mentally what I would do in this scenario half an hour previous. So I slammed the car into gear to stall the engine and pulled at the handbrake. We just managed to come to halt metres from the sheer, mountainous drop below.

That man with the flag had saved our life, stuck in a deserted road as he was, as if I had been travelling the speed I had been without having to stop there, nothing would have prevented us from going over the edge. So too had whatever put that thought in my head about what to do when the brakes failed.

We just sat there for a while, shaken up and thanking that mysterious something that was looking out for us. Then began the wondering just how we were going to get out of this mess, seeing as we were in the country illegally anyway. Suddenly though, as I had my feet on the pedals, the brakes started working again!

We continued on, crawling at the slowest pace possible down to the bottom of the mountain. There we found a garage with a mechanic who explained to us that the brakes had temporarily burnt out, which is common for cars not designed to be driven fast up and down maintains, which the Beetle obviously wasn't. The mechanic told us we could carry on, but to take it very easy. So we did, though I didn't have much confidence. Yet we still had a long drive to get to Lake Atitlan, and something was now, as it had been for a while, seemingly propelling us.

Later that afternoon, just when the car seemed to be going okay and I'd began to relax slightly, we were then stopped by the police. This was obviously a less than comfortable experience given the way we had entered the country. They pulled us over and the first thing they asked, as was normal, was to see our passports. The passports were packed in our bags in the back of the car and it seemed to take an age to find them as we rummaged around. Bizarrely, the policemen, before we had a chance to locate them, then just said okay and told us to carry on. Something strange was happening on those mountains, almost as if we had become part of a story which seemed to playing out in unexpected ways almost autonomously before our very eyes.

We arrived at Lake Atitlan in the late afternoon and it was absolutely stunning as it stretched out like an inland sea, azure blue, beneath the drama of the surrounding volcano. It felt then, with that exquisite travelling sensation of arrival; that all the adventure had been worth it. This indeed was a worthy place to be a navel of the world.

Santiago, the place I wished to visit as a kind of pilgrimage, was the other side of the lake though and we quickly came to a crossroads. To the left, the main road signalled Santiago more than 200km away around the lake. To the right, was a small track going nearly straight up the mountain labelled four-wheel drive vehicles only, where the same place was less than a third of the distance.

Our poor old Beetle was anything but four-wheel drive and had already been pushed to its limits. Yet, given the nature of the journey so far, it was kind of inevitable that we chose to turn right, hoping that it would somehow make it. Again, sense and reason weren't at the heart of this journey, something deeper was.

My travelling companion was driving now and we proceeded on a long and arduous struggle up the mountainside as the track deteriorated into little more than a rock strewn, potholed clearing through the forest. Many times we thought we would have to somehow turn back or get stuck there. Somehow though, eventually we made it up to the top, and the track levelled up and became something resembling a road, albeit a very bumpy one.

Up on the side of that volcano, with its majestic peak in the distance, the sun was gradually beginning its descent towards the horizon as people were putting in the final part of their day working the fields. I suddenly then became aware of the extraordinary journey and adventure we'd come on to get us here, to this magical moment. All the tension, the drama, melted away as I looked out of that window and became one with the immense beauty that nature was revealing. The light was golden and I felt it pour into me, like liquid honey, salving the burning intensity of my restless soul. I was at peace.

Then we turned a corner back into the forest and there was a masked gunman in the middle of the road, his weapon raised and pointing directly at us. Time froze, but my partner, instead of slowing down actually started to speed up towards him. I shouted at her: 'What are you doing, he'll shoot!' So she put on the brakes and we came to a halt right in front of him. She then wound down the window, and in what I later thought was quite an aggressive way, asked him in Spanish: 'What do you want?'

I knew this area had suffered the trauma of years of civil war, which meant that were a lot of rebellious organisations hiding out and it had several warnings in place regarding travelling through, keeping to the main highways I'm sure would have been quite high up there. My immediate fear was this could be a political kidnapping. But the man answered: 'Your money,' as he pointed the gun in the window.

It was then that time actually seemed to stop and reality took on this dream-like quality. Far from feeling scared, I actually felt immensely calm and light as I searched around for my wallet. This continued even when the man, I think realising that he wasn't going to get what he wanted out of my companion, came over to my side of the car and aimed the gun directly at my head. The only thing I could actually think of was how a bullet would fit out of the hole at the end of the barrel as, having never seen a gun close up before, it seemed so small.

I had loose trousers on and my wallet had fallen out of the pocket and down into the foot well at back of the car and try as I might I couldn't find it. It must have looked like we were stalling. I remember even having a debate in my head as to whether I should give him my camera, which was there, but it was such an old one, I reasoned that he probably wouldn't want it. All the while, he got more and more tense, waving the gun inside the window, sweat pouring down his brow.

And then, fortune, who we had been seemingly testing to her limits over the previous couple of days, again intervened on our behalf as a pick up van with a load of field workers came around the corner. They weren't going to stop to help us, probably they had learnt painfully well to keep their heads down in such situations, yet as they tried to squeeze past us on the narrow track it created a distraction. In a stroke of inspired thinking, my partner hadn't turned off the engine when the gunman had stopped us and seizing her moment, she slammed the car into gear and we sped off, coming as close as it was possible to crashing on the next bend, before she regained control.

So we were free again. As we drove away, my companion laughed in exhilaration. She really was a crazy one, but the stress of it all suddenly caught up with me and I asked her in a deadly serious tone, why she thought this was funny. 'You wanted adventure didn't you?' she replied simply, but I had gone beyond all that and suddenly felt sick.

The overriding feeling was actually then of guilt as I started questioning what I had done to put myself in such a crazy, dangerous situation and why I had been behaving so recklessly. It was as though the magic had suddenly worn off and I was stuck with the stark reality of my actions having brought me to this. It was less I was worried for my own life, but more like I felt guilty for everyone back home that I loved and how they would feel if anything had happened to me.

When we finally arrived in Santiago, the Beetle battered and bruised, as was my already fragile mind, I went straight to the church there. This church had featured a lot in the Martin Prechtel books and although on the surface Catholic, like a lot in central and South America, behind the mask of the saints were really the old indigenous gods that the people continued to worship. In that humble, beaten down church, I then prayed – for forgiveness, to offer thanks for protection, but most of all to ask for guidance of how to finally bring peace to my crazy mind that had now haunted me for nearly half of my life; since I was teenager and had been shocked out of a normal existence through being spontaneously shunted out of my body and into another world.

I was then struck by the realisation that there was a poetic inevitably in my whole journey leading me here, to the barrel of a gun. Since a child I had never been able to resolve myself to the reality of death. It used to wake me in the middle of the night and for hours I wouldn't be able to get back to sleep as the idea of being dead forever, for infinity, would seer into my bones. It had then haunted me all through my soul sickness, at the root of my mental disturbances was this simple, primal terror – that I was going to die and that meant journeying into the unknown. It was the unknown that I couldn't find peace with. Now, I had come so close to this reality twice in one day.

In his Pulitzer Prize winning book *The Denial of Death*, Ernest Becker has put forth a theory that actually most of human culture is invented through an attempted denial of death. That we are constantly running from this truth, which creates a need to defy it through creating cultures that will outlive us. The greater the fear of death and the unknown becomes, the more complex the cultures created. He states:

> The idea of death, the fear of it, haunts the human animal like nothing else; it is the mainspring of human activity – activity largely designed to avoid the fatality of death, to overcome it by denying in some way that it is the final destiny for man.[26]

Most of the time, most people suppress this primal fear, what he calls 'the terror of death'. Yet despite, or maybe because of this suppression, it unconsciously drives most people most of the time in all their activities. Whole religions and philosophies are built around this denial.

One of the main proponents of my sickness was simply the fact that the suppression system in me was faulty. It didn't work and when I was sick I had to face this animal terror on a daily basis. It consumed me for every waking hour. Yet at the same time, I spent all my energy trying to run from it, to deny it. This resulted in a thousand mental acrobatics as constantly I attempted to escape the finality of death, like a trapped animal, thrashing about in a futile attempt to resist the inevitable.

I had spent my whole life running, which had led me here, to the other side of the world, trying to crash through every border or limitation, real or perceived, that my fixed thinking had led me to feel controlled by. But the more I ran, the further away from myself I got, until there was nothing left but an empty shell. Paradoxically, of course, the more I ran away the more I actually just ran towards the inevitability of having to somehow face this primal terror. Because I had spent so much energy trying to fight, deny or escape it, quite naturally I had ran straight into its arms. This is what had brought me there to face that barrel of the gun at the end of a long journey. It was a whole initiation into learning how to die.

I knew that this was a sign for me to change this story; that ultimately as afraid as I was of dying, so I was that afraid of living also. It was my wake-up call. I resolved then in that moment, to find my peace with that spectre and to start to actually live. My sickness had kept me in a half-life for too long and that half-life meant that I didn't have to fully take responsibility for living, I wasn't committing to being here, on the earth. The catapulting out of my body that happened when I was a teenager was a natural consequence of this. It was time to finally heal my relationship with life.

A few nights later on the way back to Mexico, I was again struck with one of the convulsive terror fits that had haunted me for so long and found myself shaking violently and uncontrollably on the bed. However, in that moment, instead of resisting what was happening, I simply resolved to surrender and then focussed all of my intent into facing the black hole that would open up and step through the psychic doorway that was being offered.

I used all my training, all that I had learnt, and my new commitment to welcome life and death equally. In a moment of exquisite magic, I managed to relax and go through. I was then struck again by that feeling of ecstatic oneness and bliss that had met me spontaneously when I was 14. Finally, I was able to embrace consciously what had happened way back then and began this whole quite literally crazy journey. I knew then the purpose of it.

That was the last of those fits that I ever experienced. I knew they no longer had a power over me, but I instead had a power to welcome and embrace them, as a gift from the universe. They were simply gateways to another level of reality, a reality that was not the enemy of life, but rather its complement. This was a reality that feeds and sustains life here and one that I was supposed to be open to so that I could do the work I now do.

Many times when I am entering a trance state and communing with the invisible ones now, to bring healing, I go through a mini fit consciously. The difference is that I now have a control or mastery over it. It is the way my normal consciousness, or ego, is pushed out of the way and the denizens of the Otherworld can come through. In that moment in Guatemala I knew that the battle was over and I could return home.

My friend in this journey was the same one who would be killed at her job back in Germany a couple of years later. Her fire burnt bright in this life and we both seemed to share an attraction to those edges of reality. Hers tipped over, mine didn't; only the mystery of life knows why.

The day she died, I awoke with this incredible, indescribable grief with no idea as to why. As I was walking to work, through the busy streets of my then home town of Brighton, I was suddenly visited by what I can only describe as an angelic presence. This was strange to me as I'm not that into 'angels'. Yet, the lightness and beauty of this being was inescapably angelic, and being touched by her, in that busy city street, I had the felt experience of whatever happened to me in life, whatever I went through, this being would be there to comfort and support me. It was a beautiful, heart-warming experience, lifting the fog of sadness that I had awoken with.

Several hours later, I received the phone call from Germany, informing me of her death. Around the same time she had been killed was when I had been visited by that presence.

Chapter Twenty-Three

Returning Home and Integrating the Journey

One of the reasons the final part of my healing journey was so dramatic, was to counter the excessive self-control I had had for the whole of my life. On that crazy adventure, it was like I was seeking to initiate myself, to push myself beyond all the limits that had ever been imposed on me, both by myself and the society I was a part of. In the end though, through going out to those edges, both psychic and real, I eventually had to learn the art of surrender to those limits, in my body and in life.

At some point we have to surrender into acceptance of the world exactly as it is and not how we wish or desire it to be. In that act of surrender we then can let go of everything that stands in the way of us engaging effectively with it. Paradoxically then, we can actually garner greater mastery over ourselves and thus, over life. With nothing to lose or nothing to gain, no expectation or other trickery of the mind, we can sink deeply into the present moment, the only reality that actually exists, and from that point whole universes can be created out of our dreaming. We become the dream and can therefore guide it, as opposed to trying to force it into a model we hold as an expectation of reality. In that moment, life can become joyous again, as it is full of surprise and mystery.

Every artist understands this process well, the subtle inter-change between preparation, hard work and allowing the inspi-ration to flow in the moment – of finding the statue already there in the block of marble as Michelangelo expressed it. And what greater art is there than a human life? For a lot of indigenous tribes, a huge proportion of their time and energy is devoted to creating items of beauty. For some, this is seen as their main raison d'etre. This could be jewellery, the weaving of spectacular clothes, beadwork, or sacred objects of all kinds of different descriptions. All reflect the colour and vibrancy of their inner visions.

As we are just discovering, this was the main use of gold in a lot of South American culture. All the incredibly intricate and beautiful items they made with gold, this incredibly sacred material, were used as offerings for the gods. Gold wasn't meant for human consumption, it was far too rich; instead it was meant for the gods to eat in the form of offerings.

What these cultures understood was the subtle interplay between what you create in life and feed to the invisible world and the gods, is what will be returned back to you in your life and those that surround you. If you feed beauty, beauty will be bounced back.

The universe is then viewed as a vibrant and alive kind of information feedback loop that desires and demands our inter- action. To ensure that humans don't abuse this tool, as we have done, we have to learn the art of surrender. This keeps us humble, grounded and much closer to the source of the creative principle of which we are only a small part. Like the artist, we must at times step back from that edge, from whence the inspi- ration arrives, and bring it all back home. We must ground it in this reality. If we don't do this ourselves, nature will then do it for us.

This is where sickness can be an important righting tool that nature uses to counterbalance something that has grown too much in a singular direction and needs cutting back, closer to its roots. Thus, when we are sick, we must travel back to our roots, to discover once again that time when we grew naturally and healthily, and relearn consciously what it was that fed and watered us. From there we can regrow again. This is the nature of the heroic/healing journey with its descent into the Underworld that strips us down to our core, before we discover our true nature and are able to return home and know that place for the first time, for it is the first time we have truly known ourselves in that place.

As a culture we are obsessed with going forwards, with 'evolving'. Therefore we are inviting sickness in on a grand scale to counterbalance this. So much sickness that it is actually affecting the planet, which in turn threatens to cut us back again to our roots.

This can even be true spiritually with our obsession with 'self-development'. Everything becomes about improving ourselves, 'evolving' spiritually, moving on to the next level etc. There is nothing wrong with this per se, other than it just mirrors the cultural psychosis that is also about constant growth. Unless it is balanced with conscious withdrawal and learning the art of surrender, we will perpetuate the problem rather than help to heal it.

Instead, we could also choose to go backwards, devolve back to our roots consciously. This is why initiation is so important for us both individually and as a species right now. Traditionally, it was at the time of initiation and through its practice that individuals had the opportunity to fully discover who they were and what their true natures were. This was a fundamental part of its purpose. We must then, I believe, undertake these initiations once more, to wrestle ourselves back from the stranglehold of cultural conformity, mainstream or alternative, and instead undertake these sacred journeys deep into the depths of our souls.

Then we can return home, larger yet more humble than when we left. Gaining this wisdom means receiving the true riches of being human. It's what makes us 'fat' in a true sense rather than physically or materially. In an age where conformity is the god, to truly find and become yourself is the ultimate act of rebellion. True rebellion is something we are in desperate need of at the moment. Then, it becomes much easier to be part of a whole, part of a community, as we slot in alongside everyone else fulfilling their unique role. At least, this is just the way I see it, through my own unique lens of perception.

When we do return home, we are able to make our contribution to the whole, fully and wholeheartedly. We might discover on our voyage that we aren't who we thought we were. Or, more accurately, we might discover that we aren't who we were told we should be.

I often see in people who are reaching out and rediscovering themselves that fairly soon they can hit the glass ceiling of everyone else's expectations of them or projections upon them. Because culturally we have learnt a kind of intrinsic conformity over quite a few generations – indeed quite often in the past rebellion against this would cost someone their life – it means that it is somewhat hard wired into us. This means that as soon as you start to challenge this, you will also provoke other people's unconscious conformity and need to preserve the status quo. This can be especially true in families though usually occurs wherever you get a bunch of humans together sharing any kind of collective purpose.

If one person starts changing their role or who they are within this dynamic, it automatically challenges everyone else's supposed role and this is where you can be met with some quite potent opposition, even if you think you are just trying to change yourself and are not that interested in everyone else.

Thus, when people do go on this kind of journey, it often brings them into conflict with those closest to them, which can be incredibly painful. This can leave people with the seemingly unwanted choice of do I stay the same and therefore hold onto that person's love, or do I change and risk losing it and maybe them forever? This is when subtle and unconscious bargains can then be made: 'I'll stay the same if you promise to love me.'

This is where a lot of healing journeys can break down or falter. This might not even be with a physical person, as this bargain can be made with society itself – or at least what we perceive as society, which can often be a huge parental projection. Sometimes it is even made with God – or again what we perceive as God, which can also hold the same projection. It takes a brave man or woman to go beyond this, to truly risk the threat of loneliness and isolation that this journey provokes.

Ultimately, what I feel is beneath all of this is the fear that somewhere along the line, we might actually abandon ourselves. I know this is how it felt very often on my journey. Quite often this comes from the faint, but very real, memory of when in the past we may have lost a part of ourselves through trauma. Thus, we turn our attention now to the shamanic phenomenon called 'soul loss' and the healing tool of 'soul retrieval'.

Chapter Twenty-Four

Soul Loss, Soul Retrieval

Trauma creates loss and on a shamanic level that loss is a literal leaking away of parts of our soul. When our bodies are cut they bleed; it is the same with the invisible essence of our souls. Problems arrive when that leaking essence is not stemmed and we lose parts of ourselves to the vast expanse of nothing and everything-ness. It is then that we can suffer soul loss and it is the shaman's job to retrieve these parts of us and bring them back home. This is a major part of shamanic healing and affects our personal, Dreaming Souls.

So how does trauma affect us in this way? To begin with our Dreaming Soul, the raw essence of our individual selves, has a tendency to wander around and disconnect from our bodies. It is not as fixed as we might imagine. In fact every night, during some parts of our Dreamtime experience, this part of us can leave and explore different kinds of realities.

When this happens we call these experiences 'big dreams'. They are different in quality than the usual rumblings of our unconscious desires and motivations in that they usually have a feeling of heightened reality – the colours and sensational feelings can be intensely alive. Usually when we wake up it takes us a while to realise where we are, who we are and whether what we just experienced was 'real'.

From a shamanic perspective, what we have experienced is as real as our waking life. It is practise for where we will go to after we leave our bodies behind and die. We can also in our night dreams scout out potential futures. These are called precognitive dreams. I spent years working with my dreams, which meant to begin with writing them down every morning. The more you do this, the more you are able to recall dreams that ordinarily you will have forgotten. And the more you pay attention to your dreams, the deeper and more meaningful they become; the more they teach you. During this time I had many, many precognitive dreams, which were easily verifiable as I would have the written evidence of the dream to compare with the reality I had just experienced. I discovered also what that deja-vu feeling was about for me, as I would have that feeling, and then be able to remember the exact dream it came from. I would then go to check my notes and, sure enough, I had just been in that same landscape described in the dream.

Often, there would be some seemingly innocuous object that would be the key to me remembering. For example, a bottle of vodka would appear in the dream, and then a while later I would be in a room with some people and suddenly I would become aware of a bottle of vodka. It would jump out at me from my peripheral vision, and then someone would say something that would be word for word what had been said in the dream.

These moments are like fault lines in time, often accompanied by the deja-vu feeling. Sometimes they would be deeply meaningful and important. Other times they were just comforting reminders that I've been here before, scouting out all these potentials and must have chosen this one because I liked what I felt about it.

Over time, this can be developed into a form of lucid dreaming, whereby we can begin to direct the flow of these experiences consciously and therefore have an element of control over the reality that manifests in our dreams. This in turn can have an influence on the reality we manifest in our lives. Mostly, with this part of our soul, we are learning to do this both in our night dreams and our day 'dreaming'.

Alongside the future, the past is another favourite haunt of ours that we can explore in our dreams. I believe that often this is us searching for parts of us that have been lost to the past through soul loss, especially when they are reoccurring dreams that involve returning to the same place again and again. Our soul is constantly trying to heal itself, tracking out the future and restoring the past are a couple of ways it can attempt to do this.

But we don't have to be asleep for our Dreaming Soul to free itself from our bodies. In fact a lot of shamanic training involves putting the body under stress in order to stimulate this freeing of our souls. This could be through fasting, excessive heat, the ingestion of plants, going without sleep for long periods, all different ways we have already described, as these have the effect of bringing out, in a controlled and directed way, our body's innate survival response to trauma, which is for the Dreaming Soul to disconnect.

Again, it is no accident that the best healers or psychics are wounded ones, as there is no better training in terms of being psychically open to different realities than trauma. It literally blasts us open, especially when we experience it when young.

Viewed shamanically, soul loss is an innate survival mechanism, hard wired into our souls, a little like and connected to the flight or fight response hard wired into our bodies. When trauma occurs in our life, and the trauma is always relative to the person experiencing it (i.e. how they perceive the situation). It is like a fault line in time is created.

This is our Dreaming Soul's way of dealing with the situation. Time slows down, or even stops. Reality becomes heightened or dream-like. We can often feel like we are no longer connected to the events unfolding, but rather viewing them from a distance, like it is not us saying those words or screaming or crying. We've become a bad actor completely disconnected from the moment.

Psychologists call these symptoms disassociation. We call it symptoms of soul loss. The trauma that is occurring is simply too much to bear for our souls, which are far more delicate and sensitive than we in the modern world have been led to believe, and so a part of us escapes to protect itself from fully experiencing what is happening. You can see this very clearly, if you have been around someone who has gone through a sudden and intense shock, and you look in their eyes and you can see that they're not there anymore, they've gone somewhere else. This is huge soul loss. Or, if after an intense shock yourself you are aware of yourself losing all track of reality, and instead you become machine-like, functioning but in no way present.

Hopefully, after the shock subsides, we will return to ourselves. We will suddenly arrive back and be aware again of the reality in front of our senses. However, sometimes we don't come back. Sometimes that part of us that has left gets stuck, lost or simply doesn't want to return because the situation that caused the trauma is ongoing and hasn't been resolved. This is when soul loss becomes a problem.

A straightforward example of acute soul loss is post-traumatic stress disorder, whereby the loss of a part of our soul is so big that a person is unable to recover enough of themselves to get over the trauma. They then get caught in the fault line of time created by the trauma as it is played out again and again, in their night dreams and waking realities. People who suffer like this can also walk along in a state of constant disassociation, unable to connect with everyday life at all.

I would suggest that the symptoms of post-traumatic stress disorder are actually more common than we realise, as explored in the previous section. And they don't have to be caused by big, dramatic traumas. The deeper you go into soul loss the more you realise how subtle it can actually be. Decisions made to be a certain way and reject other important parts of yourself – painful decisions usually because there is no space in life for these parts – can cause soul loss. This is usually a response to trauma or hurt, as we say to ourselves consciously or unconsciously: 'I will only be like this from now on (to avoid being hurt again).'

Or, there can be just the gradual diminishing of our dreams as the life we encounter forces its fixed notions of how we should be onto the fragile malleability of our own souls. Again, in this case, usually we have been weakened by previous instances of trauma that may have been forgotten long ago.

If there is one thing that we do well in the modern world as a culture, it's to disassociate. I would even say that a lot of people, a lot of the time, are walking around relatively disconnected from themselves. This is part of the reason that there is such a plethora of techniques and tools, the latest being mindfulness, to try to get us back in the moment and actually experience the reality surrounding us.

Even our latest technologies are all designed to foster and create disconnection, from the TV through to the computer or smartphone screen that constantly take us away from the reality surrounding us and into some kind of abstract human-created world. It is no accident that this is what we've created. We have been fostering this kind of disassociation for a long time now, as the everyday reality we inhabit is viewed as one we need to escape from. This need to flee reality is caused by ongoing and unresolved trauma, or soul loss.

Trauma has become something of an epidemic and so has soul loss. These are big statements, yet viewed through the eyes of our soul rather than the disconnected, disassociated gaze it is now common to cast upon the world, the human societies we have created are about as crazy as anyone could imagine. They do not seem to have at their core the intention to create loving, happiness inducing societies.

Instead they seem to create ever more complex ways that human beings can tie themselves in knots and become more and more trapped. The simple existence of money is an example of this. We seem to forget that money is just a human invention, and a relatively modern one, and yet it has more power over us than probably anything else in life! The disproportionate way it is distributed is just beyond ridiculous when viewed rationally. Our societies are sick and this is a result of unresolved trauma

Even the way we deal with the problems we have created in

the world, i.e. the perilous ecological situation we find ourselves in, are themselves too symptoms of trauma, in that we argue about, deny and distract ourselves constantly from the problem instead of facing it head on. Or, if we do stand up to it head on, we feel powerless in the enormity of what we are facing as we come up against the reactions of a traumatised society in constant denial.

One of the major sources of our suffering is soul loss, the loss of parts our dreaming selves. Yet this, like anything, can be healed and it isn't as hard as it seems. To heal the planet, to heal the Body Soul, we must also heal our own individual traumas and retrieve those parts of us floating around in the stratosphere. We can then become effective agents of change in the outer world.

I did a soul retrieval on someone once that was interesting in the way it panned out. This woman had come to me in the throes of deep depression, which had been affecting her for about a year. Her spirit was very down and after doing a lot of work to remove the negative intrusions that were burdening her energy, the spirit of the depression as it manifested as an alive force inside and outside her, I was drawn to do some soul retrieval. While doing this I was taken back along a time line to when she was a little girl.

I then witnessed a scene in an underground station in London where she was with her mother. In this scene she had stepped on the train, but before her mother could get on, the doors had shut separating them, and the train then started leaving towards the tunnel. Her mother was panicking and desperately running along the platform, clawing at the doors to get in while the girl just watched in a kind of daze from inside the train as she slowly entered the blackness of the tunnel.

In the scene I was guided to retrieve the girl who I sensed had been lost in that tunnel for a long time and to bring her back to the now woman who was lying on the bed, which I did.

After the healing was over, I wondered whether what I had been shown actually happened as a literal event or whether it was symbolic of a traumatic, emotional split between the woman and her mother when she was a girl. Like with dreams of the night, it is often difficult to tell whether what you are been shown in the psychic realms are literal truths or metaphorical. The best thing to do in these circumstances is just to tell the person what you have seen, which I did.

After I had finished explaining the scene, she looked at me strangely. I asked her whether she remembered this event happening, but she immediately said no. However, she then said that what I had seen was the exact description of a reoccurring nightmare that her mother used to have when she was younger. The mother would describe this nightmare to her constantly and it was one of her abiding memories of childhood.

This was strange and unexpected yet in that moment, I understood: her mother's fear of losing her child was so strong that it had actually been passed down to the child as an overwhelming fear of losing herself. Because this 'dream' was so powerful it had actually manifested in a reality, albeit an invisible one, as the child had indeed lost a part of her soul under the relentless pressure of that fear.

The story got more interesting as it turned out her mother had actually been abandoned by her own mother in childhood and had never been able to heal or resolve that trauma. The woman, her daughter, had then inherited that fear of abandonment, and it was so deep, it actually had resulted in soul loss. When the woman had come in for the healing, one of the first things she had said was: 'I feel so lost.' This is often a sure sign of soul loss.

Six months later the woman came back into the shop where I gave the healing from looking like a completely different person. She said to me then: 'I don't know what you did in that healing, but as soon as I left I started smiling again.' It was one of the best bits of feedback I've received in its simplicity.

I've witnessed too many times to mention, literally thousands of times, the power that soul retrieval can have to completely change a person's life. This means that one healing session can actually bring a person back from deep depressions or when they are in the midst of intense psychological breakdowns. I have witnessed many times people having their whole lives turned around from one session.

This of course, is not always the case. There appears in healing to be a magical interface between preparation of the healer, intention of person being healed and a mysterious third thing that we can never predict or fully explain. Healing doesn't always work, especially instantly. For some people just one session can get them off prescription drugs and living their lives again in a way they hadn't dreamed of before. For many others it can be a long, difficult journey, with many twists and turns and take many sessions. And for some others, it simply doesn't work and they don't get better. This can never be predicted in my experience as, in the end, there are forces far more powerful and mysterious than the human, who are making this healing happen. It is magic that gives birth to life as well as taking it away and is responsible for everything in between.

Another major source of soul loss, in my experience of working with many different people, is birth. The modern birthing methods fail to take into account that being born into this world isn't just a physical phenomenon. It actually involves a delicate transition between one world and another, as delicate and with as much potential to go wrong as the journey the other way, into death.

This is why traditional cultures would always have a spiritual midwife alongside the physical one, to ensure that the whole of the person's soul enters this realm. With the ending of these practices and the at times harsh medical interventions that accompany birth, quite often a part of the person can get lost in this process.

Another instance is when a person can suffer soul loss in the womb. I have witnessed this many times too, being taken back to the person's womb experience and the loss of part of their being. As with soul loss at birth, this is invariably through a painful ambivalence that the mother has towards having the child, something that is quite a taboo subject. Often the mother may be suffering her own trauma at the time. This could be manifesting in problems in the relationship with the child's father or other members of her family. Or, it could simply be that she is unsure of the direction that this will take her life or a feeling of not being emotionally prepared.

Of course, these things may go through a lot of women's minds when pregnant. They only really become a problem when they are acute. If this is the case, the child will pick up on this and the prospect of leaving the relative safety of the womb and going through that doorway of the unknown and into life becomes too much. Through this trauma soul loss occurs.

Another factor of soul loss is soul theft, whereby one person steals another's essence through an act of jealousy or desire to control that person. This taboo subject is rife especially among that melting pot of power dynamics – the somewhat claustro-phobic modern relationship or family unit. Soul theft is carried out when a person feels weak, or is has an overwhelming need to control the other person and then steals a part of their energy, a part of their soul.

Like cursing, we disregard the power of these traditional methods of psychic warfare, which in most indigenous cultures would be viewed as the source of nearly all sickness. Yet that doesn't mean that they go away. They just become unconscious and in a way more powerful. And, also harder to heal, as we are not even aware of the possibility that these things could happen.

To get a good barometer of what is happening in the collective psyche at any one time, it's useful to look at what is popular in the contemporary culture – films, music etc. The immense popularity of vampire and zombie films and TV programmes over the past 20 years I would say hints unconsciously at the power of soul theft and also the epidemic that soul loss has become.

A zombie is someone who has suffered complete soul loss and the anxiety that most of these stories relay, is that once people become zombified, they then become hungry for the souls of the living. It creates a seemingly never ending spiral of soul loss until the whole world's population is turned into zombies. The tragedy of soul theft is that, done unconsciously, it doesn't help the person doing the stealing, as the energy they steal becomes a burden to them, and of course the person losing a part of themselves suffers. It's a lose-lose situation of the highest degree.

The genius that indigenous cultures have over us is they recognise the subtleties of existence, particularly what is occurring on the invisible level as they are far more sensitive to these realities. In the West it's hard to observe these realities in a practical way when you are conditioned from pretty much the moment you are born into believing they don't exist.

What indigenous peoples have taught us is that the Dreaming Soul, that invisible essence that makes up our being, is far more malleable and prone to jumping in and out of our bodies than we might imagine. The conflux of energy between people is also something that is occurring constantly. This means we perhaps have to be a little more aware of what we are doing with our energy at any one time. The tendency to want to give away parts of ourselves, especially in intimate relationships or any that are based on the need to 'have' the other person, can be very strong. As can be the desire to possess the other.

Human beings can survive soul loss, as they can survive trauma. The problem is that gradually in the process they can then become more and more desensitised to others and to themselves. In a way, through continual soul loss, we become less human.

If a person is prone to turning such things inwards, they will then become more and more detached from themselves and life, leading to withdrawal and loss of hope. This can lead to all kinds of mental and physical illnesses. In many ways, among other things, my shamanic illness was a journey to reclaim parts of my soul that had become lost. This is the importance of the Heroic Quest.

Or, if a person has a tendency to turns things outwards, soul loss can become dangerous to others. Trauma destroys sensitivity and also empathy. A person who lacks empathy and also lacks a huge part of themselves is then capable of doing the most horrendous things. This can be an unconscious attempt to take from someone else what they have lost themselves, i.e. a part of their soul. Abuse, emotional, physical or sexual, is a manifestation of this. The act of violence against another is an act of theft, trying to regain something lost.

Another problem is that if a person has lost a huge part of their Dreaming Soul, they become much more susceptible to the powerful destructive/creative forces of the Body Soul, which in themselves can seem inhuman, and can end up acting these out in destructive ways. This is the person who has lost their sense of self completely and is filled with the 'demons' of the Otherworld, possessing her or him and urging ever-more extremes of violent destructive behaviour, to themselves or others. A lot of this we described in the first section of the book.

There have been studies done by psychologists on many of our leaders, in the political and business worlds, which have concluded that a lot of their actions would be deemed sociopathic in everyday society and that very often they register quite high on the psychopath spectrum. The way that those at the top continually seek to take from or crush the lives of those below them, could be viewed as representative of huge cases of soul loss. It is much easier for the machine to take over those who are empty inside. Indeed this kind of constant traumatising is often deliberate in some institutions to ensure that those taught there have their empathic natures removed and are much easier then to be controlled and to control others.

Beyond the political, soul loss is something I have found that people can almost universally relate to. We have all suffered trauma of some kind at some point in our life. Many people have come to me and said things like, 'I just haven't felt the same since such and such happened,' or, 'I feel lost, like I've lost who I am,' or, 'I just can't get over that person, I feel like I'm still attached to them,' or simply, 'I feel empty inside.' Then I know that soul loss is taking its toll.

Most people have suffered some kind of soul loss to varying degrees in my experience. Usually we can adapt and get on with life. There does seem to be a critical point though, when one too many traumas lead to too much of our life force leaking away and to the place where a person can no longer just get on with it and something inside breaks. Even the smallest thing then can be the catalyst for that break.

In indigenous cultures, they would not want to leave it more than three days if a person was suspected of having suffered soul loss before getting them to the shaman to retrieve that part of them. I see people in their 70s sometimes who lost a part of themselves when they were seven.

But it's never too late to heal, and often those sessions can be the most moving. There is no greater gift in life than being a part of a process whereby a person can regain a part of themselves. I always feel immensely privileged to be a part of this process. These parts also always bring back gifts for us.

I remember doing a soul retrieval for a woman once and, as I brought back the part of her, I was struck internally by how much laughter and playfulness this part was going to bring back into the woman's life. I then blew the part back into the woman's crown, as is the technique, and she immediately burst into laughter. She then proceeded to have a laughing fit that lasted about ten minutes. I was quite shocked at the immediate impact, but joined in with her. Finally, when she could speak she apologised profusely, as she thought we were in the middle of a 'serious' healing session. She said: 'I don't know why I am laughing but can't stop.' I just smiled and then told her what I had brought back.

There are so many different permutations of what creates the trauma that leads to soul loss that it is too much to cover here. We could fill a whole book, and indeed books have been written on this subject. What is in the scope of this book, however, is to share the powerful healing potential we have at our disposal to heal the endemic level of unresolved trauma in our societies, and the individuals that make them up.

There are many practitioners who are able to offer this healing method and many more training all the time. Psychotherapy and counselling can often do similar things, but using different techniques. For whatever problems we may have, both individually and as a society, there are always ways to heal them.

This truly is the magic of nature, for every poison, there is an antidote, for every problem, a solution. We haven't been abandoned here on this earth, for whatever we need truly is here. And of course there are ways that we can call back these parts of ourselves to ourselves. Just the commitment to go on a healing journey, to commence the heroic quest of discovering who you really are beneath the layers of conditioning, to face the unknown and mysterious and to whole heartedly leap into the adventure that is life; these are time-honoured ways of retrieving these parts of our being. In the long run such ways can be more powerful than just seeking a practitioner or a shaman, as we are doing it for ourselves as opposed to having it done to us.

The best way is probably a combination of both because ultimately no one is ever really healing us, they are just assisting us in healing ourselves. It is our intention, our commitment to be

Conclusion

Integrating the Three Souls of Our Being

Life is a journey. Integrating these three aspects of our being we've been exploring is most definitely such a voyage. We're here to learn, we're here to grow, and we're here to explore and to play. And, perhaps most importantly, we're here to realise who we truly are, for when we do that, we become a part of the 'Everything'. Definition brings togetherness, separation leads to unity.

By knowing who I am, I can also know who you are, and know that we are in fact one and the same, we are all one. The paradoxical nature of the universe means that by learning who I am I can then let who I am go and no longer be caught by the definition of myself. This is the journey, this is the initiation. Then comes some kind of freedom.

Looking at our three souls teaches us how to do this. In my Body Soul I am a part of everything here on earth and in the universe. I am not separate from the forces that gave birth to the universe and continue to ensure its function and survival. I am the same as a plant, or an animal, or a rock or an element, or the gods that stand behind these beings.

The primal forces of creation and destruction continue to move through me, tugging and influencing my consciousness constantly. And if there is pain in the earth, I will feel it in my Body Soul. I am not separate from the earth's story, even if I try to distance myself with all kinds of theories that the being that makes up the earth is really just dead matter. I can justify my destructive actions and lack of responsibility with such theories or models of the universe, but deep down I will still feel it and in this part of my being I will also feel the primal pain of separation from that which I come from.

I might then create whole societies that are based around avoidance of this pain, as a kind of neurotic coping mechanism of distraction upon distraction. But it will always be there, lurking in the corners, awaiting the time when I become distracted from my distractions and suddenly wake up to the existential crisis I am carrying inside of me. That void of nothingness I must face.

Then all my rational theories will not save me, and I will have to humbly step into that void and realise that really I am just a small part of a greater whole, and that that whole actually wishes to hold and comfort me and sooth my existence anxiety, as any mother would. Then I will begin to feel whole and the societies I create will instead reflect this truth, felt deep inside my being, of deep trust at the benevolence of life. The relationship between myself and my Body Soul and the rest of creation will then be healed.

I might then wish to define myself further, to know where I have come from, in order to know in a more intimate way that greater whole of which I am a part. Then I can get to know my ancestors, as they are the first point of call for me in my connection to the invisible beings that inhabit the vast expanses of the spirit world. They have lived here and understand what it is like, understand all too well the challenges of existing in a body, and therefore have compassion for me on my journey here.

And they are also interested in my existence as I carry a part of them inside of me in my Ancestral Soul. I make them immortal and give them a continual presence in the world. So they are there to assist me, but also to show and teach me what it is like on the other side, the place I will visit when my time here is done.

That is, if they themselves have been healed of any leftover traumas or crisis from their life here. For if they haven't healed, instead of gifting me these things, as people with unresolved pain do, they will instead seek to take from me. Take my life force and energy, or load their burdens upon me, in a desperate attempt to release the trapped psychic power of their accumulated pain. Then it is up to me to assist them first, to work on behalf of my ancestors to lift off these burdens or curses. And in doing so I set free not only my own Ancestral Soul, but those of a long line of people behind me who have waited for that moment for a long, long time.

Then also, the collective Ancestral Soul of my nation or people can begin to heal. Pride can come back to us and therefore the need to dominate and oppress others diminishes. As I am able to proudly state and know where I come from, so am I able to respect and honour where you come from. And I can learn from and share in the wonder of your culture, as I share with you the wonder and beauty of my own. For, deep down, that fundamental truth that exists in my Body Soul that we are all one is there, the complexity and differences of my ancestral inheritance just adds a layer of richness to this truth. This in turn adds a layer of richness to life.

Then, knowing where I have come from, I may then wish to delineate further and finally get to know the truth of who I am, as a unique soul in this vast expanse of mystery that makes up existence. And what a journey this may prove to be. What an adventure! What a strange, wayward exploration of the depths of life through my own unique lens of perception. How crazy might I seem, what lengths might I need to go to, in an age of conformity, to confront and begin to master this aspect of my being? To realise what the sages and mystics have been telling us throughout time, that life is but a dream, and somewhere we are architects of our own reality.

Yet, when I do realise this I will already know the responsibility that comes with this knowledge, as I will already be connected to the two other souls. Thus, the fact that I can be an architect of my own reality will not mean that I spend my days cherry picking facets of reality I wish to explore, like a restless teenager in front of the latest plasma screen.

Instead I can use this newfound power to assist others and to conjoin with them, to create a living, breathing society that matches the one that exists in the grand halls of our dreaming; one that reflects the beauty and love at the heart of life. For when I get this far, I realise it's not really my dream anyway, it's just one that I can tap into. Like an artist who reveals the masterpiece already buried in the depths of the rock, so I am able to reveal the art and majesty already present in life.

Thus, when I fully know my own Dreaming Soul, I am already conjoining with and re-entering the Body Soul. The 'I' I have found then disappears back into the whole. I have learnt to die, which in a way, may be one of the main reasons I came here in the first place, to learn this most holy of all lessons. It certainly may be one of the reasons that I have undergone this initiation. For, as we explored at the beginning of this book, initiation has at its heart the relationship between the visible and the invisible. And when we are undertaking our initiations we are essentially learning how to die, so that we can then learn how to fully live.

This then brings that elusive power of healing back to the centre of our existence. Once I have learnt to die, I have no fear of it, beyond the natural bodily reactions. I am therefore free to live and thus the spirit of all of life can live, unadulterated through all of me. My life then becomes an offering, back to the whole, just in the way I live it; an expression of the beauty and magnificence that flows through me. This is then the greatest gift I can bring to the world: I exist within the Heart of Life as the Heart of Life exists within me.

Afterword

That butterfly, see it dance once again on the summer wind, see its wings flap free, unfettered by the constraints of self-consciousness. Its magnificence is its existence, no more, no less. It is here for such a brief time, yet that fact lends itself not to sadness, but instead to joy, to wonder, to appreciation and awe, in both the viewer and the viewed. Does it dance for me, for you or for itself?

These questions do not matter for, in the end, it just dances. As do we.

References

1. Mental Health Foundation (online) http://www.mental health.org.uk/help-information/mental-health-statistics/
2. Robert Lawlor, *Voices of the First Day – Awakening in the Aboriginal Dreamtime*, (Inner Traditions 1991), pages 333-337
3. Stephen V. Beyer, *Singing to the Plants – A Guide to Mestizo Shamanism in the Upper Amazon*, (University of New Mexico Press 2009)
4. Richard Tarnas, The Astrological Journal Volume 56, Number 1, page 30
5. Richard Tarnas quoting Bertrand Russell (*A Brief History of Western Thought*, Oct 5th 2012, (online) https://www.youtube.com/watch?v=2B3zm8R0dEo)
6. Richard Tarnas, The Astrological Journal Volume 56, Number 1, page 30
7. The Guardian (online) 22nd December 2010 http://www.theguardian.com/science/2010/dec/22/placebo-effect-patients-sham-drug
8. BBC.co.uk (online) 10th December 2014 http://www.bbc.co.uk/news/health-30411246
9. Martin Prechtel, TheSunMagazine.org (online) April 2001 Issue 304 http://thesunmagazine.org/issues/304/saving_the_indigenous_soul
10. Vusamazulu Credo Mutwa, *Shamans of the World*, edited by Nancy Conner with Bradford Keeney, PHD. (Sounds True, Boulder CO), 2008, page 129
11. John Fire Lame Deer and Richard Erdoes, *Lame Deer, Seeker of Visions* (Pocket Books Simon Schuster, New York), 1972, page 75
12. Terrance McKenna, *Food of the Gods – The Search for the Original Tree of Knowledge* (Bantam Books) 1992
13. Ralph Metzner, *The Well of Remembrance* (Shambhala) 2001
14. Aluna, directed by Alan Ereira, (Sunstone Films), June 2012

15. James Pennebaker, 'Disclosure of traumas and health among Holocaust survivors' Psychosomatic Medicine, Journal of American Psychosomatic Society (online) October 1989, volume 51 issue 5 http://journals.lww.com/psychosomat-icmedicine/Abstract/1989/09000/Disclosure_of_traumas_an d_health_among_Holocaust.9.aspx

16. Salon.com (online) *The Dark Legacy of Carlos Castaneda*, April 2007 http://www.salon.com/2007/04/12/castaneda/ See also Examiner.com (online) Amy Wallace on her life in the tragic cult of Carlos Castaneda, November 2012 http://www. examiner.com/article/amy-wallace-on-her-life-the-tragic-cult-of-carlos-castaneda

17. Liz Greene, *The Dark of the Soul – Psychopathology in the Horoscope*, (CPA Press, 2003, London) pages 218-319

18. Nietzsche, *The Gay Science*, Section 125, 1882, (online) http://en.wikipedia.org/wiki/God_is_dead

19. Marianne Williamson, *A Return to Love* (Harper Collins 1992) page 336

20. Lewis Mehl-Madrona *Coyote Medicine- Lessons from Native American Healing* (Fireside, 1998, New York)

21. Martin Seligman (online) see http://en.wikipedia.org/wiki /Learned_helplessness

22. Dylan Thomas, 'Do not go gently into that good night' (online) http://en.wikipedia.org/wiki/Do_not_go_gentle_into_that_good_night

23. Bob Dylan, 'Up to Me', (online) http://www.bobdylan.com /us/songs/me

24. The Guardian (online) February 2015 http://www.theguard ian.com/commentisfree/2015/feb/08/depression-drives-many-men-to-commit-suicide?CMP=share_btn_fb

25. Martin Prechtel, *The Secrets of the Talking Jaguar* (Putnam 1998)

26. Ernest Becker, *The Denial of Death*, (Free Press, 1973) preface, page xvii

Moon Books invites you to begin or deepen your encounter with
Paganism, in all its rich, creative, flourishing forms.